SOVIET SECRECY AND NON-SECRECY

Soviet Secrecy and Non-Secrecy

Raymond Hutchings

BARNES & NOBLE BOOKS
TOTOWA, NEW JERSEY

First published 1987 in the United Kingdom by
The Macmillan Press Ltd
Basingstoke and London

First published in the USA 1988 by
BARNES & NOBLE BOOKS
81 ADAMS DRIVE
TOTOWA, NEW JERSEY, 07512

ISBN 0–389–20754–3

Printed in Hong Kong

Library of Congress Cataloging-in-Publication Data
Hutchings, Raymond.
Soviet secrecy and non-secrecy.
Bibliography: p.
Includes index.
1. Government information—Soviet Union.
2. Official secrets—Soviet Union.   3. Government
information.   4. Official secrets.   5. Comparative
government.   I. Title.
JN6529.S4H88   1988   323.44′5   87–11386
ISBN 0–389–20754–3

Contents

Glossary   vi

Preface   vii

1   Introduction   1

2   Theoretical and General Considerations   8

3   The Soviet Setting   36

4   Main Features of Soviet Secrecy   55

5   Secrecy in Specific Branches   60

6   How Secrets Are Kept: I. Physical Obstacles   94

7   How Secrets Are Kept: II. The Censorship   114

8   How Secrecy Has Varied over Time   136

9   Secrecy and the Soviet Public   154

10 Cross-Frontier Relationships   167

11 International Comparisons: I. Spheres of
    Activity   191

12 International Comparisons: II. Country
    by Country   202

13 Causes of Secrecy   230

14 Consequences of Secrecy: I. Disclosure Policy   240

15 Consequences of Secrecy: II. Other
    Consequences   252

16 Final Remarks   264

Bibliography   267

Index of Names   280

Index of Subjects   285

Glossary

ABSEES	*Abstracts*, Soviet and East European Series
Aktiv	Most active part of some organisation
D.T.	*The Daily Telegraph* newspaper (London)
Narodnoye . . .	Annual statistical handbook whose title begins *Narodnoye khozyaystvo SSSR*
NFAC	National Foreign Assessment Center (US)
NYT	*The New York Times*
oblast' (pl. *oblasti*)	Territorial division and unit of provincial government and of Party organisation
SWB	BBC Summary of World Broadcasts

Preface

As usual my wife Karen played a very large role in the typing and helped in numerous other ways. The text is much the better for her comments. My son Nicholas and sister Alice also commented usefully from various angles, the former also supplying additional material based especially on his knowledge of geography and cartography. I thank Dr Heinrich Vogel, Director of the Bundesinstitut für ostwissenschaftliche und internationale Studien in Cologne, for permission to draw on my article in its *Berichte* series, issue 20–1982. I am grateful to George Schöpflin for his permission to quote clauses relating to the Polish censorship from his *Censorship and Political Communication in Eastern Europe*. I am indebted to Duquesne University (Pittsburgh), to the Mississippi University for Women (Columbus, Mississippi), the Royal Institute of International Affairs (London), and Indiana University (Bloomington, Indiana) for their invitations to lecture on the subject; to Mary Stevens (University of Toronto Library) for bibliographic support; and to Ellen Mickiewicz (author of *Media and the Russian Public*), Marianna Tax Choldin (author of *A Fence Around the Empire*), T. H. Rigby, Sidney Ploss, H. B. Paksoy, David Wedgwood Benn, and others who prefer not to be named, for useful information, comments or advice. I, of course, have full responsibility for the result.

Croydon, England   RAYMOND HUTCHINGS

1 Introduction

The twentieth century has witnessed an extension of the areas regarded as secret. Although some secrets are penetrated and many more become obsolete, new ones are coined. The complement of secrets is constantly changing: on the whole, private secrecy has declined but public secrecy increased. I mean by the latter, secrets relating to nations which are preserved, or are sought to be preserved, by national agencies. Partly this has occurred owing to the fact that a much larger number of people participate in intelligence activities, of one sort or another. What is done is sometimes regarded as secret not because it is intrinsically so but because of the person who does it. Partly it has occurred owing to the multiplication of subjects: the area of secrecy tends then to keep pace. In some degree it results from the strengthened role of information in all spheres of life, which reinforces the impact of any deliberate withholding of it. Partly it results from the deployment of incomparably more devastating weapons than ever existed before. To a considerable degree it is due to totalitarian governments which try to establish, and largely succeed in establishing, regimes of information control.

Among these latter the government of the Soviet Union has to be numbered; and yet, curiously, no book has yet been written about Soviet secrecy, or (what is closely related to it, but seen from another angle) Soviet disclosure policy. What we do *not* know about the Soviet Union because information is withheld is potentially, and in the most literal sense, of vital importance. As far as possible, it must be taken into account in any evaluation or study of the USSR. It is truly remarkable how many people, some of whom ought to know better, or do know better, take no notice of the fact that the great bulk of our information about the Soviet Union has been passed through a filter which is designed and inserted by the Soviet Union itself.

However, it might seem that the subject is one which intrinsically cannot be investigated; just as, by definition, one cannot see in the dark. But actual lack of news is only one aspect of secrecy. Secrets can be kept only in certain circumstances, and these circumstances have describable characteristics, or may betray themselves via their effect on observable phenomena.

1

Similarly, a 'black hole' in astronomy can never itself be visible as no light can escape from it, but betrays itself through what it does to adjacent bodies, or its existence is confirmed on theoretical grounds.

It is not the expectation here (although it may be a hope) to uncover the precise matters which are deliberately kept secret; this is a task beyond any single individual. The subject is Soviet secrecy (and non-secrecy), rather than Soviet *secrets*. I shall state the categories of information which are not provided, the how and when, and to some extent the where and why. The study includes reflections about secrecy in general, and comparisons are also made with a number of other countries.

Despite its intentionally restricted scope, the book took much longer to write than I had expected. Some of the reasons ought to have been clearer at the start than they actually were. Secrecy, if effective, means that certain matters are not disclosed, but these are naturally less visible than those that are, and any systematic reading programme which would uncover what was *not* visible was difficult to imagine. Substantial reliance had to be placed, therefore, on finding random references to matters which had not been reported, and this must be more time-consuming and less systematic than reading up about a topic directly.

It may be that 'all ravens are black' is equivalent to 'all non-black things are non-ravens', so that in order to prove that all ravens are black, it would be as valid a procedure to count up non-black things which are not ravens, as to count up black ravens directly (see Mackie, 1968, pp. 165–76); in actuality, counting up non-black things is too uncertain and laborious! Similarly, one cannot get very far by listing what the Soviet Union *does* disclose. Some gaps reveal themselves when one looks at what other countries disclose, but that approach too is not foolproof. At least, by approaching the subject from a number of different directions, one should get closer to the truth than if not having made the attempt.

The Times (of London) of 25 August 1982 had the following snippets on its front page:

Three A levels for the Prince
Prince Edward has passed his A level examinations in English literature, economics and political studies, also gaining an A level pass in history. At the Queen's wish his grades have not

been disclosed.
Soviet crop fails
With half of this year's crop already cut, Russia is heading for
the fourth bad harvest in a row. The harvest is so far below the
planned target that no crop figures have been released.

Thus, in Britain official secrecy covered Prince Edward's A
level grades; in the Soviet Union, the size of the grain harvest. It
would, of course, be wrong to suppose that in Britain there are
no secrets covering national totals, or in the USSR none covering
prominent individuals; this example distorts reality, as any very
simple contrast is likely to do. However, the grain harvest in
Britain would not be kept secret, unless during wartime; it is also
not uncharacteristic that *The Times* of the following day did
reveal Prince Edwards's grades, which proved to be slightly
below expectation. It is noteworthy as well that the newspaper
could confidently assert that the Soviet harvest would be 'bad',
though no total had been officially disclosed. A given total may
be (but is not necessarily) disclosed later, perhaps obliquely; it
will not be as long as sensitivity to that total persists (that is to
say, as long as it is considered that the total reflects some
discredit on the Soviet system or would create other disadvantages, if disclosed) nor will the total come from any unofficial
Soviet source. In short, there are big differences in national
attitudes to what is, or should be, kept secret. Moreover, sometimes a secret fails to be kept.

The choice of a particular nation for a study of secrecy implies
that secrecy is, or has been, important in that nation's history or
in its present-day life. It implies too that that country can be
detached from its surroundings and studied as a unit, and that it
has sufficient relevant individuality. It is presumed also that the
nation is large enough (or, perhaps, small enough), and sufficiently well organised and tightly knit to be able to keep those
secrets that it wishes to keep, at least to a large extent. Finally,
one must hope that readers will find the topic interesting and
important.

From all these angles the Soviet Union offers a good subject.
Its attitudes to secrecy are definably different from those of a
number of other countries. Soviet secrecy is intense and its scope
is broad. It has considerable influence upon how individuals and
countries view the USSR, and in other directions.

A number of theoretical issues are examined later in the book (in Chapter 2 in particular), but perhaps I should state immediately – as it must colour the entire presentation – whether I think that secrecy, and accompanying phenomena such as censorship, are necessarily evil.

Secrecy is a product of a desire to mislead, and by itself that must be reckoned unethical. In certain circumstances the result can have an ethical value which outweighs the unethicalness of the desire to mislead, and only in those circumstances can secrecy be regarded as ethical. It is also possible, and probably much more common, that the result too is unethical; in this case secrecy emerges as unethical, owing both to the intention and to the result, and therefore carries a double charge of unethicalness. In that event, activity which brings about the result that the secret is pierced can be regarded as ethical.

Some degree of private secrecy, or privacy, may be necessary for life and liberty, while some degree of public secrecy is required for the sake of national independence – if that be a good thing. In the world as it actually is, I believe that national independence is not entirely bad: for one thing, flight across frontiers affords a refuge from tyranny (cf. Gibbon, 1776, pp. 81–2). In the present century, this is an almost illimitable blessing. Moreover, both the private and the public varieties of secrecy are needed, to some extent, to ward off disharmony and conflict. Where individuals or nations hold sharply differing views which they then put into effect, it is probably better that they do not know exactly and continuously what the other is getting up to. Finally, certain aspects of secrecy, such as not exhibiting oneself as a benefactor, are morally significant.

On the other hand, secrecy involves deliberately keeping in ignorance individuals, groups or nations; this amounts to an interference with their independent judgement, and comprises an exercise of power which is frequently (and, by intention, normally) to their disadvantage. Secrecy, then, is normally bad in principle, at any rate in part, but also, in some degree at least, necessary in practice. An absolutist view may see secrecy as wholly bad and wrong, but if that view is to serve as a basis for policy, one must be aware of what the consequences of total non-secrecy would be, and these consequences would often be unfortunate. It is, of course, quite compatible with this view that the type or degree practised by a particular individual or nation might be excessive, regrettable, and unduly damaging to others and possibly as well to the individual or nation which practises it, which (simply stated) may well be the case with Soviet secrecy. In any case, if secrecy is at least in part bad in principle, one may start with the presumption that it ought not to be present unless there are justifying, explanatory or mitigating circumstances.

The duality of possible result finds some expression in English usage with the different connotations of 'confidential' and 'secret': while 'confidential', or even more 'in confidence', has an air of respectability, 'secret' has the opposite connotation. Confidentiality obviously fulfils certain important social functions (see Øyen, 1982). It imports the notions of love and of concern for a person's well-being, whereas secrecy suggests a malicious withholding of information from a deliberately disadvantaged third party. The difference is to a large extent one of viewpoint. To the extent that there is a genuine difference in meaning, it stems from the fact that 'confidential' tends to be applied to advice and opinion, but 'secret' to information.

PREVIOUS LITERATURE

It is traditional at the start of a book to mention briefly previous literature. This must, of course, reach a generally negative conclusion, or there will be no justification for making an addition to it.

Including most interesting material on secrecy, and despite its title certainly belonging in a library of international affairs, is *The Sociology of George Simmel* (Wolff, 1950). Containing chapters on 'Secrecy' and (twice as long) 'The Secret Society' this offers philosophical and psychological analyses which are often of a profound character (though a section on 'Adornment' seems misplaced in this context). Much of the emphasis is (as it should be) on individual secrecy, but some observations are also applicable to the secrecy of groups or (in smaller degree) to that of nations; for instance, 'flight into secrecy is a ready device for social endeavours and forces that are about to be replaced by new ones' (Wolff, 1950, p. 347). Simmel is strong also on the historical side. Much has been written about secrecy in countries other than the USSR, but this need not be catalogued here.

Passing on to the Russian and Soviet scenes, we find that general histories as a rule do not include any entry 'Secrecy' in their indexes. There is usually mention of the censorship, but no broader allusion; at any rate, none that is readily identifiable from the index. Vernadsky (*A History of Russia*, 1930) lists 'Secret Societies in Russia', which is very unusual. John Gunther's *Inside Russia Today* (1957) has an entry 'Secrecy', and devotes quite a lot of space to the topic. However, Gunther is in turn eclipsed by Hedrick Smith, *The Russians* (1976) which (on pp. 344–74) contains the fullest allusions to Soviet secrecy that I know of. It may be surprising that the subject should be treated most fully in books which do not lay claim to being academic; to my mind, in this respect they put to shame a number that do. As regards works by specialists, *The Russian Mind* by Ronald Hingley contains an index entry 'Secretiveness', and allusions in the text do not disappoint. Secrecy is listed in the index of *Privilege in the Soviet Union* by Mervyn Matthews, but there is no extended treatment there of the subject. The remarks of John P. Hardt, concerning the importance of Soviet secrecy, should be noted (JEC, 1977, pp. 159–66). Secrecy in international affairs has received less notice than might have been expected; various allusions will be found in the present book to Thomas F. Frank and Edward Weisband (eds) *Secrecy and Foreign Policy* (1974). Its impact in Soviet international relations does not seem to have been examined at length. There are many interesting observations about the effects of secrecy on Soviet defence innovation in Holloway's contribution to *Industrial Innovation in the Soviet Union* (1982). A useful summary and other remarks are found in James R. Millar, *The ABCs of Soviet Socialism* (1981). Finally, the subject is handled discursively and at no great length in Walter Laqueur, *A World of Secrets: The Uses and Limits of Intelligence* (1985).

It appears, nevertheless, that this whole subject is not an overworked field. I shall attempt to provide a more complete treatment of Soviet secrecy than is provided in the books mentioned above, but comprehensive treatment cannot be achieved, the subject being essentially open-ended.

Perhaps, however, the conclusion should be that this is not a suitable subject for an academic book? If one condition is that the theme should be sufficiently difficult, I believe that that condition is met. If it is stipulated that references must be adequately footnoted, this (I trust) is achieved although to a larger extent than in my earlier books it is necessary to make use of non-Soviet sources – a limitation that is inherent in the topic. One cannot quote what a particular source does *not* say. The attempt has been made to use a wide range of sources. If analytical rigour is a requirement, this will be aimed at to the maximum possible extent. Because of the nature of the subject, it is sometimes necessary to rely on analogy or collateral evidence. If the criterion of suitability is the importance of the subject, an affirmative judgement is beyond doubt.

This book is appearing at a time when the Soviet media are reporting more about the Soviet Union than they did before. The processes of book publication being unable to accommodate day to day developments, this account will necessarily be in various respects out of date. The narrative is brought up to 31 December 1986.

2 Theoretical and General Considerations

SECRETIVENESS AND FALSIFICATION

The starting point of any discussion of secrecy has to be examination of a desire to mislead, since withholding information always does mislead, whatever other effect it may have. Let us therefore consider, from the angle of any individual or authority that has a choice, whether it is more advantageous to be silent or to falsify. The discussion at this point excludes moral considerations. (In regard to Soviet economic reporting, cf. Hutchings, 1982A, pp. 249–54; also Kosta, 1973, p. 99.)

It is simpler to withhold information, as then it is not necessary to imagine some untruth. If the truth is to be revealed at some time in the future, this also will be less awkward if untrue information referring to the same matter has not been given already. The publication of false information may also be confusing to one's own people who must receive true information; even if they do receive this through confidential sources they may be confused, while the provision of two sets of information, one of which is true and the other false, risks destroying the credibility of both sets, as well as that of the authority which issued them.

Against this, suppression of information leaves to the person from whom information is withheld the choice of how to evaluate the lack. If instead of information being withheld something false is stated, this gives greater scope to sway in particular directions whomever is expected to absorb the information. A rational (if amoral) authority when deciding whether to suppress or to falsify should take into account how acutely it wants to elicit a specific response, and also whether true information will be published at a later date.

The Soviet leaders have believed time to be on their side in international affairs, and so on the whole have been prepared to await the consequences of their actions in the long term. This inclines one to suppose that they would normally prefer to withhold than to falsify. The Nazi regime, aiming at short-term

8

results, would have been more likely to come to the opposite conclusion. If the Soviet leaders came to the conclusion that time was not on their side, other things being equal they should be more likely to choose similarly.

To check out a specific falsification is usually far less onerous than to find out what happened in the absence of *any* information. This by itself would weight the balance in favour of non-reporting. The big drawback of this is that a gap is left. This might be a blank space in a newspaper or some other medium, time unaccounted for, or some other variant. With sufficient resources and access, every gap might be investigated; in practice this is almost always impossible, and even the existence of any gap may be obscured. However, as it may become difficult to conceal a gap if the enquiry is assiduous enough, it becomes important to choke off every suspicion that a gap may exist. As a rule, then, if it is vital to conceal the fact that any secret is being kept, non-reporting will not secure that result or will not do so reliably. If that dimension of concealment is not vital, non-reporting becomes a more attractive option.

The above is true in all circumstances. In national affairs it will be impossible to stifle suspicion that secrecy is present, which weakens the disadvantages attaching to non-reporting, as distinct from falsifying. On the other hand, where national secrets are concerned it may be easier to establish the content of known gaps due to internal linkages, for example of an economic nature. These two results tending to cancel out each other, any difference in the outcome, by comparison with non-national secret-keeping, is indeterminate. In other words, both nations and individuals may have recourse both to non-reporting and to falsification, though if the content of gaps cannot be established but their existence does not need to be hidden there should be a preference for non-reporting, provided that one condition is satisfied. This is that the gaps should not be mutually support-ing, i.e. that if one gap is filled it should not be immediately possible to deduce the contents of another. A would-be secret-keeping agency which is forced to yield ground here will be strongly tempted to falsify instead. This result is very relevant if one is considering the likely consequences of compelling govern-ments to provide information, by means of some freedom of information act. The English saying 'Ask no questions and you'll be told no lies' expresses essentially the same relationship.

Certain Soviet bodies have in the past purposely spread false information, for example in the form of forgeries (see Schultz and Godson, 1984, pp. 149–57 especially), and doubtless this continues. However, except where relevant to secrecy, falsification is outside the scope of this book.

Because of the special risks and difficulties of falsification, this should be on a more restricted scale than non-reporting. This is even truer on a national plane, where non-reporting is overwhelmingly the cheaper. The bias in favour of non-reporting should be stronger in larger, more complex or poorer communities; however, as on a national scale more complex usually goes with richer rather than with poorer, so that the second and third of these situations are opposed to one another, non-reporting ought not to be more attractive to a more advanced country than to a less advanced one.

In a particular sub-category, non-reporting inevitably entails falsification: this is when a framework is already defined and not deformable, so that a given space has to be filled with one thing if it is not filled with another. Cartography is one such example (see Chapter 5); another is the naming of ministries, assuming that their very existence cannot be kept secret. In fact, some Soviet ministries which produce armaments have at times been called something else (Holloway, 1982, pp. 380–1).

Is falsification less likely at certain times than at others? One recalls the aphorism 'The first casualty when war comes is truth' (Hiram Johnson, 1917, cited in Knightley, 1982, p. iv), but more recently that aphorism has sounded distinctly out of date or even contrary to the truth. It assumes Victorian standards of tranquillity in peacetime and a free press, both of which now seem Utopian. On the British declaration of war on Nazi Germany in September 1939 a measure of truth which had long been obscured made a reappearance, for 'appeasement' had tried not to cause offence to Hitler and that restraint was suddenly removed. The immediate dropping by the BBC of the 'Herr' in Herr Hitler was not merely symbolic. In the Soviet Union, a moment of truth arrived when the regime under stress of war had to mobilise reliance on traditional Russian patriotism, bolstered by the Orthodox Church. But of course there are some senses in which the aphorism is correct.

MEANINGS AND DEFINITIONS

Let us attempt a definition. Secrecy is non-disclosure of information: deliberate; selective in two respects: what is kept secret, and to whom it may be disclosed; apprehensive of penetration of the secret, and possibly also of the consequences of having even tried to keep it. It is certainly possible to venture more elaborate definitions. For example, Simmel writes about 'that aggressive defensive, so to speak, against the third person, which alone is usually designated as secret'. Without disagreeing, I shall normally allow such nuances to emerge in the course of the discussion.

We all keep secrets, not infrequently even from our conscious selves. While the subject here is the secrecy of nations, and especially of one nation, rather than that of individuals, an exposition of the ways in which the former is, or is not, similar to the latter leads conveniently into the subject.

Though in general such a claim should not be believed, an individual may claim to have no secrets, or at least to have none from so-and-so. By contrast, even if a country has nothing worth keeping secret, it is not likely ever to make such an announcement, as that would suggest that it possessed nothing of value at all; and the less important the country, the more insistently it will perhaps seek to convey the impression of harbouring important secrets.

There are important differences, and one of the most fundamental is the fact that the whole process of secret-keeping by nations has to be institutionalised. This is necessitated so that secrets can be communicated to some individuals, or to some nations, but not to others; it is also necessary to define the procedures by which secrets are created, preserved or divulged, and those for deciding which sorts of information are regarded as secret. A method of classification into degrees of confidentiality is required in the national but not in the private sort of secret-keeping. A system of penalties for failure to observe the rules has to be worked out, and also special codes and mechanical or other means of handling and transmitting secret information. If individuals make use of these means, it is on a vastly smaller scale. National secrets are usually quite different in nature from private secrets. The cost of keeping national secrets is out of all proportion to that of keeping individual secrets, and keeping or not keeping them has in the former case vastly more momentous consequences. There are a number of other differences, including that morality is closely related to private secrecy but much less closely to national secrecy.

If the fact that a secret has been pierced is itself concealed, the extent to which secrets are kept is liable to fall short of what the would-be secret keeper believes. One more of the differences between private and public secret-keeping is that the period over which a given secret is not being kept, and yet it is believed that it is still being, can be and is likely to be much more prolonged in the case of public secrets than in that of private secrets. This is because non-revelation of the piercing is potentially much more beneficial in public secrecy, if an agent who has not been unmasked can go on operating in an organisation within which he holds an important post. The reported controlling by British counter-intelligence for nineteen years of the Soviet KGB chief Oleg Gordievsky has been a spectacular example (*The Times*, 13 September 1985).

Private and public secrecy also tend to differ as regards the purposes envisaged. Secrets may relate to oneself (as an individual, nation, etc.) or to another entity (individual, nation, etc.). In either case, but especially where secrets relate to oneself, the purpose of seeking to keep a secret can be either to extend one's freedom of action, in absolute terms or relative to that of competing agencies of similar type (thus, the purpose can be served simply by restricting their freedom of action, when one's own is thereby unaltered or is reduced to a smaller extent), or to spring a surprise. For a given secret these two goals are mutually exclusive, because springing the surprise normally has the result of making the secret known, and thereby terminating the wider freedom (other circumstances being unchanged). The private sort of secret-keeping normally envisages widening freedom of action in a larger proportion of instances, and springing a surprise in a smaller proportion, than is envisaged by the national sort. This is for two reasons: nations are independent by definition and their freedom of action is already wide, being regulated by international law and treaty and by fear of reprisal (military or otherwise), but not (or not much) by domestic legislation, which leaves a smaller perceived need to widen them further than in the case of an individual, who is bound both by domestic legislation and by family ties; nations also more commonly contemplate surprising their adversaries with some new weapon. While secrets which relate to another entity exhibit this difference less strongly, these comprise a larger proportion of national than of private secret-keeping. However, an executive authority in a political democracy may feel itself to be hampered by internal constraints; the USA is an example. A one-party state, such as the USSR, can devote more of its secrecy towards gaining surprise. The share of secrecy in springing a surprise will also be larger, the more secrecy has a military orientation; advances in weaponry tend to produce that result. As regards secrecy in business, springing a surprise is almost as important as in national secrecy.

On the whole, the larger and more powerful the country, the more its secrecy is likely to envisage springing a surprise, relative to enlarging its freedom of action. This is for two reasons: its freedom of action is likely to be wide already, and it has more realistic possibilities of achieving surprise on a decisive scale. Specific small countries may not conform to this pattern: for example, a scientifically advanced nation, even if smaller than its neighbours, might gain a military advantage over them, and would perhaps orient its secrecy towards that goal. Israel possibly exemplifies that situation. The Soviet Union in this respect appears to conform to the mainstream. Geographically huge and comparatively isolated, its freedom of action is already wide apart from any extra degrees of freedom which secrecy may confer.

The importance of springing a surprise, as a motivation for secrecy, can change in the sense that a larger or smaller proportion of secret-keeping is devoted to this purpose, as distinct from the purpose of enlarging freedom of action; it may also change as a result of an alteration in the effect produced by the surprise. If the potential effect becomes much greater, the relative importance of springing the surprise is enhanced. This may be exemplified in naval armament. At the present time, warships may or may not be equipped with nuclear weapons. The difference in effective armament of a warship which is so equipped, by comparison with one that is not, is potentially far greater than, for example, the difference between two battleships, one of which included in its ammunition armour-piercing shells whereas the other did not. In this sphere, secrecy has a force-multiplying effect: if the fact that a warship is carrying nuclear weapons can be kept secret, then an enemy must consider every warship as being so equipped and thus disperse its own strength in order to combat that potential, which in reality applies to one or two warships out of a much larger number, or even to none at all. An even clearer example would have been the US project of siting MX missiles so that their position at any one moment could not be determined.

The considerable growth of the importance of secrecy is a relatively new phenomenon and may help to explain why certain governments, for example New Zealand's at the present time, are failing to appreciate its importance (see below, Chapter 12).

Secrecy adapts itself to the unit of government, particularly to the unit of defence; nowadays this usually is a nation but it can be, and at certain times or places has been, a tribe, village, extended family, or even fortified house. The tribal dimension is illustrated by the experience of the English explorer Edith Durham, who travelled through northern Albania in 1908. At one point she made a drawing of a *kula* or fortified house. A boy of 9 noticed this and went off to report to the tribe; at once stringent orders came back that 'nothing was to be written' (by which was meant 'drawn') in the tribal district (Durham, 1985, p. 318).

Secrets are found where it is important to hold them, either at or within the seats of power. This is associated with centralisation and where this is more extreme greater secretiveness is possible. It is also necessary owing to the vulnerability of the whole entity to decisions taken at the centre. Pizarro's conquest of the Inca Empire by his seizure of its ruler Atahualpa is a stunning historical example. The extent of secrecy is then determined mainly by the level in the hierarchy: the nearer the apex, the more secret. Any change in what is kept secret is therefore likely to affect the centre particularly. A sudden blotting out of visual symbols is one illustration of this. The fact that a statue of Tsar Nicholas II can be found in Helsinki, and statues of Stalin in Tirana or Shkodër (Albania), although Moscow now has statues of neither ruler, exemplifies the point. Analogously, during the Iconoclastic period of the Byzantine Empire destruction of icons, mural paintings, etc. 'was most severe in Constantinople and Asia Minor, in other words in areas that were under effective government control, less so in outlying provinces' (Mango, 1980, pp. 265–6).

In an entirely unintegrated society, if that is not a contradiction in terms, all secrets would be about others. At the other extreme, in a totalitarian regime the entire nation might comprise one gigantic secret. Though these are limiting cases, the second model has some relevance to the Soviet situation, to the extent that if companies or other non-national bodies are nationalised, their secrets become state secrets.

When secrets are gathered about others, they relate usually and primarily to one's direct competitors; however, spies (and academic people) try to penetrate the secrets of the institution to which their attention is directed. Commonly, the motive to keep secrets from one's own people is as powerful, or more so, than that of keeping them from some other country. For example, during the months when Britain was making preparations to join with France and Israel to recapture the Suez Canal, these had to be concealed not only from Egypt but from public opinion at home and abroad (Frank and Weisband, 1974, p. 215). This motive is less relevant in the Soviet case.

MEASUREMENT OF SECRECY

One may distinguish the range of items which are kept secret from how closely they are kept: these can be called respectively extent and intensity. Multiplying these two one obtains notionally the volume of secrecy, although an actual multiplication sum is not possible. The extent of secrecy might, like information, be measured in 'bits'.

The above is true from a viewpoint outside the society whose secretiveness is being assessed. Alternatively, one might consider the fraction

$$\frac{\text{State Secrecy}}{\text{Personal Privacy}}$$

as being the measure of internal relationships since, in practice, the two elements in this fraction tend to be negatively correlated. (See below in this chapter, section on 'Privacy', and also Chapter 12.) This alternative measure generates interesting results when the most recent trends are examined (see Chapter 8).

Intensity might be reckoned by the cost of keeping information secret, or possibly by the expense or time required in order to penetrate the secret. There is, however, no direct proportionality between secrets in different branches, for example in military affairs or in industry. The intensity of secrecy may depend on the sphere, with (for example) military secrets being guarded more closely than industrial ones.

Any society, when seeking to measure the volume of secrecy in some other one, will tend to exaggerate that volume to the extent that it uses a measuring rod taken from its own experience, rather than from the other's experience. The point is that each society focuses attention on the aspect of release of information which it cannot control, but which the other society evidently can.

If we should find – there are such indications in Soviet practice – that information about a certain sphere expands or contracts faster than another, this can be for four reasons, or a combination of them: altered interaction between these spheres, deliberate policy, a change in newsworthiness, or the 'principle of compensation'. Let us now consider the last reason.

THE 'PRINCIPLE OF COMPENSATION'

By this we mean that a larger extent of secrecy in one information sphere is very likely to be balanced, or partly balanced, by a smaller extent of secrecy in another sphere. This seems to be true yet is rarely stated, though Beermann claims it regarding fields of study in the Soviet Union (Beermann, 1971, p. 123). The principle should apply to societies of about the same size and type, and should hold good as long as there is any tendency for the total volume of information in such societies to be equalized. The common advance of technical means should assure a trend in that direction. If there is censorship, it will be preferred that no gaps should be left, so that if one kind of information is excluded another is more likely to be included. Again, if among rivals one releases information, this puts pressure on the others to do likewise.

Clearly, if this principle tends to operate, it does not mean that the extent of secrecy cannot differ between nations, and indeed it is obvious that it does (see Chapter 12). However, I think that the tendency towards equalisation is present, although possibly overborne by something else. Secretiveness may be entirely one-sided: for example, the veiling of women (only) in Saudi Arabia and other traditional Islamic regions. In this case, the principle has the result that the men are not veiled, except among the Tuaregs of North Africa, but there the *women* are unveiled. If within a given community *both* sexes were veiled, presumably the result in everyday life would be confusion!

OTHER GENERAL FEATURES

Like a veiled woman in unveiled company, secrecy may excite attention. Often what is kept secret seems more important than what is not. Why this should be is perhaps not at once obvious. After all, it is not what is intended. As long as what is meant to be kept secret actually is, the surmise is also unverifiable. From a journalistic viewpoint, what is made public is more interesting than what is not. Apparently some other consideration has the upper hand. In part, this should be the belief that secret information is expected to be useful as a guide to action. In addition, it is probably supposed that information is withheld in order to put a rival at a disadvantage. The withholding then takes on a competitive aspect which seems unfair, although that cannot be verified as long as the information remains secret. But imagination can have full play.

Imagination is restrained in the presence of certain sorts of phenomena, which are intrinsically non-secret or largely so. For instance, the externals of a building are in the public domain unless the building is sited in a restricted zone. Similarly, the external shape of a warship above the waterline is in the public domain, though it may be possible to conceal it from prying eyes for a while if other circumstances are propitious. Information is ineluctably in the public domain when it is associated with, or present in the midst of, physical phenomena which are not themselves controllable (such as light waves or radio waves). Now that controllable light with new qualities has been invented, i.e. the laser, the question will soon be broached about exploiting it to send information, which can be done by a laser beam along a very narrow and precise trajectory: over short distances (less than 6–19 km) this is especially suitable for safeguarding the secrecy of the transmission by comparison with the wide scatter of radio waves (Brown, 1968, pp. 81–2).

Secrecy or disclosure policy can apply to various spheres: economics, military affairs, etc. Although the intensity of secrecy may vary greatly between one sphere and another, the interaction between them tends to reduce the degree of variation.

There are always points both in favour and against keeping secret a particular item of news. Often one might ideally wish it to be disclosed to certain ears only. If that is practicable the news will be handled in a way which aims to achieve that result. I will consider first the option of enforcing physical restrictions, though at this point mainly from a theoretical angle.

In some cases a news item may be exhibited only to certain individuals, these latter being, for example, the only ones to be admitted to a closed exhibition. It may also be desired to draw a distinction between general effect (allowable) and close analysis (disallowable). Both of these possibilities are implemented in the parading of military equipment through Red Square (in Moscow) on the anniversary of the Revolution: they are seen only by physically present observers, and only momentarily and from certain angles.

The analogy of a camera shutter can help in conceptualising release of information for a limited duration and in controlled amounts. There is an instant when the shutter is fully open, while just before and after there is an extra slight exposure. Similarly, when hardware is brought through Red Square it is at a peak of visibility to observers, but it must also be brought to the Square and moved away again. These transitions correspond to the periods of opening the shutter and closing it, respectively. Instead of showing off items to an invited audience, one might allow them to stray about the city over a longer period. Observers would then not see the equipment so clearly, but would see it over a longer period. The fact that equipment is produced for observation under the observers' unhampered gaze shows that much store is placed on being able to control what is observed.

The analogy can be pushed a little further. The most effective shutters reduce to a minimum the preliminary and subsequent periods of exposure. Moreover, an efficient shutter can manage a very short exposure. It is a possible defect that after multiple use the minimum exposure may increase slightly. By analogy, a system which intended very brief exposure would need to be excellently organised. This would cut to the minimum the preliminary and subsequent exposures. Taking the parade in Red Square as an example, military units should spend the shortest possible time within the city either before or after the parade.

To decide the required exposure, we need a meter. At the level of national security policy, one would need to gauge the capacity to observe of individuals to whom the item will be momentarily exposed. It would seem that from their own viewpoint attachés should preferably convey the impression of being unobservant; they will then be granted a longer period of exposure than if they had seemed more sharp-eyed. A meter has to be adjusted to match the field of view of the lens. If objects are to be presented for viewing at a greater distance, there will be a greater risk of error in gauging what is able to be observed. One should therefore exhibit something in moderate close-up if one is going to exhibit it at all.

The above principles are expounded in terms of vision, but in all likelihood they apply also to other forms of sensory detection.

CLASSIFICATION

We will now consider means of limiting access to information which depend on classification. This refers primarily to documents, but also to photographs and sound recordings.

Material which may be seen by certain persons only is described as classified. Although the intention is always to prevent others from seeing the material, such individuals are never named, probably for two reasons: it will be impossible to draw up an exhaustive list (an incomplete list would lead precisely to the result that the material was seen by some persons who should have been excluded), and drawing attention to those who should not be informed indicates too clearly how any traitor could defeat the purpose of the classification. However, the consequence of not labelling papers in that way may be that they are not seen by some persons whom it would have been preferable to include. Though excluded individuals are not named, larger groupings (Communists, a particular country, etc.) may be.

In Britain, degrees of classification in ascending order of restrictiveness (starting with no restrictions at all) are: Open, Restricted, Confidential, Secret and Top Secret. (Open, if notified, naturally implies that a system of classification is in force in that agency.) Most Secret was renamed Top Secret during the

Second World War for the sake of agreement with US practice. Doubtless both countries also designate more specific categories, stating to which countries information may or may not be made available.

Material is classified by an official who is authorised to impose that classification. No more exact definition is possible though guidance may be offered, such as that a given classification should apply to materials which include information from certain sources. However, this does not mean that information is necessarily classified higher than opinions. In fact there is a logical problem here: opinions *are* information about what people think. Opinions can range from Open to Top Secret or beyond, depending on what topic they relate to and on whose opinions they are. If a distinction can be drawn between the official and the private persona, this can affect the classification. Persons holding an official post often claim in print to be merely expressing a personal opinion, though the disclaimer often appears precarious; it is acquiesced in because it is convenient for both parties. An individual's competence to pronounce on some subject does not in itself necessitate classifying that person's opinions, unless in some instance when it is vital to withhold that opinion from hostile persons or institutions. Einstein's letter to President Roosevelt, drawing attention to the possibility of building an atomic weapon, would be an illustration. The classification of information tends to be more stable over time than that of opinions.

The highest grades of classification are likely to apply to military and political matters, though there is no rule about this. Due to the somewhat arbitrary basis of classification, documents which are classified similarly will include items of extremely varying importance.

Known categories in the USSR are: *Ne podlezhit oglasheniyu* ('Not subject to being made public'), *Sekretno* ('Secret') and *Strogo sekretno* ('Strictly Secret'). Must this mean that *Sekretno* is equivalent to the British Secret, and *Strogo sekretno* to Top Secret? That need not follow, as usages might be different in the two countries. Moreover, the three Soviet grades cannot stand in one-to-one relationships to four British grades. The two higher Soviet grades are used in regard to decisions taken within the Party organisation (Voslensky, 1984, pp. 155–6). *Strogo sekretno* is stamped on a document which confirms the appointment by the Party of a member of the *nomenklatura* (defined as appointments which must be Party-approved) (Ibid., p. 164). As *nomenklatura* appointments do not exist in Britain it is impossible to be sure what classification would be applied here in such a case, but Top Secret seems excessive. Basing oneself on this illustration, *Strogo sekretno* might correspond roughly to Secret, while Top Secret would be equivalent to a Soviet grade which was higher than *Strogo sekretno*. *Ne podlezhit oglasheniyu* would then correspond roughly to Restricted. Apparently the special position of the Party does not receive explicit recognition in the system of grading, probably because the Party is already so deeply involved in classified matters. A local Party secretary would receive papers of local importance, probably up to quite a high level of grading.

It makes a great deal of difference precisely who is allowed to receive information. In general, the higher the grading, the higher the rank of person who is so authorised (within a given hierarchy). Thus in effect the classification can be changed simply by varying the list of authorised recipients. This may also be the reaction to breaches of security, though another possibility is to introduce new and still more limited categories. For example, in Britain a new 'super secret' classification bearing the letters CMO, which is believed to stand for 'Cabinet Ministers Only': each document will be limited to two copies (*The Times*, 30 May 1983, p. 1).

The higher the grading, the more carefully the information will be protected. This means as a rule that physical means are more secure and that information is made available to fewer persons. The number with access to each successively higher grade would diminish rapidly; perhaps by an order of magnitude, or somewhat less. Only the limits of this system are readily definable, through *reductio ad absurdum*: information which was not graded at all could be made available to everyone, while information which was infinitely secret could be made available to nobody. Indeed, information of this type could not even be gathered, unless in such a way that the gatherer could not inspect it himself; in that case, however, the classification would have to be based solely on the means used in gathering it (if it were known that *anything* had been gathered). While this seems ridiculous, it was approached in Judaism where the initials YHWH, as the name of God, were considered too sacred to

pronounce, or it might be said from the present viewpoint, too
secret; though those initials would have had to be known to the
priests, so that they could tell when the rule was being violated.

Two forces, which are mutually opposed, affect the classification of material which is regarded as confidential. Its originator
will incline to wish that it should be kept as secret as possible, so
as to minimise the risk of leakage; hence he will tend to overclassify. By contrast, the more secret the information the less is
the opportunity to make use of it (because of the risk of disclosure of the secret); hence the user will tend to underclassify.
Ordinarily, the originator makes the decision, so that as a rule
there is a tendency to overclassify; though the balance might be
shifted by a superior authority which took into account both
supplier and user interests. Thus, over time material might be
reassigned, and would possibly reflect a shift in the balance of
intelligence and user interests.

DISTRIBUTION OF CLASSIFIED MATERIAL

As there are fewer recipients, more highly classified information
is transmitted through fewer stages than less highly classified.
However, some of the final recipients in the former case are then
likely to be relatively remote, both organisationally and perhaps
geographically, from the despatch point, which suggests a risk
that information will not reach its intended destination. Furthermore, the choice of final recipients of classified information has
always to be made in the absence of direct instruction from
potential recipients that they require that particular item. Recipients can merely indicate in advance that they require to see
certain *categories* of information. Thus on either count there is a
risk that information will be maldistributed, and this applies
especially to the higher grades. The fact that intelligence-
providing agencies have to make detailed decisions about what
information should be supplied to whom places them in a
strategic position.

The larger the community, the more difficult it will become to
decide to whom a particular message should be addressed. In
some circumstances there will be a reason to advertise, that is to
say to use channels which may not be entirely secure against

information falling into the wrong hands; this risk can be mini-mised, but not entirely removed, by careful choice of the adver-tising medium. Here is one illustration where the message went astray. Late in 1941, in Nazi Germany, the SS *Bulletin of Budget and Construction* included an invitation for bids for building cre-matoria in a camp (Belzec) south-east of Lublin. This was to be one of the extermination camps, where the gassing chambers were completed in March 1942, at which time these crematoria were still under construction. This notice was seen by Oskar Schindler, who was subsequently able to save a large fraction of his Jewish workforce from the gas chambers, although when reading the announcement he had not guessed exactly how the crematoria would combine with other elements of the extermina-tion plan (Keneally, 1982, pp. 116, 130–1). In general terms, advertising media which are read by specific groups comprise a more effective, but less secure, alternative to the supply of information via closed channels. The fact that this alternative is poorly developed in the Soviet Union places a heavier load on those channels.

STORAGE OF SECRET INFORMATION

Following distribution, secret documents are either destroyed or stored. It is impossible to make any general statement about what proportion is destroyed, except that this is likely to be smaller in a country where there are more ample facilities for storage. The United States should be one example, and as described in 1976 the LBJ Library in Austin, Texas, contained one million classified papers (Divine, 1976). In the Soviet Union, such repositories are probably less conspicuous, perhaps less large, yet large all the same. It would thus be correct to suppose that mountains of secret information already exist and, of course, their bulk increases continuously.

The expansion is doubtless posing the problem of what to do next, a problem which is confronted also by libraries which house non-confidential data. It is likely that the former must tread the same path as the latter, that is to say, of placing more emphasis on microfiche and computers, and on retaining only data for which one can foresee some future use; thanks to their

inherent secretiveness, repositories of confidential data can go
faster and farther along that road than is allowable to libraries
holding non-confidential material.

The question of how long secrets need to be kept is also
relevant, and can be approached by asking oneself whether a
nation should need to keep secrets for a longer or a shorter
period than an individual needs to do. At first glance one might
think for a longer period, since a nation, unlike an individual,
has a continuous existence: at any rate (in some cases) one
extending over centuries, by comparison with human existence
lasting one century at most. I think, however, that the correct
answer is the contrary: as a rule, though with some exceptions, a
nation can be satisfied with keeping its secrets for a shorter span.
The reasons for thinking this are the following.

First, some nations have only a short life. Secondly, a nation
has – what a human being does not – a procedure (institutionalised at regular intervals in a political democracy, though that
is the exception) for replacing its government. A new administration may still wish to preserve some of the secrets of the
outgoing one, but it is likely to be willing and eager to disclose
others. We shall see that this has substantial importance in
Soviet practice. A nation is more susceptible than an individual
to scientific and technical change. Though (and to increasing
degree) people during their careers are retrained or gain additional skills, they remain partly within the envelope of skills
acquired previously. The faster is technical progress, the shorter
(other things being equal) is the span over which secrets need to
be kept. This ought to influence Soviet practice, but it is not
clear that it does.

The alliance systems and patterns of international relations
within which nations form and implement their policies tend to
be more volatile than the web of relationships that surround an
individual, although there are exceptions to that rule, of course.
The more volatile the circumstances, the shorter the period one
should find it necessary to keep a secret. More common divorce
of individuals, and increasing stability of alliances, would bring
those periods closer together; these trends have not as yet closed
the gap. The fact that an individual may need a longer span of
secrecy than a nation is illustrated by the argument that, in
Britain, the period prior to release of confidential information
should not have been reduced to as little as thirty years, because

that period is often shorter than that of a person's career (see Chapter 12). However, the Soviet Union seems to be one of the exceptions to this argument. *Its* alliances over the past forty years have not greatly altered while its system of government remains essentially unchanged through successive administrations.

PERPETUATION OF SECRECY CLASSIFICATION

Despite the comparative volatility of governments, material that is classified tends to remain so, while what is unclassified tends, similarly, to remain unclassified. This is for several reasons. A system of classification, once established, goes on functioning, its procedures tending to become permanent. Moreover, if information passes through stages 1 and 2, secret information which has passed through stage 1 is unlikely to be declassified at stage 2, as the fact that it had previously been classified would then be disclosed; while not an absolute bar, this might cause embarrassment. Non-secret information which passes through two stages will not be made secret at stage 2 because it will already have been revealed at stage 1. Thirdly, what is communicated illegally must be kept secret in order not to compromise the source. If counter-intelligence has not detected any leak, that body will not be eager to disclose its mistake (cf. Pincher, 1984). Finally, when secret papers are superannuated they will probably be destroyed (see below). For similar reasons, the *degree* of classification is unlikely to be altered (though the likelihood is slightly greater).

This perpetuation illustrates a situation which is of broader extent. For example, among the English middle classes it remains normal not to enquire into a friend's income (i.e. it is tacitly agreed that this may remain secret), though that income has to be divulged to the inland revenue. Similarly, it is still felt that 'an Englishman's home is his castle' although in actuality a variety of officials can insist on entry. In Turkey, veiling was discouraged by President Ataturk (1925) yet still today, in rural districts of Anatolia, women are swathed to an extent that is by no means demanded by the climate, even if the strict veiling which is enforced in Saudi Arabia is no longer practised (Lewis, 1974, pp. 102–4, and own or others' observations in Turkey and Saudi Arabia, 1985).

While the tendency is for a given classification to be preserved, if any change does take place it will be the new classification that thereafter tends to be perpetuated. This might be called a 'ratchet principle'. The example of this happening which is likely to have most importance is if the classification is reduced to Open, which due to the factors mentioned above will most probably result from action by persons who are outside the classification system and who wish to subvert it. If that happens, there may be no choice but to continue to reveal that type of information, at least in part. The publication of the Russian budget from 1861 onwards, following disclosures by émigrés of the unpublished figures (Hutchings, 1982A, pp. 16–17) is an illustration. As this example shows, people who want to bring about such a result should try to bring to light data which are of a type that is collected periodically.

SECRET SHARING

Nations share certain of their secrets. There are obvious difficulties in writing about the subject but some conjectures are possible. The pattern of secret sharing will be related quite closely to that of alliances, but may extend a little farther although, naturally, not including any country which might be suspected of sharing such information with any country belonging to an adversarial alliance. Secret sharing requires a degree of stability in an alliance, and confidence that it will not be disrupted. It may require a certain similarity in intelligence communities and even some congruity in the governmental and administrative structures.

If secret information, something that is believed to be particularly important, is exchanged, this is a signal mark of confidence and friendship and will be so understood by both parties. The sharing of secret information will therefore help to make an alliance last longer. Conversely, if among alliance partners the interflow of confidential material ceases, this is a sign that the alliance has suffered some severe blow and is probably on the way to dissolution. Of course, it is not likely that a country will exchange *all* information with another one: if it did, it might in some sense cease to be sovereign, even to the extent that it would be otherwise. Some secret information may be passed to non-alliance governments with its origin disguised, such as 'Ultra' material which was passed directly to Stalin from the British ambassador (*Sunday Times*, 20 July 1980, p. 2). The sharing of secrets has to be distinguished from a situation of dominance by one country of another, which results in the former knowing the secrets of the latter but the latter not knowing those of the former.

PRIVACY

Where secrets are shared, problems may arise owing to different criteria of secrecy, differing estimates of the value of the shared information, or different understandings of what is meant by privacy. By one formulation, privacy is 'the claim of individuals, groups or institutions to determine for themselves when, how, and to what extent information about them is communicated to others' (Westin, 1971, p. xi). Certain writers in the volume from which this citation is taken would have extended the concept even further. My own interpretation is narrower: to me privacy signifies merely freedom from observation when performing activities or functions, the general nature of which is known and publicly approved, or at least is not criminal, and it applies to individuals more than to groups or institutions. If this is, as I think, the more common understanding of the term in Britain, it differs from the American formulation quoted above. It can then be very readily imagined that there is also a difference between the British and the Soviet conceptions, and even more between the US and the Soviet ones. This is supported by what has (or has not) been done in legislation: it has occurred to the Americans to legislate in favour of privacy, and they have done so; it has occurred to the British, but we have not done so; while to the Russians it has probably not occurred. The difference must reflect in part degrees of affluence: privacy is expensive, so is likely to be correlated with living standards generally. Social *mores* are influential too. The result is that as regards the mass of the people, there is less privacy in Britain than in the United States, and less in the Soviet Union than in Britain.

But it is important to note that at top political levels these relationships are exactly reversed. The personal life of the President of the United States is to a large extent non-private; in other

Western democracies the leadership can enjoy somewhat greater privacy, while in Eastern Europe and the USSR the leadership enjoys total privacy. Thus, replying to a question from a British listener about Jenoe Fock, at that time Prime Minister of Hungary, Budapest English language programme observed that his wife was a talented painter and his daughter a noted biologist: 'One would have to put a lot of effort into finding out this much about the Prime Minister's family, because the socialist mass media work on the principle that the issue of everyone's private life is their affair' (SWB EE/4904/A1/5, 15 May 1975, Budapest in English 21:30 gmt 13 May 1975). The same, or an even greater, degree of privacy surrounds the Soviet leaders: they live in seclusion, protected by tall fences, armed guards, anonymity of residence. Thus, at the top level, extent of privacy as governed by comparative affluence of the different countries is stood on its head. At this level, considerations which determine privacy are absorbed and overridden by those that decide the degree of the secrecy.

The example shows that to award an extreme degree of privacy can result in an overall deprivation of rights rather than a conferring of them, because it constricts possibilities of investigation and comment. In Eastern Europe this deplorable result is concealed behind a smokescreen of self-righteous concern for individual privacy.

HOW TO KEEP A SECRET INCONSPICUOUS

Various illustrations have already been provided of what are evidently attempts to keep secrets inconspicuous. More generally, in any circumstances (such as spatial circumstances) where there is more than one dimension to be considered, there is often a choice between out-of-the-way-ness and multiple alternatives. (One may, however, resort to both.) If a secret is not fixed in one place, it will often be easier to preserve it. Where (as with time) there is only one dimension, concealment becomes less easy and it therefore becomes more important to behave in an unpredictable manner. Also, there should not be many people in the know; indeed there should be as few as possible. What is not revealed should be important but known to few, and not carrying a high incentive to reveal it. However, a clear contradiction and possible clash is embodied here: the fewer the people in the know, the larger can be the potential reward to whoever discloses the secret. If it is not revealed, one must suppose that this is overborne by a still stronger disincentive. Apart from loyalty and honour, this may be supplied by the fact that *if* one has made an illicit disclosure, the likelihood of avoiding detection is reduced approximately in proportion to the reduction in the number of people known to be aware of the secret.

If intending to keep secret a general situation, when others are interested in ferreting it out, one must aim to do more than to keep secret specific facts and circumstances. As Thomas Carlyle put it: 'He that has a secret should not only hide it, but hide that he has it to hide' (Frank and Weisband, 1974, p. 224). Of course, the fact that one is aware of this maxim and acts upon it should itself be concealed.

Clearly, this is a difficult task. The more effectively gaps are filled in, the less possible it may become to keep the whole operation free from observation; yet if the operation becomes non-secret, its purpose may ultimately be frustrated. It is true that in one case secretiveness about keeping a secret can make that easier to penetrate: this is where 'jargon' is used, i.e. a code which replaces only certain key words by others: if the true equivalents are discovered the whole message at once becomes readable (Kahn, 1969, p. 520). Against this, and more generally, demonstrative secrecy stimulates efforts to penetrate it, which adds to the fun of intelligence work. Almost certainly, no country has ever been studied from the outside as intensively as the Soviet Union has been since the Second World War, and its almost ostentatious secrecy has undoubtedly been among the reasons. The Russians never seem to have fully realised or acted upon Carlyle's maxim, or perhaps they simply fail to appreciate what an impression their attitudes make on the outside world.

In principle, and therefore in practice, secretiveness and secrecy may change at different rates, or even in different directions. The relationship between secrecy and range of secretiveness is positive over a wider scale than that of secrecy to intensity of secretiveness, owing to the mutually reinforcing effect of blacking out one area after another, so that fewer and fewer clues are left. But extending the range of secretiveness also tends to dilute attention and facilities for keeping secret any specific matter: safes and lockable filing cabinets run out, occasions for accidental laxity are multiplied, and the justification for keeping secret a particular thing is liable to appear less. Above all, if there is any chance that one was not suspected of harbouring a secret, extending the range of secretiveness will diminish that chance or extinguish it. In private life, therefore, it may be best to try to keep nothing secret except the secret one really does want to keep, provided that this is not encroached on by the rest. The principle should also apply in national affairs, but probably less strongly owing to their wider ramifications. Below its lower limits, if secretiveness decreases, although secrecy continues to decrease (until zero level is reached), the novel directions being opened up are liable to be not immediately relevant to the subject under discussion – though they may open up other avenues.

DECLASSIFICATION

A high proportion of secrets is intended to be kept for only a limited period. Here the policy to be followed is partly governed by disclosure policy, such as in the phenomenon of the 'release date'. When a programme has reached a sufficiently advanced stage, it may be deemed permissible for the secret to leak out. The French began to show off their *force de frappe* in 1974 probably because it had by then attained a degree of credibility (Rutherford, 1974, p. 7). Though its results are normally published at the beginning of August, in 1982 British Airways chose not to publish them until 8 October. It was perhaps the intention not to disclose the size of the 1981 loss until its impact could be lessened by the improvement expected in the first six months of 1982 (*The Times*, 9 July 1982, p. 1).

Where a decision to declassify must consider only the importance of the information, it usually is taken more readily, and at an earlier date, than where the method of obtaining the information must also be considered. An important corollary of this is that secret information relating to another country is less likely to be declassified than that relating to the country which is considering whether to declassify. Correspondingly, we find in Soviet practice a much greater variability in release of data relating to the USSR itself than in release of data about some other country; in fact, this difference is especially marked.

Declassification is often undertaken after deliberation, but sometimes it is precipitate. The rather arbitrary basis of classification allows scope for declassification for special purposes. Thus following the resignation of Michael Heseltine as Defence Minister (in Britain) various relevant papers were promptly declassified, in support of one side or the other. (See *The Times*, 10 January 1986 and immediately following issues.) This example would not be followed in the Soviet Union as there the dramatised resignation is unknown.

If compelled to reveal a secret, should one do so all at once, or only in part, so that part or all of the rest may have to be revealed, and may in fact be revealed, later? In favour of making a clean breast is the fact that the likelihood of the rest being ferreted out is increased by the disclosure of only a part of it. Against this, what is not revealed may be much more worthwhile keeping secret than what is; releasing the part may also divert attention from the more important fraction that still remains. A formal answer might be that disclosure should be halted at the point where the importance of keeping secret the remainder is increasing, while the likelihood of discovery is declining; in practice, the situation may be less clear-cut.

It appears to be especially difficult for the Soviet Union to make a clean breast, and several reasons, which are explored in later chapters, can be imagined: these include the concentric barriers against release of secret information and a preconception, ingrained over centuries when modern technical means were not available, that Russia can keep secret whatever she wishes.

Revealing a secret often creates a powerful impression, which is due partly to the news itself and partly to its timing. The timing will probably aim either to soften the impact or to sharpen it. The effect of the revelation is cushioned if no conflict is present between the person or agency which reveals the secret and those to whom the secret applies. Generally, the timing of any revelation of a secret which relates to the same agency as reveals the secret is likely to be somewhat forced, due to realisation that if the secret is not revealed now it must be shortly – and with even more unpleasant results.

It is, of course, unlikely that a party which is guilty in a particular instance will take the initiative in bringing the facts to light. This obvious relationship can sometimes be helpful: for example, it becomes unlikely that the Nazis, who discovered and publicised the Katyn murders of Polish officers, were themselves responsible for them. However, over a sufficiently long time-span disclosure of secrets by the authority that first decided to keep them secret is probably not uncommon (the composition of that authority in terms of individuals having perhaps altered in the interim). If disclosure is restricted to a finite group about disgraceful actions of members of a given body, other members of that body are likely to be the first to hear about them. Khrushchev's secret speech in February 1956, which revealed to current Communist Party members the crimes committed by Stalin against past members, exemplifies the point.

A sudden revelation of what the *other* side had intended to keep secret can have an explosive impact, so its timing is important. Khrushchev's secret speech at the XXth Party Congress, which fell into American hands, illustrates this too.

VALIDITY AND UTILISATION OF SECRET INFORMATION

The value of unauthorised access to another nation's secrets depends on which nation gains access to them and when. It is usually greatest to whatever nation is mentioned directly, and is likely to be much greater in wartime, or in a period of active preparation for war, for two reasons: the most valuable items relate to defence, and such material becomes rather quickly out of date. A classic example of a document which was especially valuable to a nation that was actively preparing for war was a British Chief of Staff report which admitted British military weakness in the Far East: in 1941 this fell into German hands and they brought it to the notice of the Japanese, who as a result sharply upgraded their estimate of the probable success of a Japanese attack in a two-front war against the United States and Britain (Andrew, 1986, pp. 2–4). I am not aware of any such coup by Soviet intelligence, though there may have been one, or indeed more than one.

A decision whether to make use of secret information must hinge on whether it is believed. If it originates from unique access, by definition no other verification can be obtained. There is then a sort of trade-off between the unexpectedness of the information and its reliability: if the information is not unexpected its reliability is higher, but its usefulness is less, while very unexpected information might be much more useful, yet one may not be able to rely upon it. The only way out of this dilemma is to obtain information by means which do not require unique access.

The exploitation of secret information, by whatever country, frequently encounters a further dilemma. If the information has not been gathered for the sake of amusement – and though it must be pleasant to know things that others do not, this indeed is not the purpose – it must have been gathered for the sake of its usefulness as a guide to action. In other words, it must be possible to take action on the basis of secret intelligence which is different from, and more advantageous than, the action that would have been taken otherwise.

However, even if gathering and processing secret intelligence has not drawn attention to itself, action taken on its basis may well do so. Should one then risk compromising the means, or not do so and as a result possibly lose an opportunity for gaining a victory, or averting a defeat? During the Second World War, from the British side, this dilemma was encountered a number of times in practice. Thus, Mr Churchill knew from secret sources that Coventry would be the target of the next massive German air raid. It would have been possible to order more radical measures, such as evacuation of the city, but since that would have revealed that the British had this foreknowledge, and it was considered paramount that that should not become known, it was decided only to alert all civil defence services; the RAF also had time to put their counter measures into action (Winter-botham, 1974, pp. 94–5). Similarly, Churchill knew from 'Ultra' what the German response would be to the British despatch of food parcels to the Channel Islands. but was obliged to wait for the German official response (Ramsey, 1981, pp. 43–4). As regards Soviet experience, one example of a link between infor-mation and its use as a basis for action has been the way that Soviet space research became more secret as the opportunity to use it for military purposes increased. In general, one would expect the USSR to be at least as sensitive as other countries to the possibility that injudicious use would enable its sources to be compromised.

If secret information is intended as a guide to action, and yet action cannot in fact be taken, of what use is the information?

The usefulness of secret intelligence is indeed diminished as a result, but not to zero. The following considerations are relevant.

It must not be concluded, from mention of specific occasions when it was not reckoned allowable to take action, that this is how things are either invariably or normally. In the nature of the case, occasions when action *was* taken on the basis of secret intelligence are themselves very likely to be kept secret, at any rate as far as possible, or at least one will hide the fact that secret information had been the trigger. As we now know, various decisions were in fact reached during the Second World War on the basis of secret information, although this was not disclosed at the time or indeed for long afterwards. It is then but a small step to conclude that, in all probability, there were other occasions too which have not yet been disclosed.

Again, necessary decisions are of many different sorts, and a number will not draw attention to themselves. A decision to take action may be conspicuous; one to take no action is much less likely to be noticed, but is a decision nonetheless and might be just as momentous. There can be occasions – one hopes these may be rare – when the importance of taking action overrides, perhaps by a wide margin, the importance of not compromising the source. If the fact that information from a given source is being gathered becomes known to a possible adversary and that fact in turn becomes known to whatever agency would take the decision, inhibitions on using the information will disappear and the likelihood of action is consequently increased. This needs to be realised by whoever imagines that by giving publicity to some form of secret information they will diminish the likelihood that action, based on that information, will be taken: exactly the contrary is true.

Another use of secret intelligence is to confirm or deny the correctness, hence the reliability, of open sources. This may be of substantial use if there is no other way to evaluate them. It may sometimes be possible to ascribe foreknowledge, which actually had been gained from secret information, to open sources – if, for example, these had been interpreted with special acuity. Much information is useful as background, rather than as instigating any specific action in the immediate future. Here again, secret sources can play their full part. Much of the information that is gathered by foreign offices would fall into that category. Finally, if action is seen as indispensable and yet as not permissible by oneself in order not to compromise the source, it may be possible to share the information, or certain conclusions drawn from it, with a nation that is not so inhibited.

The general conclusion is that secret information can and does play a very important role, despite the limitations which are sometimes imposed by the perceived need not to compromise the source.

OPPOSITION BETWEEN COVERT AND OVERT ACTIVITIES

In their foreign policies, nations sometimes pursue over short or medium length periods an overt policy and another that is secret, and which is partly or even wholly in contradiction to the overt policy. The supply of US arms to Iran (revealed late in 1986) is an illustration; the Soviet Union too is capable of pursuing contradictory policies, for instance one in pursuit of state interests and another that envisages ideological goals. The circumstances when such contradictions may occur could form the subject of an interesting enquiry, but one that mainly falls outside the scope of this book. In one respect, however, such a situation is relevant: the overt pursuit of a different policy helps to keep covert actions secret, because it tends to head off potential investigators into alternative directions. This benefit is gained at the expense of possibly rendering nugatory one of the policies or even both of them!

This chapter has looked at a number of issues relating to secret-keeping, primarily from a theoretical angle but with various allusions to experience, including Soviet experience. Chapters 3 to 10 now look directly at the case of the Soviet Union.

3 The Soviet Setting

The origins of secretiveness are embedded deeply in Russian and Soviet history and other circumstances, including geography and the intellectual sphere.

HISTORY

Throughout history Russia has been a prey to invaders, despite which Russian (now Soviet) territories have been almost continuously expanding, and yet, except over the past forty years, the invasions have not stopped. Russian attitudes to secretiveness were formed in the earlier period, so the latest experience of domination of weaker neighbours is irrelevant. During the period of defeat and withdrawal, secretiveness was a defensive tactic. The Mongols, having extended their direct rule over the Ukraine, acted as suzerain but not as direct ruler of the less accessible forested lands to the north; there, Muscovy established itself, first as a principality and then as the nucleus of a relentlessly expanding empire.

If the habitable part of European Russia may be divided into a steppe zone and a forest zone, the victory of the Mongols in the thirteenth century, at a time when the boundary between these zones was more clearly defined than it is today, signified in effect the victory of the steppe over the forest. By contrast, the subsequent expansion of Muscovy signified the victory of the forest zone over the steppes. The forest being inherently more capable of guarding secrets than the steppe, Muscovy's triumph in effect meant the victory of the more secretive region. If a geographical basis is required to explain the importance of secrecy in Russian history, this sequence may supply it.

Some of the most notorious episodes in Russian history and literature are connected with secretiveness. When Catherine the Great visited the Ukraine, her viceroy, Potemkin, had erected façades along her route which concealed the squalor in which the peasants actually lived. In practice, perfect secrecy and complete ability to observe are impossible to combine and the more secret the observer tries to be, as a rule the more imperfect will be the observation. Thus, in the Forbidden City in Peking the Chinese emperors would know little about how their subjects lived, and the Potemkin villages exemplified how the Russian Tsar might be deceived. Gogol's *The Government Inspector* hilariously portrayed the supposedly incognito visit of such an inspector to a small provincial town. His 'Dead Souls' described how an enterprising speculator made a profit, or tried to, out of mortgaging serfs who, though dead, remained on the books until the next census, that is to say whose deaths had been kept secret. In general, serfdom – which was not abolished until 1861 – strongly impelled towards secretiveness, among the serfs to protect themselves, among the serf-owners to preserve the system, and so far as the state was concerned to put the best face on the system's oppressiveness.

The non-formation of a powerful and responsible middle class is another important reason for a secretive tradition. The habit of being able to demand information from the government had little chance to develop. Although the Duma (set up after the Revolution of 1905) did useful work in publishing accounts and statistics (Hutchings, 1982A, p. 17), this came too late to expunge the ingrained tradition of secretiveness. A Russian civil service rank was 'secret councillor' (*taynyy sovetnik*) – probably taken over directly from the German *Geheimrat*. Finally – as will be explored further below, in Chapter 11 – the conspiratorial experience of the Bolsheviks was still another powerful influence.

To sum up, the Soviet Union inherited a double or treble dose of secretiveness from its national history.

THE OUTSIDE WORLD

This was compounded by the hostility of the outside world, much of which treated the Soviet Union as a pariah. In its extremest form this did not last very long, even if events such as the Communist uprising in Hungary, led by Bela Kun who was financed by Russia (1919), are disregarded. The Treaty of Rapallo between Russia and Germany (April 1922) constituted the first real break in the *cordon sanitaire* drawn by the Allies to contain Bolshevik Russia. It did not so much diminish Russian secretiveness as afford it a wider scope, for a secret provision of the treaty provided for German aviation training within Russia, out of reach of inspection authorised by the Treaty of Versailles; naturally, Russia also benefited. Throughout the inter-war period the world, with the sole exception of Outer Mongolia (1924 onwards) remained stubbornly un-Communist, and this tended to intensify Soviet secretiveness. Only after the Second World War did the international situation alter, and that was chiefly due to Soviet expansionism.

GEOGRAPHICAL EXPANSION

It has to be noted that over the centuries Russia has encroached upon the outside world. Whenever a certain type of governmental system is diffused into other regions, attitudes to secrecy which are conjoined in that polity are also likely to be diffused. This is illustrated in the spreading overseas of the British type of parliamentary government (see Chapter 12). Similarly, the expansion from the nucleus of Muscovy into the Tsarist Empire stretching right across to the Pacific Ocean, to the Pamirs and the Caucasus, in the absence of any fundamental change in the system of government, resulted in a corresponding territorial extension of Muscovite attitudes and practices in regard to secrecy. The inaccessibility of Siberia and its use as a destination of exile brought the result of making secrecy in these outlying regions still more intense.

BACKWARDNESS

The concentration on territorial expansion at the expense of other objectives is one of the reasons for Russian backwardness. Russia is chronically backward in many respects by comparison with the most advanced countries, and this contributes a strong motive not to disclose features or events which would create an unfavourable impression or an impression of weakness. However, harsh oppression needs to be concealed from visiting foreigners of liberal persuasion, yet at the same time, lest it lose its deterrent effect, it must not be concealed from those whom it is intended to oppress – which is an enduring complication.

INSTITUTIONS

The Tsarist censorship (which is considered in a little more detail in Chapter 7) was officially brought to an end by the Bolshevik Revolution (Choldin, 1984, p. 9). If that happened at all in practice, any period during which no censorship existed in Russia was exceedingly short. The Decree on the Press, adopted on 27 October 1917 (Old Style), only two days after the Bolsheviks seized power, was the first Soviet measure of censorship – though it was declared to be temporary. (As the French say, nothing lasts like the temporary.) The decree described the 'bourgeois press' as 'one of the most powerful weapons of the bourgeoisie', being 'no less dangerous than bombs and machine-guns' (Matthews, 1974, pp. 18–19). The 'Chief Administration for the Preservation of State Secrets in the Press' was set up in June 1922 – in advance of the USSR itself. This body is the strict successor to the Tsarist censorship. Of course, we cannot as a general rule expect decisions relating to the censorship to be made public.

The last published statute on the subject was a Decree of the People's Commissars of the RSFSR of 6 June 1931, which set up the Chief Administration for Affairs of Literature and Publishing (the Soviet title in brief being Glavlit) and its Local Organs. Its function was 'to effect political, ideological, military and economic control of all kinds over printed works, manuscripts, photographs, pictures, etc. as well as radio programmes, lectures and exhibitions, which are intended for publication or distribution'. ('Control' here has more of the sense of supervision.) Only publications of the Communist Party and of the Academy of Sciences were not subject to political and ideological control, but for these as well Glavlit and its local organs were 'charged with ensuring the complete preservation of state secrets by means of preliminary perusal of them'. Glavlit representatives would be installed in publishing houses and maintained at the latters' expense (Matthews, 1974, pp. 71–3). There is every reason to believe that this organisation still exists and that it carries out approximately the same functions.

Disclosure of information by people who are not authorised to disclose it is forbidden. This is a tautology, but in the USSR the enforcement is especially strict. According to a Law on Criminal Liability for State Crimes, which was approved by the Supreme

Soviet on 25 December 1958, handing over a state or military secret may be treated as High Treason, and punished by death or by deprivation of freedom for ten to fifteen years, in either case with confiscation of property; or as Espionage, with similar penalties except that deprivation of freedom may be from seven to fifteen years; or as Divulging a State Secret, which is punishable by deprivation of freedom for two to five years, or if it has grave consequences for five to eight years; while Loss of Documents Containing a State Secret is punishable by deprivation of freedom for one to three years, or if with grave consequences for three to eight years (Matthews, 1974, pp. 283, 285).

In contrast (and in brief, as arrangements in other countries are examined in Chapter 12), United States laws normally require disclosure of information; according to some views this ensures a 'flow of secrets to Russia' (*D.T.*, 14 January 1984, p. 6). The USSR also lacks any regular arrangements for terminating secrecy. In the USA or Britain, government bodies may well try to act in secret but in the course of time this may be exposed by some independent agency. In the Soviet Union this is either impossible or far less likely, there being there no constitutional division of powers. Less simply, the political stability of the Soviet Union tends to inhibit effective secrecy in relation to foreign observers (which enables greater continuity in study of the USSR) but also to intensify it (there is less movement of persons into or out of government, as well as within government posts). However, while this circumstance may operate in either direction, on the whole secrecy has been promoted. The fact that previously confidential information has tended to be revealed immediately following a change in the leadership supports this conclusion (see Chapter 8).

To monitor with complete effectiveness the writing of history, one needs to control the availability of source material. It is believed that this requirement came to a head in the political infighting following Lenin's death in January 1924, which led to the discrediting and subsequent exiling of Trotsky, with Party members being ordered to transmit to the Central Committee of the Soviet Communist Party all materials which were in any way related to the Central Committee archive and to Party history (Ploss, 1972, p. 32).

THE PRESS AND EDUCATION

The Soviet press, under strict Party management, is docile and makes no attempt to ferret out secrets, in sharp contrast to the Western press which tries to do just that. The absence of a free press is an enormously important aid to maintaining secrecy. In Western countries the press almost invariably supports individuals who challenge state secrecy, irrespective of party. How useful it is, when seeking to preserve official secrets, not to have a free press was well illustrated in the efforts of the US government to keep secret Space Shuttle Mission 51-C. Although at the Pentagon's request NBC, the Associated Press and *Aviation Week & Space Technology* held off stories about the mission, *The Washington Post* soon reported that 51-C would launch a satellite which was able to intercept signals intelligence (*Time*, 31 December 1984, p. 16). Under the Soviet systems there is little scope either for raising voluntary funds. It was raising funds by popular appeal that led to the disclosure of the then still continuing airlift to Israel of Ethiopian Jews (*The Times*, 5 January 1985, p. 9).

The Bolsheviks with a large measure of success set out to abolish illiteracy, their main purpose being that workers and peasants should be able to read the Bolshevik decrees, orders and proclamations; according to Lenin's possibly apocryphal remark this was even the sole purpose (Annenkov, 1966, p. 270, cited in Taylor, 1980, p. 65).

The growth of literacy has doubtless had beneficial effects of great importance for education and scientific research, *inter alia*; however, it is our business here to notice its impact on the censorship, which must have been to require a broad extension in its scope, coupled with a shift of emphasis away from intellectual publications towards the mass media. The educational system too has been developed with an eye to conformity and, as one aspect of conformity, to the preservation of secrets. The compulsory grounding in Marxism–Leninism is the clearest expression of the ideological basis of Soviet education.

The tremendous expansion of Soviet education over time, to include far larger numbers of people, educated for a longer span and embracing a much wider range of subjects, must still have been in many respects antagonistic to the preservation of secrets. In relation to a given universe of knowledge the possible frontiers of confidentiality have been contracted. At the same time, that universe has greatly expanded both in fundamental knowledge and in innumerable details, so that perhaps on the whole the scope for secretiveness has not been reduced.

About a third of the Soviet population is claimed to be undergoing instruction of some kind. Its scientists have multiplied more than a hundredfold since 1913. The system must evolve if it is not to be swept away by an advancing tide of unsupervised information, engulfing more and more people. As Roger Bacon wrote, 'he who will not apply new remedies must expect new evils'. In these evolving circumstances, to maintain an even partly effective information control has been no slight achievement.

INTERNAL ECONOMIC POLICY

The adoption in August 1921 of the New Economic Policy (NEP) was favourable to some relaxation of secrecy, as the new policy extended some opportunity to both domestic and foreign enterprise, which could flourish only in conditions when an adequate volume of information was available within the public domain. Also in 1921 the State Planning Commission (Gosplan) was set up, and NEP was eventually succeeded by the era of long-term economic plans (October 1928 onwards). The directive planning system, which over time embraced successively larger segments of the economy, has brought the result that certain data are published about plans and their fulfilment, which under a system of private enterprise there was no occasion to report. On the other hand, a whole range of information connected with private business has totally disappeared. Various transformations in the economic scene, in particular industrialisation, also modified the picture. Quantity of output became the chief goal. At the same time, in both industry and agriculture, the average size of units increased, and hierarchies were formed, so that it became normal to rely to a large extent on information which was transmitted within hierarchical networks – information which was not made public.

Soviet industrialisation may have included as a by-product developing the ability to build complicated coding and decoding machines, and other apparatus required for recording, transmitting and guarding secret information. It is less likely that the ability to design such machines was developed, both because Soviet design ability in general has tended to lag behind Soviet manufacturing ability (Hutchings, 1976) and because other prototypes were already available. By the early 1920s, three types of encyphering machine had been developed; since they were offered on the international market (Rusbridger, 1986, p. 7) it is likely that the Soviet government bought examples of one of more types.

GEOGRAPHY, TERRAIN AND VEGETATION

Soviet geography is on the whole well adapted for secrecy. The Western frontiers are not protected by any mountain barrier (though the Pripet marshes are an obstacle to movement in one sector); the Caucasus present an obstacle to entry from the south. Mountain areas within the USSR are extremely extensive but mainly remote from inhabited areas. On the other hand, the country is huge – 22.4 million square kilometres, which is 2.4 times as large as the entire United States, for instance. This confers substantial advantages in preserving secrets: there is more territory for any observer to scan, and it is probably longer from the borders to any specific place. Hence the opportunity to hide any particular site or base tends to be great. On the other hand, if breadth of territory is accompanied by sparsity of transportation routes, as is rather likely, this limits the areas to which an object can conveniently be transported and consequently makes it harder to keep the secret, as observers can focus on places which are accessible.

The principle can also apply when the Soviet Union is a starting point or a destination. One illustration is to be found in the deployment of Soviet submarines. The squadron in the Mediterranean receives submarines not from the Black Sea Fleet, though this would be nearest, but from the Northern and Baltic Fleets: the reason is the Montreux Convention, which restricts the passage of submarines through the Turkish straits (Schoelwer, 1986, p. 179). Surveillance can therefore be focused on the exits from the base areas of the Northern and Baltic Fleets.

However, on the whole, size, isolation and remoteness from frontiers make for unusually favourable circumstances for secret keeping.

The relatively compact territory is also of assistance, in that messages or consignments need not as a rule cross foreign borders; however, the generous geographical dimensions of the Soviet Union entail a sizeable time-lag (and expense) if one is to rely on physical transmission of information to far-flung outposts. We find during the Soviet period a rapid growth of aviation, including the number of passengers carried on internal routes. This, of course, is not peculiar to the USSR, yet the growth in air passenger traffic in the USSR has been remarkable: between 1940 and 1981 the number of passengers carried rose by 272 times, passenger-kilometres by 860 times (*Narodnoye* . . ., 1982, p. 352). The volume of information transmitted by this medium should also have increased enormously, though probably not by quite so many times. The volume of freight, including mail, carried by air over the same period increased by 54 times, the freight times distance by 133 times (Ibid.).

For transmission over shorter distances one would expect an increase in overland traffic, which would be even harder to relate directly to information transmission. One would expect too a considerable augmentation of numbers of units for disseminating information – typewriters, duplicating machines and so on. One would expect a multiplication in numbers of radio transmitters, including microwave transmitters, which lend themselves less readily than others to interception. As far as my limited information extends, microwave installations have indeed become more numerous.

If a larger area is conducive to secrecy, a larger population is more likely to be inimical to it. For in this case the number of people who get to know about a particular secret project is likely to be bigger than in a country with a smaller population. (That number may, however, be a smaller *proportion* of the total population.) Hence, the advantages of a large country in keeping secrets apply particularly to fixed installations in relatively remote locations. It is perhaps noteworthy in this connection that Novosibirsk, where the regional science centre Akademgorodok was established in 1963, and which for the first few years after its foundation was out of bounds to foreigners (Hutchings, 1976, pp. 22–3) is about as far from the Soviet state frontier as it is possible to get. On the other hand, the larger country that wishes to preserve its secrets would be well advised not to concentrate them too obviously within a few remote regions.

There are other factors which operate against the ability of the bigger nation to keep its secrets. If the country is important, its secrets will be considered to be important also, so other countries will devote more effort to trying to penetrate them. If it is large in population, this probably means that more individuals outside the country speak its language. The bigger country is likely to have more complicated and wide-ranging links with foreign countries, through trade and otherwise. The bigger country is more likely than a smaller one to be 'normal' statistically in regard to indices which can be reckoned both for itself and for other countries. For example, the ratio of males to females born in the Soviet Union is much closer to the world ratio than is the Albanian one. Finally, a larger number of quantities relating to the bigger country can be compared with quantities relating to other countries.

Let us now consider the question of terrain. The great Russian plain is featureless and monotonous; for instance, Leningrad *oblast'*, which is one-third the area of the whole of Britain, is entirely of uniform aspect. This may help in concealing sites, such as airfields, which do not demand much modification of the landscape; in contrast, among the Alps airstrips stand out 'like Band-Aids' (McPhee, 1984, p. 21), though to an untrained observer, even from quite close quarters, one may look like a river bed (private source). There may be a risk that the natural cover will provoke slackness in adopting more deliberate precautions, as in June 1941 when air force planes were drawn up 'in parade formation' on aerodromes, in gleaming aluminium, as nobody had given any thought to camouflaging them (Salisbury, 1969, p. 76). However, in an otherwise uninhabited landscape any installation will stand out the more clearly: for example, American astronauts had no difficulty in identifying the Soviet missile launching site at Choybalsan in Mongolia, which is a focus of activity in the middle of otherwise empty plains (Francis and Jones, 1984, pp. 55, 57).

The vegetation too is highly important. In general, secrets are hidden much more easily in forest or jungle than in open ground. This has great importance even today, as the Vietnam War showed. In the Second World War, the guerrilla movement in the USSR was much stronger in the forested areas in the north of European Russia than in the treeless vicinity of Odessa. Among physical features of an economy, one of the most visible from above is field patterns. The transition from long strips, at right angles to the St Lawrence river, to larger square fields marks the transition from the areas of French settlement in Canada to those of British settlement. In countries with a collectivised agriculture, fields are large and with squarish or more irregular shapes, in distinction to the smaller, longer and narrower strips which characterise peasant agriculture. One can see this difference when overflying the frontier between Bulgaria and Turkish Thrace. (My own observation.) However, along the border between the USSR and China along the Amur river, a difference is no less visible: both sides of the river are Marxist but the Chinese, with more mouths to feed but with less mechanical equipment, have retained a network of peasant cultivation which has been abandoned on the other river bank (Francis and Jones, 1984, pp. 55–6). For almost half the year (roughly mid-November to mid-April) a large fraction of the USSR is under snow. The effect of snow to aerial observation depends on how thick it is and on the feature being observed. A light dusting of snow brings field patterns and transport routes into clearer relief (Short et al., 1976, plates 76, 163).

SECRECY AND ATHEISM

I now start to consider non-material instrumentalities. The English words 'secret' and 'sacred' come from the same etymological root. In either case, the original notion would have been of something that is apart from and loftier than the mass of mankind. In present-day Britain this affinity is no longer felt, but in countries where the prevailing attitude remains that government is apart from and higher than the mass of the people, the notions sacred and secret continue to be close. People there seem to acquiesce that there are some things which they cannot be told. Where that attitude has been outgrown, 'sacred' becomes attached to religious agencies and 'secret' to secular ones. It would seem to follow that an ampler interpretation of what should be kept secret would be found in societies which do not offer an opportunity to hive off what is sacred into a different department of life. In these societies a larger fraction of secrecy can be identified with secrecy in public affairs.

The emergence of Communist ideology as the only politically acceptable ideology in the Soviet Union was taking place at about the same time as a supersession of religious beliefs among substantial numbers of the population, and accompanying this transition the connotation of 'sacred' was transferred to the doings of the Communist Party which is the mainspring and channel of that ideology: this at least is the causal relationship that I envisage. If 'secret' and 'sacred' are considered as diverging at some point in time in Western societies, in the Soviet Union this divergence has, in consequence, not taken place; their time-scale in this respect seeming earlier to us than it does to themselves.

The instrumentality that brings about the result that religiosity and secrecy tend to be negatively correlated is institutional as well as conceptual. A religious hierarchy is a ready-made instrument for uncovering secrets (within limits) and for spreading information. The latter we see today in Poland. As regards the former, in the Philippines the Catholic Church possessed a better intelligence system than anything the Marcos government could muster (*Sunday Times Magazine*, 3 March 1985, p. 44). As regards fiction, Father Brown suffices as a parallel. Albania, where all institutional religion was declared terminated in 1967, is one of the most secretive of all the East European countries. In present-day theocratic Iran, under Khomeini, the religion is the state, so naturally secret and sacred are rolled into one, making an unusually tight package.

Secular states, such as the Communist ones, are in fact more secretive than Western ones where institutional religion is not deliberately disadvantaged. That might be coincidental, and nothing is more certain than that secretiveness is affected by multiple influences; the suggested link between state secrecy and repression of organised religion is at least not dramatically violated. So far as the USSR is concerned, the theorem holds good: here is a secular state, where indeed atheism is the official religion. More generally, plurality in decision-making is a factor which makes for the spreading of information, and which militates against secretiveness. The fact that in Communist states (excepting Yugoslavia) plurality, with the exception to some extent of religious bodies, is limited places these latter in the forefront of this issue.

Various other relationships between religion and state secre- tiveness should be mentioned. The extent to which religion is practised in atheistic countries is itself a state secrecy, but probably it is in excess of what is officially suggested. At one extreme Albania claims to have abolished religion altogether, but the fact that lamb and beef are eaten in Albania in larger quantities than pork, in contrast to everywhere else in Eastern Europe – eating pork being forbidden by Islam, the faith to which most Albanians used to belong – suggests that religion in this matter remains not without influence. The Albanian press still complains that pig production is undervalued (e.g. *Zëri i popullit*, 10 December 1983, p. 1). This may also be a problem in Soviet Muslim areas. Soviet practice as regards access by visitors to religious institutions is not uniform: the Trinity Monastery of St Sergius of Zagorsk, 72 km north-north-east of Moscow, is regularly on the itinerary of foreign tourists and diplomats, whereas a Sufi (Muslim) temple on the outskirts of Bukhara is out of bounds to foreigners (Owen, 1985, p. 12).

If on the whole, in more advanced countries, religion is antipathetic to public secrecy, it certainly helps to uphold priv- acy. An abatement of religion is therefore likely to bring in its train an abatement of privacy, which has in fact been the consequence in the Soviet Union. When the practice of a religion is very time-consuming, or the religion prevents women from going out to work, activity of an intellectual kind by the latter is discouraged and state secrecy thereby perhaps prom- oted; on the other hand, the privacy of the family is intensified.

FEMALE EMANCIPATION

In general terms, I am inclined to think that female emancipa- tion must tend to be inimical to the preservation of secrets. For one thing, if women are entrusted with them as well as men, the number of people who are privy to secrets is roughly doubled. Perhaps, too, women are less inclined to keep secrets than men are, but this result would be secondary, and is not needed to maintain the proposition.

H. V. Morton in his account of travels in Italy at one point links Venetian secrecy with the fact that women in Venice were far from being emancipated. 'Venice did not trust its women: it had too many secrets' (Morton, 1964, p. 381). I wonder whether Russian or Soviet secrecy might not also be linked with limitations in Russia or the USSR upon female advancement? The Soviet Union claims to have achieved equality of women with men, but the lack of women in the upper reaches of the Communist Party and the Soviet government remains notorious, as does the fact that wives of public men do not ordinarily take part in state visits or ceremonies: Raisa Gorbacheva is in this respect an exception. Noteworthy too is the role assigned in espionage stories to Russian *femmes fatales*, of being entrusted with wheedling out secrets.

SECRECY AND MORALITY

Although sexual or everyday morality (honesty, for instance) is not particularly emphasised in Soviet ideology, it is supposed to form part of socialist principles; also morality plays a significant part in that the motivation of the authorities (apart from single individuals who may be admitted to be blameworthy) must always be presented as praiseworthy. There may have been shortcomings in performance, but these must not detract from the motive. Or if there have been defects in the motives of lower levels, these should not cast aspersions on those of higher levels. Even if there had been bad consequences, there must have been good intentions. This at least has been the normal state of affairs, until Gorbachev brought with him a wind of criticism. However, still the Soviet state, and of course the Communist Party, is never admitted to have done anything wrong. This attitude spills over into the contemplation of other national authorities, as witness Soviet attempts to play down Watergate and to show President Nixon in the best possible light, or more recently the precipitate congratulation of President Marcos, of the Philippines, following his supposed electoral victory (*The World Today*, April 1986, p. 59). It is important from the Soviet angle not to denigrate authority, not only Soviet authority but to some extent even authority in general. As the Soviet leaders realise, a spirit of anarchy might spread.

SECRECY AND MARXISM

The Soviet Union is secretive, atheistic (at least, among its governing strata) and also Marxist; so there might be an affinity between secretiveness and Marxism. If so, what would that be?

Marx wrote his *Das Kapital* apparently without making any use of his own powers of observation: all was compiled from evidence discovered by others, and then transcribed within the walls of the British Museum Reading Room. So, it might seem, any secret could have been kept from Marx, provided only that it had not been written down. Like Marx, Stalin (according to Khrushchev) in his later years never set foot inside a village (Kaser, 1970, p. 75). Marx wrote about a country other than Russia, although in his later career he did become very interested in the possibilities of a revolution in Russia. He wrote too about conditions of a hundred and more years ago, so nothing which occurs today can refute him – a useful characteristic of a philosophy which is presented as infallible. But this means too that if one confines oneself to citing Marx, whatever has happened during the past hundred years is held in deepest secrecy. The focus on a century ago, again usefully, distracts attention from what has happened since.

The above features illustrate a certain affinity between secrecy and Marxism. They show a high compatibility of Marxism with secrecy. If the Soviet Union had adopted a more liberal and sceptical philosophy, one which emphasised arriving at one's own generalisations or which permitted a broader eclecticism, that would have been much less compatible with a secretive approach. However, there is one important consideration to be set on the other side: to the extent that Marxism influences Soviet behaviour, the behaviour becomes more predictable and, therefore, effectively less secret.

MARXISM, THE RUSSIAN LANGUAGE, AND PRIVACY

At least, Marxism as such does not invade privacy, the governing role in social transformations being ascribed not to individuals but to classes. However, this aspect of lack of curiosity into individuals' opinions, except to the extent of investigating their class affiliation, is seriously modified by the Russian environment. (In this case I say Russian, not Soviet: the busybody element in Soviet life is a Russian phenomenon.)

There is, in fact, no word – none at least that I can discover – in the Russian language with the meaning of 'privacy'. The translation given in *The Modern Russian Dictionary for English Speakers* is *uyedineniye*, but this, being derived from *yedino* or *odin*, meaning 'one' or 'alone', signifies 'solitude, isolation, solitariness, aloofness', which are the renderings given in Segal's *Russian–English Dictionary*, and none of these has the same meaning as privacy. Similarly, 'in the privacy of my own house' is translated by *The Modern Russian Dictionary for English Speakers* as *u sebya doma*, but that would mean 'by oneself at home', or 'in one's own home': privacy is not mentioned. Again, *lichno* means 'personal' in the sense of a letter addressed to a particular person; 'private' is not connoted. Although a word *privatnyy* exists, this means 'unofficial' and is equivalent to 'private' in the phrase 'in one's private capacity'. The abstract noun corresponding to *privatnyy* would be *privatnost'*, but no such word exists and even if one did and it meant 'privacy', it would be a Russianised foreign word. By contrast, there does exist a single word meaning 'to keep silent' (*molchat'*)

THOUGHT PROCESSES

For preference, in this exposition, Soviet secrecy should be linked with any special features of Soviet thought processes. Any attempt to uncover these must seem ambitious, though books such as *The Russian Mind* (Hingley, 1977) and even *The Russian Mind since Stalin* (Glazov, 1985) do exist. Although it is impossible to supply sources for the principles asserted below, dedicated readers of Soviet material will, I hope, recognise them as being at least broadly correct.

The Soviet concept of public information is intensely serious, in that enormous attention is paid to science, for example in popular education: bookshelves which might contain occult writing are filled instead with scientific texts, though also with the Marxist classics and the speeches of Soviet leaders. Karl Marx's works are, of course, not noted for any humorous content.

As regards analysis and research, the following elements seem to characterise Soviet attitudes:

(a) All research must be approved by authority.
(b) It must be pursued within a theoretical framework which is compatible with Marxism–Leninism.
(c) Only certain subjects are legitimate objects of study. (This follows from (a) and (b), singly or jointly.)
(d) Originality in analysis or interpretation is not a virtue. (If the theme must be approved and the theoretical framework is given, the possibility of different interpretations is severely restricted.)
(e) Only a specialist is qualified to arrive at conclusions which may be regarded as true. The only exception is the tiny band of Marxist 'classics', who are in effect licensed non-specialists. Their role is to supply the obligatory theoretical framework.
(f) Nobody may be a specialist in more than one subject.
(g) Whenever a factual situation is described, huge importance is attached to a complete listing of all the components of a given entity. (Criticism of non-completeness in this respect is a stock-in-trade of Soviet reviews of non-fiction books.)

It would be reasonable to see in several elements of this list an adaptation to secrecy. This applies clearly to (a). In the list, (b), (c) and (d) follow directly from a Marxist approach, but are also very suitable to a situation where factual information is scarce and slanted: shortage of facts can then be made up by dogma. As regards (e) and (f) they are attributable to the circumstances of a hierarchical society; whether the supreme ruler is Autocrat of All the Russias or General Secretary of the Communist Party of the Soviet Union is irrelevant at the moment. Only (g) comes unequivocally down on the side of non-secrecy.

To a quite large extent, knowledge is disseminated within the USSR, and especially within hierarchies, on a 'need to know' basis. Hence compartmentalization of knowledge, occasioned by centralised dissemination of information, is typical: for example among scientists (where it leads to excessive specialisation) and in the armed forces. One Western expert believes that there is extraordinary compartmentalization of knowledge within the Soviet armed forces, including to an extreme degree in the General Staff. (Mackintosh, 1985, p. 180; however, this view was apparently not shared by Rice, 1985). Remarkable ignorance has occasionally been shown by high-ranking officers, like the

Black Sea admirals who even in the late 1950s were not aware of the existence of guided missiles (Khrushchev, 1974, p. 29). 'Need to know' also tends to govern Soviet relationship with other countries; for example, the French were not told *how* their laser reflector would be placed on the Moon (Daniloff, 1972, p. 186). However, sometimes foreign countries are not informed even when they *do* need to know.

Specialisation is readily consistent with secrecy, it being so easy to transform an attitude that someone who has specialised does not need to know anything outside his own specialisation to an attitude that that person *ought not* to know about it. That is not inevitable, as is shown by the example of the United States where specialisation is narrower than in Britain yet secrecy is much less. Still, I believe that specialisation predisposes to secrecy, and that in America this relationship is outweighed by something else whereas in Britain it is not.

It is also arguable that secrecy is not so much derived from specialisation as specialisation is derived from secrecy. If one may receive only certain sorts of data one must *ipso facto* specialise. Approximate parallels can be found in the restrictions imposed on Jews in the Middle Ages in Christendom and in the Hindu caste system.

Pursuing this approach, one might derive secrecy in Russia at least in part from the rigid class system of Muscovy. Analogously, more intense secretiveness in Britain than in America might be related to the stronger and more rigid class division in the former country. On the other hand, in India the caste system is still strong and the country vast enough to permit a high degree of specialisation, yet the cult of secrecy is not so far developed as in the USSR. This might be for several reasons, including that during the centuries when secretiveness became entrenched in Russia, India remained under imperial rule and consequently lacked a ruling group within which secrets might be generated and concentrated. That situation may be contrasted with the situation in the ruling country, Britain, where the two departments most characterised by secrecy, the Foreign Office and the Treasury, were staffed chiefly from the upper classes. Another difference between India and Russia was the fact that in the former country 'secret' merged into 'sacred', the influence of religion being vastly greater in India.

As regards (g), this is partly conditioned by a hierarchical

society, since implementing a command requires that it be addressed to all intended recipients without exception. However, it seems right to emphasise the fact that exhaustive enumeration may counteract an attempt to keep secret specific elements within a given grouping.

Thus secretiveness is compatible with Soviet habits of thought (if these are correctly set out above), as affected by Marxism. This does not mean that secretiveness has been generated directly by Marxism. Rather, it may be deemed a product of, or symbiotic with, other traits in the Russian character in conjunction with the nation's history, circumstances and institutions.

This chapter has mentioned in outline a number of general features of the Soviet context which seem to be relevant to secrecy, and to the degree to which secrecy can be pierced. It is now necessary to focus more precisely on the categories of information which are not disclosed.

4 Main Features of Soviet Secrecy

Owing to the nature of the subject, these categories cannot betray themselves directly; however, one can have recourse to indirect means.

A formal definition of state secrets is provided in a law of 1956. Secrets are divided into military information and economic information, but a clause states that the Council of Ministers of the USSR may add other items. Dated 28 April 1956, the law is published in *Ugolovnyy Kodeks RSFSR*. (A full translation is given in JEC, 1977, pp. 159–61.)

Under military information, the law classifies mobilisation plans and other overall information about the armed forces; storage places and stockpiles of reserves and of certain products having defence significance; operational plans concerning locations and numbers of troops and arms; general information about training; overall information about numbers of military reserves in the USSR as a whole and in military districts; plans of fortified bases, warehouses, etc. and their armament; overall information about the airfield network and information about airfields' condition and capacity; construction of bases and special construction; plans for local anti-air defence; and information about the state of defence of the frontiers.

Under economic information, it classifies location and capacity of military industrial enterprises; overall information about production of non-ferrous, noble and rare metals, and about capacities and production plans for radioactive elements; reserves of non-ferrous, rare and noble metals, titanium, diamonds and piezo-optical minerals; discoveries and inventions having considerable military significance; ditto for those of scientific or economic significance, until department heads give permission to publish them; currency stocks and balance of payments information; government codes; and other information which may be added.

This list is on the whole not distinctive, except in the inclusion of an unusually wide range of economic information, such as in relation to currency and the balance of payments, and in the implied assessment that it is as important, or almost as important, to preserve economic secrets as to preserve military ones. In general, the completeness of the measures to protect secrets in the Soviet Union is more distinctive than the law itself. This law was to supersede the decree of the Council of Ministers of the USSR of 8 June 1947 (no. 2009). The new law was possibly less rigorous than the one it superseded; this would fit with other features of the Khrushchev period (1955–64) as described below (Chapter 8).

However, in practice what is kept secret extends appreciably farther than this list. To illustrate this, the paragraph which follows comprises my own summary of what is kept secret in economic matters, and was drawn up independently of the secrets law. While the law provides more detail in some directions, the greater scope on the whole of the independently derived list emerges clearly.

First, the output of certain items, especially military goods and strategic materials, is not published. Material reserves and foreign exchange reserves, including gold, are secret. The balance of payments is strictly secret. Invisible items in trade are never quantified. Nothing is reported about arms exports. High salaries are secret, and various arrangements for benefiting privileged groups. Most prices and all data about the money supply are confidential. Only summary data are published about the budget, and even less about any overall financial plan. Non-socialist aspects of the economy tend to be concealed or minimised. Different years are reported unevenly, and the coverage of items shifts frequently and usually without explanation. Comparatively little information is provided about capital construction, despite its propaganda potential. Most information about forced labour is secret, as well as all details about forced collectivisation in the early 1930s. Alternative economic plans are not published, nor is there any systematic breakdown of plan non-fulfilment. Regional differences tend not to be reported. Various occupations, especially domestic service, are not listed in statistical handbooks, and there is no mention of unemployment or of seasonal underemployment, with much else relating to seasonal performance also being obscured. The real economic burden of defence is carefully concealed, and in appearance is minimised below both possibility and credibility.

As regards the scope of secret-keeping with respect to all

subjects together, any simple and comprehensive formula is difficult to find. Perhaps one would get nearest to such a formula with the statement that most unofficial events and circumstances are classified.

At an intermediate level of generalisation, the following propositions may be found helpful, both in providing evidence that Soviet secrecy indeed exists and in helping to characterise it.

(1) Statistical handbooks provide much less new data than their bulk would at first sight suggest. For instance, annuals covering the whole USSR consist to only a small extent of new information. The handbooks lavishly waste space by continuing to report events of long ago which have been reported many times already, while not telling us important things about the current year. For instance, the 1977 statistical handbook reported to the nearest 1000 metric tonnes how much cheese was produced in 1940 (thirty-seven years before!) but nothing at all about any weapons which might have been produced or sold in 1977.

(2) The degree of detail in reporting is extremely uneven. Here are two illustrations: numbers of scientists in different scientific branches, and amounts of spending on the economy from the annual budget. Published totals of numbers of scientists allocate them to seventeen branches of science, the size of which varies from 0.2 per cent of the total to 45.9 per cent. The biggest subdivision therefore amounts to almost half of the total. On 31 December 1972, scientists in the 'technical sciences' comprised 484 968 out of a total of 1 056 017 (Hutchings, 1976, pp. 263, 265). Again, within spending on the economy from the budget during the Ninth Five-Year Plan (1971–5) 'other expenditures' made up 50 billion roubles out of 101 billion, whereas another of the listed subdivisions amounted to less than 1 per cent of the total. It is obviously not possible to say anything very detailed about the composition of a total when its largest subdivision, which is not divided further, amounts to half of that total.

(3) Certain kinds of society during a time of international tension engage in periodic crackdowns on unauthorised leaks of information. The Reagan administration was doing so at the end of 1984 (*Time*, 31 December 1984, p. 17). The same phenomenon is visible periodically in Britain. Societies which do *not* make such crackdowns must either be highly secretive (so that no leaks

occur) or not secretive at all. The Soviet Union is one such society and clearly belongs to the first group rather than the second.

(4) In general, when the aim is to withhold information, this will be released eventually – if it ever is released – after periods or irregular length; by contrast, where secrecy is not present the periods are of standard length. By this test, the USSR is partly secretive, partly not. However, the attempt may be made to get the best of both worlds, via the publication at regular intervals of reports which are similar in general form but dissimilar as regards their precise content. This practice is characteristic of Soviet published plan results, and one may then conclude that secrecy is present, or is likely to be present, to the extent that the same items are not reported regularly.

(5) If totals are reported when, if the larger the better, they are above a certain limit, or if the smaller the better they are below such a limit, we may conclude that a reporting threshold is present. This is in fact true of Soviet reporting in various spheres (see Chapter 5).

(6) A reporting threshold applies also in some circumstances to the time that has elapsed since a given unfortunate event: the longer this is, the more permissible it will be for the event to be criticised. However, in a situation where history can be rewritten to reflect contemporary preferences, this last rule will not be adhered to consistently; here again, Soviet practices are relevant. The concept of a reporting threshold applies also within an institutional framework. In this case, the threshold has to be defined by distance from the vitals of the system: the nearer the vitals, the less criticism can be permitted.

(7) A very important category of Soviet secrecy relates to definitions. That of 'defence' (the Russian word is *oborona*) is an example. The Russians do not allow information about one sector of national affairs to shed unwanted light on the situation in another sector. Naturally, therefore, quantities or relationships along the margin of two sectors – for instance, military and economic – are shrouded especially closely.

(8) Secrecy is expressed in one-sided reporting which mentions only the virtuous and favourable aspects of Soviet activities.

Whatever external entanglements the Soviet Union is involved in, the entanglements, if reported at all, are reported optimistically and self-righteously.

(9) Whatever happens outside the Soviet Union is treated as secret so far as Soviet citizens are concerned, in that they may be told about them only what the authorities want them to hear. Any exceptions to this rule are rare, extremely limited, and strictly reciprocal – by agreement reached at a top-level meeting.

(10) Only the Party and government decide what is to be kept secret. Soviet enterprises function inside 'glass walls' in the sense that they are not permitted to have business secrets from other Soviet enterprises (Hutchings, 1982A, p. 254). The commercial secret of which the formula of Coca Cola is the archetype is therefore not present. (Regarding the Coca Cola secret, see *The Times*, 22 August 1985, p. 5.) Soviet patent law also testifies to the intention to avert business secretiveness. The secrecy of voting by citizens is guaranteed by law, but voting cannot topple the government, and in any case it is unlikely that even the secrecy is universally believed. (In regard to Albania on this point cf. Gardiner, 1976, p. 18.) But changes of address by Soviet citizens have to be registered with the authorities, i.e. must not be kept secret from them. On the other hand, if any danger is perceived to the state or the ruling Party there is no limit in practice to the extent or intensity of secrecy which is claimed and enforced.

Although the Soviet Union is a socialist state, information there is far from being common property.

5 Secrecy in Specific Branches

In this chapter I examine secrecy in certain specific branches of activity or study in the Soviet Union.

INTERNATIONAL RELATIONS: SECRET TREATIES AND PROTOCOLS

The archives of the world's foreign ministries doubtless house innumerable secrets. As a general rule, only military defeat will bring about the result that everything is revealed, and neither the Soviet Union nor any of its allies have been defeated; what may have been agreed to secretly remains therefore hidden, apart from any results which become known because they are conspicuous. For example, the Soviet launching site at Choybalsan in Mongolia must have been agreed by treaty between the two governments (see above, p. 45). A secret protocol was included in the Treaty of Rapallo, signed by Russia and Weimar Germany in 1922 (see above, p. 37). Another secret protocol in a treaty with Germany, this time to the Non-Aggression Pact signed by the USSR and Nazi Germany on 23 August 1939, helped to clear the way to war through its assignment of various territories to the spheres of interest of the signatories: for example, Lithuania was to be within the German sphere of interest but other Baltic states within the Soviet one (see Deutscher, 1949, pp. 437–9, and Spring, 1986 p. 207). Other secret treaties or protocols must have been signed but have not come to light.

GOVERNMENT, PERSONALITIES AND POLITICS

The Soviet Union is governed by the Politburo of the Soviet Communist Party, but what happens at Politburo meetings is unknown: no foreigner has ever attended such a meeting, nor are they described in Khrushchev's memoirs (Pipes, 1986, p. 2). Not only is governmental decision-making, for instance in foreign policy, secret (Hoffmann and Fleron, 1971, pp. 63 and 77); the opinions of individual policy-makers are not expressed clearly in public, although nuances of view can sometimes be detected. The fact that the true opinions of secondary personages cannot be reliably discovered until the death or deposition of the leader has the result that to foreign governments, the policies to be followed by a successor administration are in effect shrouded in secrecy, which may be either complete or almost so, until the first policy statement of the new administration appears.

The private lives of Soviet leaders are secret or very largely so (Arendt, 1967, p. 373; cf. also above, Chapter 2). The Soviet Union is the only developed country which does not make freely available anything in the nature of a *Who's Who* (*The Times*, 31 May 1977, p. 15). Secrecy is also manifested on city streets, in the blinds drawn across the rear windows of official limousines, and in the extreme rarity of amputees in cities despite the very large numbers of war wounded: evidently they must as a rule remain out of sight (see *The Times*, 7 September 1985, p. 7; Barman, 1968, p. 167; Hutchings, 1982A, p. 116). This may apply also to beggars and down-and-outs (cf. Barman, 1968, pp. 143–4).

Certain individuals must not be mentioned in print; they are unpersons in the language of Orwell's *1984*. Trotsky is the most notorious. To be consistent, erasure must be, and is, performed also in photographs, with appropriate adjustments so as not to leave any gap in the pictorial composition.

No statistics of an economic nature are published about internal politics (such as the affairs of the Communist Party, the finances of individual politicians, or the costs of convening the Supreme Soviet).

SCIENCE, TECHNOLOGY AND DESIGN

Despite large achievements, especially in enlargement of the sums spent on science and technology and of the numbers engaged in research, developments in this sphere have tended to fall short of expectation. In particular, they do not match achievement in the United States. The USSR does relatively best, though not often absolutely best, in science relating to military affairs and in certain spheres of pure science (cf. Hutchings, 1982A p. 247).

Expectations at first had been very high, and had partly been based on what would result from the abolition of business secrets. Non-Soviet Communists enthused about the 'new socialist economies, freed from the restrictions and secrecy of rival commercial exploitation of minerals' (Bernal, 1969, p. 798). Russian Communists had similar expectations. They were destined to be disappointed, and the arrangements they inherited in regard to patents were eventually in part reinstated, as the following sequence of events shows. Pre-Revolutionary Russia had awarded patents mainly to foreigners (Garmashev, 1962, p. 11), a patent being the only form of protection for an invention. Following the Bolshevik Revolution a decree of 30 June 1919, signed by Lenin, introduced a lesser sort of acknowledgement, the 'author's certificate' (*avtorskoye svidetel'stvo*). All laws relating to patents issued previously in Russia were annulled. However, this radically altered situation lasted only five years. A law of 12 September 1924 revived the patent as a form of exclusive right to make use of the innovation, and from April 1931 onwards an innovator was allowed to choose whether to receive an *avtorskoye svidetel'stvo* or a patent (Ibid., p. 19). Successive high-level bodies were set up to handle patents, culminating in the formation late in 1955 of a Committee for Matters of Inventions or Discoveries, attached to the Council of Ministers of the USSR (Ibid., p. 21).

Although this history suggests a transition to a manner of treatment of innovations which is not very unlike Western practice, Soviet society remains untypical owing to the fact that 'knowledge which in a Western society would pass more freely between the military and non-military spheres in the Soviet Union can be confined to the military sphere while, by contrast, it cannot be confined to the non-military one' (Hutchings, 1982A, pp. 242–3). This leads to a different distribution of knowledge, and in general expertise is likely to be higher in the military than in the non-military sphere.

This is added on to the more widely observable fact that science does not in practice, or in all respects, welcome dispassionate re-examination. If, within the scientific world in general, there is 'deliberate concealment of the "obscurity which envelops the *principia* of science"' (Ravetz, 1971, p. 18, quoting Pearson, 1937, p. 3); in the Soviet case there must also be added on the substantial incubus of the Marxist–Leninist approach, when this is interpreted so as to require specific results: Lysenkoism has been the best known and clearest example. On the whole, there has been an almost unlimited belief in the potentialities of science, a recent catchphrase being the 'scientific-technical revolution'. Secrecy in scientific matters which is not related to ideology or to basic principles is likely to relate to the margin of scientific knowledge, which other countries putatively have not yet reached. A number of organisational aspects of Soviet science and technology also remain obscure, and this apparently is intentional.

Science Policy in the USSR (Paris, OECD, 1969) provided a surprisingly large amount of detailed information about the organisation of Soviet science, but also left large gaps in knowledge of the subject (see Hutchings, 1969, pp. 179, 181).

The national security motive is the principal factor which introduces secrecy into Soviet science, technology and design, which on the whole are kept in tighter secrecy than the Soviet economy. At least since Archimedes' engines routed the Roman attack on Syracuse – and including the centuries when 'Greek fire' gave 'the Byzantines a powerful advantage, particularly in naval warfare' (Browning, 1980, p. 78) – science and technology have had military importance, but until comparatively recently the direct relevance of science to military matters has been fairly limited. In the eighteenth century scientists were permitted freedom of passage even as between warring nations. In the 1980s, the importance of science to defence has become enormous.

There are occasional explicit Soviet allusions to observing scientific secrecy. For example, the State Committee for New Technique (*Gostekhnika*) was authorised to 'Publish the "Industrial Economic Gazette" and also bulletins of scientific–technical information. When disseminating and publishing materials it must strictly observe secrecy and furnish information about matters which are not for publication through the classified press'. (From instruction no. 669 of the Ministry of Higher Education of the USSR, dated 18 June 1955, clause 2b (Karpov and Severtsev, 1957, p. 220).) It was insisted that 'expertise and the keeping of depositions with regard to innovations must be carried out in the procedure laid down for documents which are not for publication' (from the statute confirmed by the Council of People's Commissars of the USSR of 5 March 1941, no. 441, clause 16 (Karpov and Severtsev, 1957, p. 238).) Correspondence relating to innovations where certificates of ownership had not been issued had to be safeguarded in the same way (Ibid., clause 28). Any state organ might declare an improvement or innovation 'Secret', and special premises had then to be provided for the inventor to work in (Ibid., section V).

On the other hand, armaments comprise an element in a country's technical equipment, and their historical evolution in Russia can be studied from concrete examples. Museums illustrate particular branches of the history of technology, for instance railway equipment. Several are devoted to military or naval equipment: the Central Museum of the Armed Forces (Moscow), the Naval Museum (Leningrad), the Artillery Museum (Leningrad). (At different times I have been able to visit all of these.)

In up to date technology, however, secrecy continues to be stricter than it normally is in pure science. The 'secret' of the atom bomb was technical more than scientific. Where technique has or could have military applications it is regarded as confidential information. This is clearly illustrated in the comparative attention given to different branches of metallurgy in a volume published in the USSR entitled *Mining and Metallurgical Technique*, part of a five-volume work on the history of Soviet technology. Whereas a description is provided of current and future tendencies of development in steel-making no such description is furnished in regard to technique of non-ferrous metallurgy and rolling processes. 'Entirely absent from examination are such branches of metallurgy as the production of titanium, molybdenum, niobium, tantalum, that is to say materials without which it would be impossible to create present-day rocketry and cosmic apparatus' (Parkhomenko, 1968, p. 37).

The increasing dominance of the 'technical sciences' as shown in Soviet data is making it difficult to see what really is the distribution of scientists among branches, and this is probably deliberate (Hutchings, 1976, p. 39; cf. also p. 117). Some ministries, such as the Ministry of Radiotechnique and the Ministry of Aviation Technology, award degrees secretly. (Ibid., p. 41). The exact number of research institutes is no longer published (Hutchings, 1982A, p. 242). On the other hand, it may be noted that Soviet military bodies have published a considerable volume of scientific literature. The military interest has naturally been prominent in photography and map-making. The participation of military personnel in some university faculties has been very noticeable (e.g. Vere-Jones, 1964, p. 56).

Epidemic situations receive minimum publicity in published sources, though Asian 'flu is common in Moscow in winter; AIDS is still on an extremely tiny scale. Information is not provided about the distribution of scientific manpower (Korol, 1965, pp. x, xvi, 4); various areas of science are censored (Vucinich, 1963, p. 249); the home addresses of scientists are not given (Medvedev, 1971, p. 307). Data are not provided about some aspects of the space programme (Sheldon, 1969, pp. 8–9), such as the weight of mooncraft (Vladimirov, 1971, p. 160). Certain technical requirements such as military or space standards or testing and certification (Campbell, 1972, p. 598) are not given.

Generally speaking, in design secrecy is either very important or not important at all. The TU-144 is an example of maximum secrecy in design. 'Although a number of British firms, including Plessey, English Electric, Marconi and Cossor, have supplied parts for the aircraft, great secrecy has surrounded its construction, and no foreign journalist has ever been allowed to see inside its construction hangar' (*The Times*, 1 January 1969, p. 1). Similarly, Americans might not see the site of the Kama river motor vehicle plant, although $27 million had been spent on the design. Likewise, the Japanese were not allowed to see the Nakhodka port which they had designed (Goldman, 1972). Partial use, or adaptability, for military purposes may perhaps be one reason. Where civilian and military equipment is partly interchangeable, data about the civilian version may be withheld as well. For instance, the Ministry of Defence would not release noise levels of the TU-114, as this plane is a civilian modification of the TU-95 (Bear) bomber (Heymann, 1972, p. 33).

Designers are only in certain circumstances recognised as public persons. Whereas the identity of the 'Chief Designer' of space vehicles was hidden as closely as if he had been head of the secret intelligence service, designers of aircraft were granted a public projection that their colleagues in the West would have envied: their abbreviated names were prefixed to their creations, so that one was constantly reminded of AN (tonov), TU (polev), YAK (ovlev), IL (yushin) and so on. In contrast, the designers of motor vehicles were hidden in obscurity: cars were named for example Volga, Pobeda (Victory), Moskvich (Muscovite), or after the factories where they were made, such as ZIL (*Zavod imeni Likhacheva*) or ZIM (*Zavod imeni Molotova*). Obviously relevant here are considerations of secrecy (the birthplace of the spacecraft was kept secret doubtless owing to the strong military connections of the space exploration programme with defence establishments and objectives, while names of factories producing particular types of aircraft would also come under the military censorship), while there existed no independent firms producing motor vehicles, aeroplanes, or indeed anything. The role of the designer *is* emphasised in situations where it is desired to draw attention to the end product but not to the medium of production or to intermediate agencies. Whether to mention the *name* of the designer would then be considered separately, and the decision would be affirmative only where the project was not secret.

SECRECY AND ART

'Secrecy and art' seems at first an incongruous combination because one thinks of art in exhibitions, where obviously secretiveness is the last thing to be desired, or of berets, smocks and easels, which seem the psychological opposite of secrecy. Nevertheless, 'secrecy and art' is a quite real conjunction under Soviet circumstances, but only when, from the viewpoint of the authorities, the art is from the wrong side of the blanket: it is entirely a question of hushing up 'dissident' art. *That* sort of art has indeed been kept secret, perhaps on the whole almost as effectively as topics more obviously connected with national security. There is, however, this distinction, that dissident art is kept away from the Soviet public more assiduously than from the outside world, or more exactly this has recently been the trend. Whereas in 1971, when an exhibition of Soviet art and design was held at the Hayward Gallery in London, an 'abstract room', composed of murals and sculpture, was sealed off for ideological reasons (presumably) on Soviet orders (Hopkirk, 1971, p. 2), in 1977, Soviet unofficial artists held an exhibition at the ICA Gallery in London. According to Mr Alexander Glezer, who left Russia with half of the 170 paintings on show, when a similar exhibition was opened in Moscow forty artists were refused permission to show their works. They decided to go to Leningrad to show in private flats, but on arrival were detained by the police and sent back to Moscow (*The Times*, 19 January 1977, p. 16; cf. Glezer, 1975, p. 40). Certainly, policies in the artistic sphere have sometimes been inconstant: thus, in 1975, an exhibition of non-orthodox art which at first had been banned, indeed 'smashed by the authorities with the aid of bulldozers, fire-hoses and plain-clothes militia' (Brown *et al.*, 1982, p. 182), did finally open, including some items which were 'so far out' one wondered how the authorities had passed them (Stevens, 1975, p. 1). Yet many artists have been forced into emigration (Brown *et al.*, 1982, p. 182), so that although Soviet dissident art has become better known abroad, within the Soviet Union it remains chiefly underground, and in effect is kept secret from the mass of the people.

For purposes of consideration here, religious art can be regarded as a special sort of dissident art. The specifically Russian form of religious art is the icon. The Soviet attitude towards icons has evolved in a commercial sense – from selling them for only a few pounds to a lively awareness of their value to foreign collectors. Icons today are handled by the all-union trading association Novoexport. However, previous neglect may have resulted in the destruction of substantial numbers, both in the earliest Revolutionary period and during the 1960s when about half of all working churches were closed (*Sotheby's Preview*, October–November 1980, p. 5). The general result is the same as in the case of other dissident art: that it has become relatively better known abroad than at home.

EXTRAORDINARY SITUATIONS AND CATASTROPHES

There are no statistics about fires or fire-fighting, or about the amounts (which must be enormous) of snow shifted from city streets (cf. Hutchings, 1971B, p. 155).

As a general rule, accidents are reported only when the foreign press would be likely to get to know of them anyway (for example, if foreign nationals were involved or they occurred within the capital city). For instance, according to *Vechernaya Moskva* (the Moscow evening paper) an escalator at Aviamotornaya underground (subway) station caused an undisclosed number of casualties (*D.T.*, 19 February 1982, p. 30). Sometimes too a report appears if exclusively natural forces are responsible (e.g.

an earthquake – this can, of course, also be detected by instruments), if the event can be made the occasion for reporting some heroic deed (e.g. *The Times*, 21 January 1965, p. 6), and in some other cases. The high accident rate on internal waterways has received some publicity, drunkenness being often blamed (e.g. Krayushkin *et al.*, 1983, p. 2; cf. Pushkarev, 1985, p. 3). These combined circumstances not amounting to very much one might think that accidents occur rarely, which would certainly be mistaken: for example, I was a witness or near-witness to three street accidents, two of which may have been fatal, during one two-month stay in Moscow in 1963. Road accidents are rarely reported in the press and there are no national published statistics of them, though information is provided occasionally about local road accident totals, or affecting particular social groups (SWB 4971, broadcast in May–July 1975, or *Literaturnaya gazeta*, 17 January 1973, reported in *Osteuropa*, 11/73 pp. A782–A785. Cf. Wells, pp. 15–16). Non-reporting of traffic accidents in the local press occasionally causes annoyance: see Kotelevskiy and Golub 1971, cited in *Soviet Analyst*, 1 February 1973.

Until Chernobyl, the biggest nuclear disaster in any country in peacetime occurred in the Urals in late 1957. This must have resulted in heavy mortality (Komarov, 1978, p. 103). The facts were and are secret in the USSR, and were revealed by Zhores Medvedev who pieced together fragments of evidence (Medvedev, 1978, pp. 232–44). They are now accepted although they were initially discounted by the (then) chairman of the British Atomic Energy Authority (*The Guardian*, 10 October 1979, p. 16). Some hundreds of square kilometres were affected. A hundred kilometres from Sverdlovsk, on a road from near Chelyabinsk, a road sign warned drivers not to stop for the next 30 km and to drive at maximum speed. According to the eyewitness, on both sides of the road the land was 'dead' (*The Times*, 8 December 1976, p. 1). (On the Urals nuclear waste disaster see also *Sunday Times*, 7 November 1976, p. 3.)

The disaster at Chernobyl nuclear plant, not far from Kiev (26 April 1986) was more serious still, but at the time of writing (15 May 1986) its full consequences cannot be gauged; indeed, these may never be known. For the same reason, comment here has to be preliminary. The fact that the accident occurred in the Soviet Union is significant, as bearing witness to the fact that less heed had been paid than elsewhere to accident prevention; the fact that the accident was not immediately announced, although pounced on by the Western press, may be less significant, as it appears that the top leadership genuinely did not realise at once the scale of the disaster. The effort subsequently made by Gorbachev to provide information about the disaster confirms his commitment to diminish secrecy, a conclusion already reached in Chapter 8, below (see also in this connection Chapter 13).

Among five crashes of Aeroflot flights in the USSR during 1976 (up to 30 November) two had not been officially confirmed. A spokesman at Sheremetevo airport confirmed that a TU-104 crashed on a flight to Leningrad on 29 November 1976, but would not give a casualty figure. According to Western airline sources, all seventy-two people on board were killed. (*N.Y.T.*, 30 November 1976, p. 12). According to one apparently well-informed traveller, among the major airlines Aeroflot has the worst safety record, while the airlines of certain satellite countries, flying Soviet Ilyushin and Tupolev aircraft, have a particularly bad one (Harrington, 1982, p. 70; cf. *The Economist*, 6 July 1973).

Soviet officials confirmed to visiting French industrialists that a TU-144 supersonic airliner crashed on a test flight early in the summer of 1978. When informed Western sources said in September that such a crash had occurred, an official of the Civil Aviation Ministry denied the reports (*San Francisco Chronicle*, 27 October 1978, p. 18). On the other hand, although there have been stories about Soviet cosmonauts being killed in space and their deaths not reported, these are not confirmed and were discounted by a Pentagon 'expert' (*The Washington Post*, 13 April 1973). A survey of Soviet space flight gives the dates of Cosmonaut Komarov, but without mentioning the fatal end to his last mission (Kosmodem'yanskiy and Ostol'skiy, 1969, p. 449).

The most serious accidents in the USSR often seem to involve defence establishments. Those which have come to outside notice in recent years include a massive explosion which took place at Severomorsk, north of Murmansk, late in May 1984. This is believed to have destroyed a huge quantity of naval munitions. The explosion was detected by satellite (*The Times*, 23 June 1984, p. 1). An accident, said to have killed several hundred people, occurred in an underground defence industry plant in the Kuzbass in mid-December 1983 (*The Times*, 9 January 1985). A catastrophe to a space rocket, which ignited prematurely, killing the Commander-in-Chief of Soviet missile forces among others (October 1960) must also be mentioned here. Such accidents either are not reported at all or only with concealment of the true circumstances (see Medvedev, 1978, pp. 98–100).

It is also probable that even when accidents are reported, the casualties resulting from them are liable to be understated. The Tashkent earthquake of 1966 and a flood in Tbilisi on 7 June 1972 are illustrations, also fires around Moscow which in August 1972 led to the city being filled with smoke (*Soviet Analyst*, 1 February 1973). Similarly, the following news about Romania, though vague, struck me as reliable: one summer in the 1960s a collision at Chitila, near Bucharest, of a passenger train from Galati with a local commuter train heading towards Bucharest must have caused hundreds of deaths, possibly (a guess) up to 800; the Romanian press reported a total of twenty-five deaths only (private para-medical source).

PURGES AND WAR LOSSES

The immense numbers of deaths during the great purges of the 1930s or resulting from the Second World War are 'accidents' of a different order of magnitude, yet so far as secrecy and disclosure policy are concerned, the treatment is much the same as that of road accidents or other catastrophes. No total of deaths during the purges has ever been released. As regards wartime deaths, the only Soviet official total, 'two tens of millions' (Khrushchev, 1961, p. 8) could hardly be less exact; obviously it is rounded, but is it rounded upwards or downwards? This problem has usually been approached via examination of the probabilities of natural increase had the war not taken place, as compared with what actually did happen, in conjunction with other available facts (cf. Hutchings, 1966).

If one approaches the subject solely from the angle of disclosure policy, the lack of data concerning population development in the first five years after the war becomes relevant. 'For these years only crude birth rates have been published, and only for 1946 is the death rate mentioned' (van den Berg, 1985, p. 179). No population total was provided until the estimate of '200.2 millions' as at 1 April 1956 (*Narodnoye khozyaystvo SSSR*, 1956, p. 17); 200 also is a 'round' figure, and the announcement was apparently delayed until that round total had been reached. When this total was published it appeared to Western specialists to be too low: 215 millions was thought more likely. Subsequently it has been suggested that either this total is too low or that 191.7 millions for 1940 is too high (Gottinger, 1968, p. 154. Gottinger incorrectly ascribes the report of 200.2 million to 1955). Unless the second of these conjectures is correct, the Soviet authorities must have been wishing to conceal how far the population had declined. Surely then they would also have preferred to minimise the amount of losses, i.e. 'two tens of millions' was probably less than the correct figure. This lends support to Newth's implied estimate that wartime losses had actually been within the range 22–27 millions (Newth, 1964, p. 347; cf. van den Berg, 1985, pp. 179–85).

MILITARY AND NAVAL MATTERS

The Nazi invasion in 1941 could not be kept secret! Yet the Soviet government not only stifled news of the German preparations, but held up for several hours the first news of the attack (Hingley, 1977, pp. 94–5). It appears not entirely convincing to explain this as being wholly due to a fear of provoking Hitler; as Stalin must have been well aware, provocations can if necessary be invented. As noted elsewhere (see below, Chapter 10) it has recently been suggested that the Soviet Union was itself preparing to attack Germany in the summer of 1941. If that had been so, extreme reticence in supplying news about anything happening along the Western borders would have been more understandable. Alternatively, the news black-out may have been primarily a manifestation of ingrained secretiveness. Similarly, when the war in Germany was coming to an end, and for more than twenty years afterwards, the Soviet Union kept secret the fact that Hitler's body had been found, thus engendering here a quite unnecessary mystification (*The Times*, 2 August 1968). Analysis of the reports of the censuses of 1959 and 1970 shows that these did not include Soviet troops based outside Soviet territory (van den Berg, 1985, p. 184).

A great deal has now been disclosed about Soviet military history, including the campaigns of the Second World War, although the importance of other fronts, and the contributions of the Western allies, are minimised. But secrecy about contemporary military matters is intense, and as regards equipment sometimes complete. National defence is illuminated to the minimum degree that is consistent with projection of the image of a superpower. The likely realities of nuclear war are concealed from the public.

In military matters, special heed is paid to preserving the anonymity of units and individuals. Any military unit is called the 'Nth' and its members are not identified by name. If a personal name is given, then the unit to which he belongs must not be identified. Thus we find an allusion to 'senior seaman Sultan Khankhodzhayev, serving on one of the ships of the Red Star Black Sea fleet' (*Pravda vostoka*, 7 February 1984, p. 3). The fact that a given unidentified person belongs to the armed forces is not hidden, though (unlike the US forces) names are not worn on tunics. The centre of Moscow has a remarkably large number of officers in uniform: in the centre of London (far fewer I believe than in Moscow, even if one could identify them all) they are mostly (naval officers invariably) in mufti. Special heed is also paid in the Soviet Union to keeping locations secret, a propensity which even – although vainly – goes so far as to try to keep secret the address of the Ministry of Defence.

But secrecy in defence matters may conflict with the aim of impressing foreign nations with Soviet armed might. The way this contradiction is normally solved is to permit occasional and fleeting appearances of the bulkiest, physically most imposing and outwardly least revealing weapons, such as heavy tanks, artillery and rockets, on ceremonial occasions such as May Day or the Revolution anniversary. The solution to a not completely different problem of the Indonesian authorities has been analogous, though manifested more crudely: 'For several months, the press have been prohibited from reporting about this operation [the killing of criminals]. At the same time, to scare people in order that they learn the lesson, it is necessary that they know criminals are being executed brutally. Thus the solution is to expose the dead body in a public place' (*Fijar*, December–January 1983–4, p. 23).

The same need for exceptions from absolute secrecy crops up again and again. Why, for example, did Soviet planes based near Alexandria which were scrambled to intercept Israeli planes on 18 April 1970 send out all their communications in Russian?

Presumably the Soviet Union intended Israel to get the message that the Russians had arrived in Egypt (Heikal, 1975, p. 34) – unless indeed we choose the less machiavellian explanation that this was the only way the pilots had to communicate with one another!

Soviet sailors' capbands indicate only the fleet to which the wearer belongs (such as *Severnyy Flot* – Northern Fleet). By their nature, naval forces are stationed remotely from the capital and at comparatively few ports which are not included in tourists' itineraries. Vladivostok and Sevastopol are anyway off-limits to foreigners, perhaps especially because a higher proportion of Soviet warships stay in port, or if away from their home base, at anchor, than is the case with the US Navy or the Royal Navy. Whereas army or strategic forces detachments can parade down Red Square and aircraft overfly it, naval forces cannot be deployed there to impress foreign observers. These circumstances lead to the result that among all the Soviet armed forces the navy is particularly secretive. This is true in another sense which is unattainable by the other services: an unusually large fraction of the Soviet navy consists of submarines, which it is hard not to see as in some sense a manifestation of secrecy.

Secretiveness in NATO navies, even in undersea operations where it is invariably more intense than in relation to surface vessels, is more discriminate. For example, the existence of the NATO SOSUS system (Surveillance of Submarines Under Sea) in the Atlantic Ocean is no longer classified, although it is classified *how large* an area of the Atlantic is observed (Friedman, 1985, p. 66). Again, while the top speed and maximum diving depth of Royal Navy submarines are secret, many other things are not. The USSR reveals little about *its* submarines except human interest aspects (e.g. Verstakov, 1986, p. 6) and generalities of threats and tactics. An example of protecting of their secrets was a guard maintained for five years over the wreck of the 'November' class submarine which sank in 1970, 550 miles south-west of Land's End (Britain). This guard was abandoned only in 1975 (*D.T.*, 22 March 1975, p. 5).

However, the Soviet navy no less than the other services needs to create an impression of being formidable to an enemy. If one does not include under this latter intention the noisiness of Soviet submarines – which is so marked a drawback that it must be unintended – there are two other ways in which such an impression can be generated. Soviet warships *look* ominous – in fact considerably more noxious than their Western counterparts, thanks to their aggressively sleek lines, multiple bristling weapons and spiky uncovered radars (Roach, 1979, and Hutchings 'Soviet Design and its Influence on Soviet Naval Design', 1979, unpublished). Surface vessels detailed for the purpose may behave in a way that draws attention to themselves: close shadowing of the envisaged adversary and engaging in dangerous manoeuvres. This too has been very characteristic of Soviet naval behaviour, in the Mediterranean and elsewhere, and it also can be understood as stemming essentially from a perceived need to appear formidable, even if that has to entail revealing more than would ideally have been preferred.

However, manoeuvres in close contact of Soviet and US warships have come to be regulated by the INCSEA (Incidents at Sea) Agreement between the US and Soviet navies, signed on 25 May 1972. Probably the Russians thought that by then they had made their point, and should take more account of the very real dangers of collision in such circumstances (Hilton, 1985, pp. 30–7).

The Soviet Navy engages in an extensive range of visits to foreign ports: in 1975 alone, fifty countries and eighty-two ports were visited. The majority of visits are 'official', and substantial political dividends have sometimes been gained; the maiden voyage of the aircraft-carrier *Minsk*, en route to take up station with the Soviet Pacific Fleet, is often cited in this connection. To observers on shore, such visits offer an opportunity for a closer look at the warships and their crews, and therefore secrecy is to some extent sacrificed. It has been the practice that visits to foreign ports are not made by the newest classes of Soviet ships until several years after their commissioning, probably with the aim of minimising this result; perhaps for the same reasons, visits to Western ports are never made by Soviet submarines (Tsouras, 1986, pp. 270, 272–3).

As regards other defence forces, naturally the operations of a secret service are secret. The Soviet secret services are not to be found in published telephone directories – which themselves are not readily obtainable.

GEOGRAPHY

All maps on a scale greater than 1:500,000 are secret (Mellor, 1966, p. 109, quoting French, 1961, p. 163), while publication of the co-ordinates of any town in the USSR is forbidden (Vladimirov, 1971, p. 49). 'Some places, such as spacecraft launching centres or nuclear-weapons sites are omitted from Soviet maps for security reasons' (Shabad, 1971). It is probably due to secretiveness, at least in part, that maps of Kamchatka are very sketchy, lacking even contours, roads, a scale or north point: the peninsula has great strategic importance for the Soviet Union, as it gives access to the Western Pacific (Francis and Jones, 1984, p. 117). Certain scientific centres are not shown on any maps, such as the Baykonur space centre near Tyuratam (Vladimirov, 1971, p. 164). The exact alignment of the BAM railway is never indicated. Geographical falsification is also probable, the aim being deliberately to distort the geographical representations of the USSR' (Milsom, 1970, p. 8). According to Vladimirov (1971, p. 49), not a single city or town in the USSR is shown in its correct position with regard to latitude and longitude. It has been claimed that a decision to deform the entire map of the USSR was taken between 1964 and 1967, when the second edition of the Soviet world atlas was published (*D.T.*, 19 January 1970, p. 26).

It is right to react with scepticism to reports of this nature. In my view, they are supported by the integral connection in this case between reticence and falsification: not to specify exact geographical co-ordinates will achieve nothing if positions are shown correctly on maps. However, one must then presume that correct charts are issued to airline pilots among others.

How should one explain the fact that sites do not appear on maps although they have already been extensively photographed from satellites? There is a possibility – though as expertise in interpretation improves, it becomes slighter – that a satellite picture may not be recognised for what it is, or that it may be linked with some other installation. In the case of Baykonur, it may have been thought that there were two installations, one in the place photographed and the other in the place named. At least, there is conflict between the two types of information, which may generate confusion and lack of confidence in one or both sources. Then there is habit and administrative routine: if a location has not been revealed precisely on a map it will continue not to be revealed, even if the objective reasons for not revealing it have disappeared.

An *Ukazatel' k skhematicheskomu planu Moskvy* (Legend to a Sketch Map of Moscow, dated about 1971 – which also was the year when the experiment referred to below was made) was constructed to different scales, the centre as far as the Sadovaya ring road being magnified and the rest reduced. As one would expect, and as was discovered when wandering about map-in-hand in the southern outskirts in the outer areas, angles and distances are distorted.

The comparative lack of geographical sense among Western Sovietologists may have made a contribution to this falsification, in that senses were not alerted here to the possibility as quickly as they might have been. Textbooks on the Soviet economy are available which make almost no allusion to geography, for instance *Soviet Economic Structure and Performance*, by P. R. Gregory and R. C. Stuart (1974). Where maps of the USSR *are* included in Western texts, these are occasionally inaccurate (such as Dev Murarka, *The Soviet Union*, 1971, pp. 40–1 and 140–1; the Caspian Sea is not shown to have shrunk, the Volga–Don canal – opened in 1952 – is not shown nor any other canal, while the Karelo–Finnish SSR which was abolished in 1956 *is* shown), or are almost completely lacking in detail, such as the map of Moscow in Pallot and Shaw, 1981, figure 11.1, p. 262. Talking about Soviet geography, one should briefly note the extensive renaming of places in Russia since the Revolution. This may not have had any aim of intensifying secretiveness about locations, but if anything, that must have tended to be the result.

ECONOMICS

The role of published information in the management of the Soviet economy is much slighter than in a market economy, as is shown by the little or no correlation between the performance of the economy and the amount of data published in the Soviet Union about it. For example, whereas over time the share of industry in the Soviet gross national product has greatly increased relative to that of agriculture, relative numbers of industrial and agricultural tables in the annual statistical handbooks have altered in the opposite direction (see Hutchings, 1982B, Appendix VII). The Soviet economy does not react automatically to changes in the rate of interest, profit, exchange rates, the balance of payments or the money supply. The interest rate is invariable but the money supply and balance of payments are secret, while a change in exchange rates signifies only a change in payments into or from the budget.

The exchange rates of the socialist countries used to be based on a fictitious gold content, which was fixed with a propagandist purpose. When economic policy began to emphasise an intensive kind of development, this ceased to be workable: the information role of the exchange rate has to be strengthened, but for propaganda purposes it was considered improper to abandon the official exchange rate; instead, 'foreign currency coefficients' were introduced which expressed the degree of devaluation relative to foreign currencies (Bakule, 1983, pp. 955–64).

Although it is a difference of principle between planned and market economies that the former compose official forecasts, and as a rule publicise them at any rate in part (this referring especially to five-year or longer term plans), not infrequently the contrast between the two systems is not that the market system reports what has happened, and the planned one also what is forecasted: rather, a planned economy may *not* report what has happened (or is happening). Secrecy may extend to the state-controlled sector of a market system, though probably in less complete degree than if the entire economy is planned. Thus, while the USSR releases no information about the total money supply, the British Treasury in one instance refused to make any information available about the government's expectations of the growth of the money supply (Lamont, 1975, p. 16).

Soviet outputs of certain items are not published. These include synthetic rubber and various chemical products, as also their raw material base (Amann *et al.*, 1977, pp. 255, 249). Arms production is, of course, secret. Aluminium is classed as a defence industry, and production statistics are secret (as previously noted: also Wilczynski, 1974, p. 277). Shipbuilding statistics are not published, although some information is provided about shipbuilding specialisations in Comecon countries (Ibid.). All figures relating to Soviet gold – both production and reserves – have been state secrets for more than half a century: the last officially published figure was in 1934, when reserves were put at 3500 tonnes (*The Times*, 4 February 1980, p. 18). Other state reserves, such as oil (*Staff Report of the Senate* . . ., 1978, p. 12) also are not made public. The machinery data in value terms are scarce, and references to the radio-electronic industry, its costs and other parameters even more so (Treml *et al.*, 1972, p. 283).

High salaries are secret, as well as arrangements (the 'packet system' and closed dining-rooms) for supplementing the salaries of Party workers, etc. (Matthews, 1978, pp. 127, 129). What is believed to be the very first reference to these in print is appearing at the time of writing (*Pravda*, 13 February 1986, p. 3). There is an embarrassed silence concerning the privileged position of élites in socialist societies, to which the Polish Marxist scholar Adam Schaff has drawn attention (Fischer 1967, pp. 36–7). Concerning foreign trade: a proportion of regular deliveries is not reported (Hewett, 1974, p. 67). Food prices are confidential (Schapiro and Godson, 1981, p. 14). In Stalin's day and indeed for some years afterwards an indignant crowd would surround any foreigner who was apparently writing down retail prices, and compel him or her to desist. In particular, 'the prices for which the Soviets supply various materials and equipment for military purposes are considered a secret in the USSR' (Birman, 1984, p. 45). Similarly, rates of Turnover Tax are secret (cf. Asselain, 1981, pp. 74–5), and 'the Soviet Union publishes no figures about money supply in any of its definitions' (Nove, 1974, p. 16). The last officially published figure for the absolute amount of currency in circulation related to 1 January 1938, all later figures remaining a state secret (Grossman, 1985A, p. 29).

As regards other topics: according to a 50-year-old reference, comparatively little information was provided about capital construction (Ioffe, 1935, p. 204). Much more recently Hanson, when attempting to assess the share of imported Western investment and know-how, found it handicapping that branch investment series existed for only twelve industrial sectors and three non-industrial ones, and that these were not regularly broken down into equipment and other forms of investment (Hanson, 1981, p. 134). Comparatively little information is provided about environmental pollution; according to Komarov, even nothing about oil pollution (Komarov, 1978, p. 36). I have never seen any reference in Soviet publications to production of funeral goods (cremation equipment etc.), though reticence in this matter is neither uncommon nor surprising; there are shops entitled *pokhoronnyye prinadlezhnosti* (funeral appurtenances). Secret from other private citizens are deposits in savings banks. Though surely not proof against any determined investigation these could also be hidden from the State Bank (Gosbank), which in 1931 was reported to be one out of many ways of infringing credit and payment regulations (Prutkin, 1931, pp. 13–14. Many other ways of infringing investment regulations are described in Hutchings, 1984.)

STATISTICAL ANNUALS

From 1956 onwards annual statistical handbooks began to be published, and these are now available in many regional divisions and for various branches of the economy. While no comprehensive and authoritative catalogue of these handbooks exists, according to records published in *Soviet Studies* up to July 1979 1106 had been published (Hutchings, 1982B, p. 3); by now (1987) the total would just exceed 1500 (Rees, 1980 *et seq.*).

The interest afforded by this multiplication to the outside world per statistical handbook has shown very sharply diminishing returns: the world is chiefly interested in statistics relating to the whole USSR, only to a much smaller extent in republic statistics, and even less in those relating to smaller territorial divisions, with the exception of the largest cities. Interest is also focused on certain branches or areas, especially those which have military or economic significance. Many of the statistical handbooks, and a great deal of the information released since 1956, shed no direct light – or no light at all – on these two areas. Looking at this more closely, one inclines to make distinctions. Certain sorts of economic information have much greater value, in shedding light on other activities, than other sorts. Thus, what would chiefly shed light on military matters is the output of weapons or weapon systems; the output of particular kinds of consumer goods in individual small regions sheds either no light at all on this, or so little as not to be worth pursuing. And in fact as a general rule the release of information in a given major sector has been so regulated that it sheds minimal light on other major sectors. Thus, release of economic information as a rule sheds no, or very little, light on military or political matters.

This no doubt is one of the chief concerns of the authorities in deciding whether or not to release information. For example, the complete absence of Soviet literature about defence industry conversion in the USSR (Leitenberg, 1979, pp. 263–4) is doubtless deliberate.

REPORTING OF PLAN RESULTS

An example of a rigid reporting framework is provided by the timetable of reporting by plants to their superior authority: regularly every ten days, every month and every three months. On the other hand, it is not less certain that the reporting of plan fulfilment is incomplete. For instance, data on the basis of which economic plans are compiled are not released, and the same applies to any alternative plans which may have been considered. There is no quantitative presentation of numbers of units which fulfil or do not fulfil economic plans (Strumilin, 1952, p. 42).

There is no standard reporting list of what is achieved in economic results: this varies according to the year, or even the quarter. It must be supposed that this is not accidental, and various signs indicate that the selection is made deliberately with the aim of creating a favourable impression. If performance is bad, quantitative results are likely to be withheld, as in the case of the grain harvest of 1981 (*D.T.*, 25 January 1982, p. 5). Indeed, non-disclosure of such data is an almost certain indication that performance *was* poor.

Similarly, a 'reporting threshold' is apparently present in the reporting of quarterly output totals. This is shown by the behaviour of output series, the reporting of which is interrupted. When the seasonality of a quarterly series is reckoned (according to the formula devised in Hutchings, 1971B, called log S), in five cases out of seven this index was rising immediately before the series was interrupted, while the index immediately after the gap was lower than it had been immediately before. (This is based on Hutchings, 1982B, pp. 304–5.) The results which were covered by this comparison were: output of prefabricated concrete parts; (output of electric motors AC); output of motor-cycles and scooters; output of steel tubes; output of agricultural machines; catch of fishing and whaling; (output of butter); output of whole milk; output of conserves; (output of caustic soda); output of soda ash; and output of forging and pressing machines. Within this group, items for which there is insufficient data to trace the evolution of seasonality immediately prior to the gap in reporting are shown here in brackets (Hutchings, 1971B, Appendix XI). This suggests a tendency to interrupt the reporting of a trend of increasing seasonality, and to resume reporting of it only when seasonality in that series has again fallen.

A partly, but not wholly, similar picture emerges from consideration of gaps in reporting of output items in the annual all-union statistical handbooks. A total of twelve items are available for examination. The items covered by this comparison were: output of caterpillar-tracked tractors; output of furniture; electricity consumed in agriculture; the entire agricultural sown area; the area of vineyards; rail goods turnover; length of hard-surfaced roads; basic funds brought into operation, excluding collective farms; training and raising of qualifications of workers and employees; budget expenditures on defence; budget expenditures on science; and savings resulting from innovations (Hutchings, 1982B, pp. 14, 32).

On average, the rate of growth of output from year to year was no lower during the gap, when there had been a gap in reporting, than where there had been no gap. However, when the gap was between two and six years (the duration of gaps which were chosen for examination), the longer the gap in reporting, provided that reporting was resumed eventually, the more likely was the rate of growth in the year immediately following the gap to fall short of the average annual growth rate during the gap, and also this difference became larger. A possible scenario which would bring about this result could be that reporting is interrupted for as long as may be necessary to ensure that the average growth rate which can eventually be implied is not below normal, but that the longer the period until this result can be claimed, the more likely is the effort of achieving it to provoke the sequel that the growth rate in the next year becomes abnormally low. One might then conjecture that the longer the gap, the more substantially the growth rate in the year immediately following the gap would fall short of the average growth rate in *all* the post-gap years, and this is in fact the case. It would appear that reporting thresholds were present in these series (Hutchings, 1982B, pp. 32–4).

Some topics in economics may fail to be reported because they are so familiar. Seasonal influences in the Soviet economy in part fall into this category (Hutchings, 1971B, p. 9), though another reason for not reporting them in detail can be that they are seen as a reminder of uncontrollable influences, inconsistent with a planned economy.

AGRICULTURAL HISTORY AND FORCED LABOUR

No account has been provided about the forced collectivisation campaign or the purges of the 1930s, which makes any attempt to be systematic, objective or complete. A number of dissertations on agrarian history written in the 1940s and early 1950s have not been published (Keep, 1977, p. 414). Nothing definite, still less reliable or complete, has been made public about the forced labour 'archipelago'. Solzhenitsyn, whom Khrushchev once allowed to publish 'One Day in the Life of Ivan Denisovich', a fictionalised but realistic account of the forced labour system, was eventually expelled from the USSR. The contrast with Academician Sakharov's forced retention is absolute, and almost certainly to be chiefly explained by the fact that Solzhenitsyn, unlike Sakharov, had not known any military secrets.

The Soviet statistical handbooks – and Soviet published information generally – tend to conceal non-socialist aspects of the economy. For instance, the fact that production of potatoes, vegetables and eggs depends largely on the private plots of collective farmers has to be extracted from series indirectly. Regional differences, for example in gross product or national income, also tend not to be reported. Various occupations, especially domestic service, which may still be quite widespread (Hutchings, 1982A, p. 91), are missing from statistical handbooks (Sacks, 1981, pp. 251–63). Officially there is no unemployment, though in 1966 the presence of unemployed labour in various constituencies of European Russia and Central Asia was disclosed (Hutchings, 1982A, pp. 110–11), and current policies of labour saving may well produce the result that it emerges on a significant scale. Different years are reported with an unequal degree of detail. The coverage of items shifts frequently and for unexplained reasons. A summation of components of a total, subtracted from that total, often leaves a substantial gap: this is the problem of 'residuals', which has attracted attention in the West especially in Soviet foreign trade statistics and the annual budget.

Among the principal levers of Soviet economic development, Soviet literature has focused chiefly on the planning mechanism; much less attention has been paid to foreign trade, the price mechanism, the budget, financial arrangements, or technological imports. The first systematic revelation outside the USSR of the extent of Soviet technological borrowings from the West was constructed not from Soviet sources but primarily from the US State Department Decimal File and German Foreign Ministry archives, supplemented by journals (Sutton, 1968, p. vii).

FOREIGN TRADE

To the outside world, what a country trades in and how much it trades are great giveaways, so far as information is concerned. A country which aims to be maximally secretive should therefore reduce foreign trade to a minimum, though that *would* reveal that it could produce within itself everything that it needed. If it is assumed that information is collected solely by the country which is traded with directly, this information is fragmented, and the larger the number of countries with which it trades, the more so. (Decolonisation has brought about this very result.) On the other hand, the larger the number of countries, the more detail might potentially became available, and the smaller the likelihood that all trading countries will keep secret the transactions. Gathering information from the large number of sources will demand a wider intelligence network, hence bigger expenditures on it, unless some other body will do the job free of charge.

'For a long period, under Stalin, the USSR did not publish statistics about its foreign trade. The Russian example of secrecy was imitated by the satellites, and one of these, Romania, maintained secrecy for much longer' (Hutchings, 1982A, p. 209). Invisibles (tourism, shipping, etc.) still are not included, nor are goods comprising unrequited assistance to foreign countries or goods which do not bear a commercial character. Arms exports too are not itemised, but may well be included under the global totals of trade with particular countries (Ibid., p. 219). However, it may go too far to assume that *all* non-reporting items are military. As regards arms statistics the USSR is not much more secretive than other arms-exporting countries (Ibid., p. 223), but there is no official publicity either about principles guiding supply, which may be illuminated in parliamentary debates in Western countries (SIPRI, 1975, p. 77), or other analyses or investigations by individual Soviet researchers; thus, on the whole, the Soviet Union provides substantially less information about its arms sales than Western countries do about theirs. It appears possible, however, to gain some understanding of the processes of decision through analysis of the rhythms of Soviet arms exports to the Third World, or particular regions of it, in relation to the periodicity of Soviet five-year economic plans (see Hutchings, 1978A and 1978B and 1985, and Abouchar, 1981).

Stoppages of trading activity and the reporting of such stoppages do not necessarily take place at the same moment, judging by the fact that Poland suddenly stopped reporting its imports of tobacco from Bulgaria, in 1967, but stopped reporting before it stopped buying (Hewett, 1974, p. 67).

Strictly secret quantities include the balance of payments in negotiations for the CSCE. Western countries tried to obtain information about this, 'but met with a stone wall' (Lascelles, 1975, p. 5).

The United States being the ideological enemy, trade with that country is a particularly sensitive topic. *Vneshnyaya torgovlya* for 1973, the annual foreign trade handbook, omitted statistics of grain imports. There had been only three mentions on domestic radio of grain imports from the the USA. As reported in July 1974, since 1972 grain purchases had been concealed from the Soviet public, the last mention having been made in the statistical handbook *Foreign Trade of the USSR for 1971*. The subject was referred to only in indirect allusions by specialised periodicals, or by provincial radio stations with limited audiences (Radio Liberty Research, 9 July 1974, RL 202/74). Because the Russians did not supply basic and vital information about their grain harvests, in 1972 and again in 1974 the US Agricultural Department was caught very much by surprise regarding their requirements (*International Herald Tribune*, 9 October 1974; cf. Wolf, 1983, pp. 32–3). Similarly, 'Soviet exports to the US rose by 80 per cent in 1973, but the published breakdown omits the bulk of the commodity composition. A fair guess is that it consisted of oil – a matter about which silence is preferred' (*The Times*, 17 July

1974). There is always an orchestrated attempt to keep secret the actual terms of Soviet foreign trade. If some item becomes highly important in Soviet foreign trade, it may disappear from the relevant Soviet statistics. Thus, large-diameter pipe is invariably mentioned in surveys of recent Soviet–Western trade, but as reported in 1981 it had disappeared from Soviet published trade returns since 1975 (Hanson, 1981, pp. 132, 140). Soviet imports of equipment for the chemical industry have been very import-ant, but are not disaggregated usefully by Soviet trade returns (Ibid. p. 170).

Naturally, foreign-made goods bring with them information about those goods: first of all, the fact that such things exist. This cannot be prevented, if they are to go on general sale; however, certain items are reserved for distribution through special out-lets, and those outlets as well as the goods themselves must as far as possible be kept secret. In general, the authorities do not wish knowledge of the existence of specific goods to be disseminated, unless the goods themselves can be supplied: otherwise, desire would be evoked when there was no intention of importing those items. No doubt this is why foreign firms may only advertise in Soviet publications (obligatorily under arrangements with the foreign trade association Vneshtorgreklama) goods which are already on sale within the USSR. A small exception to this rule, no disclosure without availability, is made at exhibitions of foreign-made goods, such as for example the American Exhibi-tion in Sokolniki Park in Moscow in 1959; perhaps the objective here is to stretch the imagination and fire the mettle of potential Soviet producers. There must be important reasons for allowing such exhibitions, as they are considered to be occasions also for Western espionage activity (Sergeyev, 1970, p. 17). Ample data about new foreign-made products will be reaching the foreign trade agencies, but via their own private channels. The pre-existence of those channels – originating normally in a Soviet trade mission in the other country – then also supplies a possibility of using that agency, and those channels, for trans-mitting information which has been gathered less legitimately. Out of twenty-five Soviet officials expelled from Britain for spying in September 1985, seven had been based in the trade delegation (*The Times*, 13 September 1985).

In the main, of course, a Soviet trade delegation is engaged in trading activities. As such, it comprises an element in the network of Soviet foreign trade agencies, which consist of (a) a Ministry of Foreign Trade and (b) a number of foreign trade corporations. These latter 'arrange imports, exports, or both, of anything classifiable within a specified rather broad group of items' (Hutchings, 1982A, p. 235). They constitute an additional stage between sellers and purchasers, and on the principle that additional stages are undesirable it can be argued that the system is far from being optimal. Indeed, that comment is frequently made by Western traders who engage in East–West trade (as the Soviet system has been adopted also by other Soviet bloc countries, though by now Hungary and to some extent Poland have departed from the Soviet model). The pattern of corporations is in principle rational and easily surveyable (Ibid., p. 236), and doubtless in many instances the Soviet representatives make a vital contribution to trading arrangements. The chief factor that makes any system of organisation work better than one might at first sight expect is the knowledge, energy and conscientiousness of its employees; if the system works reasonably well this is therefore no cause for particular surprise. However, since the existence of an intermediate stage is *a priori* disadvantageous it might have been expected that experiments would have been conducted with other organisational forms. In fact, although the system of foreign trade organisation attracts, and has always attracted, much more widespread and unanimous criticism from Western sources than the organisation of the domestic economy, Soviet foreign trade organisation has been far less variable than that of the domestic economy. A reorganisation, aimed at improving efficiency and not affecting basic principles of structure, occurred in 1978 (see below). This could well lead one to suspect that some factor other than economic efficiency was involved, but although I had previously concluded that the organisation of foreign trade observed the principle of State monopoly too rigidly (Ibid., p. 235), until starting to approach the problem from the standpoint of information control it had not struck me that that too might help to explain the form of organisation.

If we view the Soviet system of foreign trade organisation as intended also to satisfy the demands of a system of information control, the remaining pieces fall into place. The fact that a State monopoly of foreign trade was one of the first measures to be adopted by the Bolsheviks, although at the time there was no foreign trade worth mentioning, becomes explicable. The subsequent extension of the system to other Soviet bloc countries appears natural too. The even greater centralisation of the Ministry of Foreign Trade than of the Ministry of Foreign Affairs, since there are no republic ministries of foreign trade whereas some republics do have a ministry of foreign affairs of however nominal significance, becomes understandable. The role of the foreign trade corporations and of their representatives in offices around the world is to supply information about foreign demand or supply, but only within the closed channels of the foreign trade network. The subsequent work of negotiation and signature of contracts adds to this role but is secondary to it, although according to the respondents in one survey the stages of negotiation and inspection (which tend to be especially protracted) are themselves useful in enabling valuable information to be gained by the Soviet purchasers (Hanson, 1981, p. 199, citing a survey of UK machine-tool exporters). Although state control of foreign trade sometimes confers the advantages of monopoly or monopsony and this must be among the reasons why this system of organisation has been preserved, an explanation from the side of information control also explains restrictions upon foreign advertising, as well as the existence of foreign trade corporations even in areas where there would be few or slight advantages from monopoly or monopsony. In other words, I see the principle 'State Monopoly of Foreign Trade' to be included under a broader rubric of a 'state monopoly of information about foreign trade'.

One fairly important reorganisation has taken place, in 1978. Although all foreign trade corporations remain subordinate to the Ministry of Foreign Trade as regards authorisation of contracts, some now operate within other ministries or other high-level governmental bodies. This should improve direct liaison with these bodies and would not affect the principle of a monopoly of foreign trade information. An extension of this trend, which enabled 'more than 20' ministries and departments plus 70 of the largest enterprises to enter foreign markets freely without having to refer to the Ministry, was announced in September 1986 (*Pravda*, 24 September 1986, p. 1), during a phase of more liberal release of information.

THE STATE BUDGET

It is partly due to the gaps and bias in published data that Western studies of the Soviet budget have been comparatively few, while in a related sphere a systematic examination of the influence of the pricing system upon Soviet economic development has yet to appear. (Regarding the budget, see Hutchings, 1983, pp. 17–19 and Wanless, 1985, Introduction and p. 1.)

The Soviet national budget integrates about 55 000 republic and local budgets, but is promulgated in a law which occupies only a few paragraphs – enactment of which is preceded by a 'debate' which is heavily propagandist. The law too is rather uninformative. As no Soviet source provides lengthy continuous series of budget figures, these have to be laboriously built up from numerous individual sources. The degree of detail in the available data is highly uneven. Revenues are indicated in less detail than expenditures. A large fraction of budget revenues is not itemised, which permits Birman to deduce that part is actually contributed by bank credit (Birman, 1980, pp. 96–7). Among expenditure clauses the detail is fairly considerable in Social and Cultural Measures, very much less in Finance of National Economy, and entirely lacking for Defence. Certain principal totals are missing for 1952, 1954 and 1964. For most other items, series without gaps cannot be constructed. For example, budget allocations to centralised capital investments from the budget, enterprises' own funds and bank credit are known for only twenty out of the thirty years 1952–81 inclusive, and those years are irregularly distributed (Hutchings, 1983, pp. 107–8). Breakdowns of Finance of National Economy into industrial and non-industrial, and (approximately) into capital and non-capital expenditures are available for certain years, but never for the same year – which can hardly be accidental (Hutchings, 1983, pp. 11–12).

If a topic, which fundamentally is treated as confidential, has nevertheless to be illuminated from some angles for general pedagogical purposes, the usual choice is to explain general principles, making use mainly or entirely of hypothetical examples, without resort to naming names or quantities in specific instances. The treatment of turnover tax, which provides about one-third of budget revenues, is an illustration. A chapter allotted to this topic in A. M. Aleksandrov (ed.) *Gosudarstvenniy*

byudzhet (*The State Budget*), 1961, has the following subheadings:
The essential nature of the turnover tax; Trade turnover; Payers
of turnover tax; Calculation of the taxable turnover; Calculation
of turnover tax; Procedure and terms of payment of turnover tax;
Exemptions or reductions (*l'goty*) in turnover tax; Peculiarities of
taxation of turnovers in the sale of commodities in certain
branches of the economy; and Planning of payments of turnover
tax. (This is apart from lesser subdivisions.) Within altogether
forty-eight pages it provides only the following apparent examples of rates of turnover tax: fish 42.9 per cent (inclusive of a 'tax
difference' which seems to be peculiar to this branch), cotton
cloth 85.2 per cent, goods sold at agricultural retail prices 66.7
per cent, men's chrome shoes on leather soles 66.7 per cent,
cotton wool 80.4 per cent. (These rates are reckoned relative to
the retail price minus turnover tax, whereas the Soviet practice is
to reckon turnover tax rates relative to the retail price *inclusive* of
turnover tax.) It does not make clear whether these rates are
representative. The chapter does not give average rates, either
on the whole or in regard to particular groups of commodities, or
attempt to describe or quantify the importance of turnover tax
within total budget revenues. The chapter does, of course,
provide a good grounding in the calculation of turnover tax in all
circumstances (with the possible exception of generalities which
may be too secret to disclose), when the precise quantities are
supplied.

It may also be occasionally possible for a talented researcher
to make use of such a theoretical framework into which he
interpolates what he believes to be the actual figures, as is done
by Wiles in his detection of the actual distribution of income in
the Soviet Union (Wiles, 1974).

While much of the Soviet budget is veiled in secrecy, this is
even more true of the 'national financial plan' (including also
enterprises' collective and personal revenues and expenditures),
in which the budget is included. 'The lack of systematic elaboration of the non-budgetary parts of the unified financial plan
cloaks that document with an extra veil of secrecy, as is probably
the intention' (Hutchings, 1983, p. 16). Elaboration of a proposal in a doctoral dissertation that the role of the unified
financial plan should be increased was halted apparently in
mid-career, possibly following outside intervention on grounds
of security (Ibid., pp. 16–17).

INPUT–OUTPUT ANALYSIS

Input–output work in the USSR was at first conducted in complete secrecy, its veil being lifted in 1960. The published results exhibited interesting gaps: while the lack of data (and of explanation) for defence and for non-ferrous metals was not unexpected, most gaps (according to the American authors) were not related to areas of traditional Soviet secrecy (Treml *et al.*, 1972, pp. 17 and 21). The end-product, reconstruction of a 76-sector *ex post*-table of the Soviet economy, demanded that over 13 per cent by number of items and about 50 per cent by value of the total flows in the quadrants should be estimated by the American researchers (Treml *et al.*, 1972, p. 5), who also claimed that 'more descriptive information and data are available on *ex post* tables than on planning tables, and more information and data are being released on *ex post* tables in physical value terms than on those in physical units' (Ibid., p. 69). Various omissions or obscurities are noted in the structure of the economy, as presented in input–output tables: Soviet economists themselves are sometimes uncertain where items are located. For example, the situation of forestry is ambiguous: 'apparently it is included with other branches of material production' (Ibid., p. 217).

> The 1959 input–output table, never published in complete form, included seven categories covering private and public consumption in its final demand quadrant . . . After the table itself was completed, Soviet input–output statisticians undertook a major study of private and public consumption for a period of five years, 1959–63, using the 1959 input–output commodity classification. The results of this study were published in the 1964 statistical yearbook. (Ibid., p. 345)

Omitted industrial flows in the published matrix amounted to 18 390 600 thousand roubles, representing the sum of sixty-nine cells in the eighteen-sector table (Ibid., p. 393).

The same concealment techniques were used in publication of the 1966 input–output table as of the 1959 one, i.e. some original sectors were aggregated and others omitted. The original 110-sector table was transformed into one of 85 sectors by means of aggregating 29 sectors into 10 and omitting 6. Also, the published flow table contained no data for the final demand or value-added quadrants and gave nothing on the total outputs of any of the sectors (Ibid., pp. 89–90).

CRIMINALITY AND SOCIAL DEVIANCE

The Soviet press conceals the fact that Soviet citizens have in reality diverse opinions about the Soviet Union and about the outside world. No statement from any dissident is ever published. Similarly, unrest within the USSR is another of the taboo subjects, for obvious reasons. Departures from this rule are very rare, and until December 1986, when 'nationalistic' riots were acknowledged to have occurred in Alma Ata (*Izvestiya*, 20 December 1986, p. 6), always avoided any admission that disorders were nationalistic. For example, 'some violations of public order' in Estonia in 1980 were ascribed to unruliness and criminal hooligans, although that origin was denied by unofficial sources (*D.T.*, 18 October 1980, p. 8).

Absolute numbers of crimes and criminal sentences have not been given during the past fifty years, though sentences have been given for certain periods, regions or categories (van den Berg, 1985, p. 9). Of course, criminality exists, as witness the exhibition 'Krimtekhnika 74' which was to be held in Moscow in August 1974, and which appeared to be intended to cover the whole gamut of methods for crime prevention and detection (Zand, 1974, p. 8). The total number of executions is secret (*Soviet Analyst*, 6 April 1978, p. 7), though probably large, as it was even in the years of NEP (van den Berg, 1985, p. 87). Homosexuality and drug-taking in socialist countries are taboo subjects; drunkenness is admitted (it could not be hidden) but its full extent and the damage to health have to be pieced together from scattered references (Treml, 1982). Data have not recently been published on the size of the adult population, which makes it impossible to calculate the numbers in corrective labour institutions or other forced labour camps (van den Berg, 1985, pp. 185–6).

Racist behaviour in any of the socialist countries is never mentioned, whereas if it occurs in a capitalist country it is given full publicity. Any suggestion that the socialist countries do not specially favour women is barred.

RELIGION

The Russian Orthodox Church has been stripped of the main part of its political role. Spiritual literature does not exist except in extremely limited circulation (plus rarities such as Bourdeaux, 1976), Marxism being materialist and idealist philosophies being banned (cf. Komarov, 1978, p. 73). Religious instruction to children is forbidden. A few seminaries exist, but no publicity is given to religious events, unless these have some other significance as well (for instance, a papal election: in the case of Pope John Paul II, this could not possibly be ignored). It is uncommon, though not entirely unknown, to see a priest outside a church in his priestly robes; in the countryside, one might encounter a priest-led funeral procession. High ecclesiastics may attend diplomatic functions; on one such occasion (it was in fact the Danish National Day, probably in 1957) my wife and I had the opportunity of conversing with the Metropolitan of Moscow. As some churches in city centres have not been demolished, but renovated and flanked by modern buildings of very different style and scale, the effect is sometimes to make the church more conspicuous; in New Arbat Street, in Moscow, this effect is most striking. Moreover, as churches are few and small, at major religious festivals such as Easter the main part of the congregation must perforce spill into the street, so that the entire occasion becomes very non-secret. However, all this is superficial: except in theological materials mention of God is censored, even if the utterance is by the General Secretary of the Soviet Communist Party! (see *The Times*, 3 September 1985, p. 6).

SHORT-TERM SECRECY

The foregoing relates mainly to secrets which are to be kept for a long period. Temporary secrecy is less diversified, but includes in particular prohibitions on travel to specified areas. For example, in 1932 Uzbekistan was barred to foreigners, though neighbouring Kirghizia was open, doubtless because of the 'tremendous shortage' of food there which was the consequence of decisions that cotton should be grown in Uzbekistan rather than grain (Maillart, 1985). Cotton was to be grown for the sake of the industrialisation plan. 'In September 1970, for example, the Party imposed a temporary ban on the discussion of environmental problems, and *Izvestiya* was forced to cancel a series on the pollution of the Volga. By early 1971 the ban had been lifted, apparently after discussion among top leaders' (Kelley, 1978, p. 93). In such cases the intention must be to hide the appearance of things, or the views of the inhabitants, within the area that is closed and during the period of closure.

Temporary secrecy also typically surrounds any function to be attended by the top leaders, such as the assembly in Warsaw with the aim of renewing the Warsaw Pact (*The Times*, 26 April 1985, p. 32). When in June 1982 CMEA prime ministers met in Budapest, the Hotel Duna-Intercontinental, the venue of their meetings, was shut to other visitors for the duration.

Much more characteristically, before the national leader dies the economic situation or contemporary life generally are painted in rosy colours; how bad things really were will be made known (if at all) only after a new leader has taken over. The 27th Congress of the Soviet Communist Party (February 1986) again illustrated this sequence, with former President Brezhnev, although not named, being in effect one of the targets of Gorbachev's strictures. It was not until December 1986 that Brezhnev was criticised publicly by name (*Pravda*, 19 December 1986, p. 5), in the course of a review (timed for the 80th anniversary of his birth) of Brezhnev's life and career which devoted about equal space to his positive achievements; the contrast between this measured evaluation and the uncritical praise heaped on President Brezhnev during his lifetime was indeed great.

6 How Secrets Are Kept: I. Physical Obstacles

In this chapter and the next I shall consider the means by which secrets are kept in the Soviet Union: first of all, physical obstacles.

BARRIERS TO EXIT AND ENTRY

The practice appears to be to attach great importance to physical, including especially geographical, barriers. These are disposed concentrically. Moving outwards from the interior of the USSR, one encounters first the frontier zone: residence within this zone is permitted only with specific permission, which is indicated on one's internal passport, and authorisation is required for entry into or transit of it. Next, adjacent to the frontier, is a fortified zone, 100 metres wide on average, which is equipped with various harmful devices, including man-traps, and then a 'neutral zone', which is patrolled by frontier guards, in pairs, with dogs (Voslensky, 1984, pp. 417–18). Just back from the border are observation points, comprising elevated covered-in platforms which are supported on splayed-out wooden struts; this design is the same opposite both Finland and Turkey. Arnold Toynbee, when describing the valley of Arpa Çay, which forms the frontier between the Soviet Union and Turkey just to the east of Ani, mentioned a 'fence of electrified wire, equipped with observation posts – miniature Eiffel Towers– at intervals of about a quarter of a mile and with the ground raked over to take the impress of footprints. I had seen all this from Iran, on the Western shore of the Caspian. I had seen it again from Afghanistan across the river Oxus' (Toynbee, 1969, p. 45). So it appears that this system of barriers and observation posts is standard all along the Soviet land borders. There are similar arrangements (with slight differences to the architecture of the towers, which appear more of a prefabricated type) on the north bank of the Danube where the river forms the frontier between Czechoslovakia and Austria. The aim along all the

94

borders of the Communist countries is evidently to prevent the passage of individuals, rather than to offer resistance to an invading army.

The Soviet frontiers are patrolled by a force of 300 000 to 400 000 border guards belonging to the KGB (Committee of State Security – Schultz and Godson, 1984, pp. 31–2). The perimeter of the Soviet Union being almost 60 000 km long (Hutchings, 1982A, p. 1), there can be about five to six guards on average per kilometre, or somewhat fewer taking into account leave, training, and supervision of airfields. These are élite forces, green-capped, whose allegiance to the regime has to be unquestionable.

Although the system of barriers along the borders is intended to prevent crossing of the frontier from either direction, its emphasis is clearly upon preventing unauthorised exit from the Soviet Union, which in fact is how it is understood by the mature population though propaganda, or course, dwells upon the supposed need to guard the USSR from foreign spies and 'diversionaries'. This bias is clear in the construction of the 'Berlin Wall' (see below). As Khrushchev put it, Soviet border policy was designed 'for the sake of keeping the dregs and scum inside our country' (Khrushchev, 1971, p. 553).

On exiting from the USSR by air, the last thing that happens before one boards the plane is a scrutiny of one's passport and one's face by a frontier policeman standing at the base of the stairway. Doubtless there is an analogous inspection when one leaves the Soviet Union by any other means of transport, but as far as I recall the formalities when crossing the Soviet–Finnish border by train were less prolonged than when a train crossed from Hungary into Austria: at Hegyeshalom, there was a delay of one hour while Hungarian border guards scrutinised every possible space where either person or contraband might be concealed. (Own observations in 1959 and 1981.) Probably the reason for this difference is that in the former case one is crossing into a country from which refugees are returned, whereas into Austria they might be free for ever. In effect, Finland acts as the goalkeeper on this important sector of the Soviet border, in proximity to the Soviet Union's second largest (and most Westernised) city. No doubt it was because they were aware of Finnish complaisance that two Soviet soldiers, hiking to freedom from the Murmansk area, did not give themselves up until they had crossed both the Finnish and the Swedish frontiers (*The Times*, 16 October 1985, p. 1).

On top of this, though on a much smaller scale, countries adjacent to the USSR also maintain their own border forces. Any Soviet citizens who crossed and were caught would be returned to their own country. Given the tightly organised life in these countries, not to speak of linguistic differences, the likelihood of remaining undetected would be small. If that is deemed necessary, additional restrictions are imposed on travel between the USSR and an East European country, or (it can be presumed on Soviet instigation) between one East European country and another; for example, between the GDR and Poland between 1980 and 1983, when Solidarity emerged in Poland and subsequently (December 1981) was outlawed.

From the maritime borders of the USSR it is naturally easier to prevent egress, but this is not left to chance. According to Zhores Medvedev, 'armed high-speed large frontier protection launches' are permanently on watch at twelve miles from the spring-tide low-water mark (Medvedev, 1971, p. 245). He explains that the sea frontier is why there are almost no Soviet yachts to be seen. Along the Baltic coast, across from Finland, a roller traverses daily, so as to make footmarks visible (Ibid). The Soviet Navy has a large number of small patrol craft – many more than the US Navy has. Their functions probably include preventing illegal cross-border movements (cf. Brown *et al.*, 1982, p. 432).

The prevention of escape from East Berlin is obviously the predominant reason why the Berlin Wall was built by the East Germans in 1961. There would otherwise have been no need to enclose so elaborately as enclave which offers no military threat; rather, defensive works should protect *West* Berlin, yet in fact there are none. The perimeter of West Berlin is 100 miles long and on the East German side it is permanently manned by 14 000 troops. The Berlin Wall, thirty miles long, comprises not only a wall but other physical barriers, dogs, watch-towers, etc (Shears, 1970, p. 9, and *Encyclopaedia Britannica, Macropaedia*, 1980, vol. 2, p. 853). In fact this should more accurately be called a fortified zone, which is perhaps modelled on the Soviet frontier zone although within a much more compressed space. As regards the numbers who may have been killed or arrested along the Soviet frontiers, there are no complete published figures. But in a certain sense, the Berlin Wall, and other barriers along the frontiers between Eastern and Western Europe, are the true external boundary of the Soviet Union. Up to March 1983, 3082 East Germans had been arrested at the Berlin Wall and seventy-one people had been killed.

The violence gradient leaps up at the borders of the Soviet empire, as these totals show. On a smaller scale, the same applies to boundaries between zones of lesser and greater security within the Soviet empire, as witness the shooting of Major Nicholson, a member of the US military liaison group based in Potsdam, on the border of the Ludwigslust restricted area inside East Germany (*Time*, 8 April 1985, pp. 26–7).

It might be arguable that prohibitions on emigration are motivated not so much by the desire to preserve secrets as the desire not to permit the loss of manpower which would certainly occur if all restrictions on emigration were removed. This has clearly been one of the most important motives behind the erection of the Berlin Wall. So far as exit from the Soviet Union is concerned, I consider that this motive is less weighty than that of preserving secrets, but that it comprises an important secondary motive.

EXTRA-TERRITORIAL MOVEMENT OF MILITARY EQUIPMENT

Secrecy regulations are doubtless extended to countries to which secret equipment is supplied. For instance, at a Cairo military parade which included Soviet-made rockets the warheads were covered by a screen (*Armies & Weapons*, no. 27, 1976, p. 48). Soviet military hardware which goes out of control outside the frontiers of the Soviet Union must be relieved of secret items and if possible returned intact. For example, if a Soviet naval vessel runs aground not in Soviet waters, items are quickly offloaded on to other Soviet ships and papers burned, as in the case of the naval auxiliary *Negriz*, which ran aground in the Sea of Marmara in January 1972 (*D.T.*, 21 January 1972, p. 17). If a missile or other item of military hardware strays into foreign territory it must be recovered if possible, if necessary by requesting the unintended host country to return it, and by paying for the search. Thus, the wreckage of what was apparently a Shaddock

missile, modified to be a target drone, which crashed in Lake
Inari in Finland on 28 December 1984, was returned by the
Finns to the Soviet Union, which paid the bill of 560 300 markka
(£74 000) for recovery costs, although it is unlikely that this
obsolete weapon would have provided any significantly useful
intelligence (*The Times*, 9 February 1985, p. 6, and other reports,
e.g. *Daily Express*, 7 February 1985, p. 6).

RADIO JAMMING

From time to time, both in the USSR and in other countries in
Eastern Europe, certain foreign broadcasts are blotted out by
radio jamming. The raucous roar, of uneven pitch, of the *za-
glushka*, like a medley of car horns, was regularly heard in
1957–9 whenever one twiddled the knobs. Jamming applies to
broadcasts in Russian or some other vernacular, and is effective
especially in urban areas, where no doubt most jamming aerials
are situated. To black out rural areas, less effective skyjammers
are used. It is believed that radio engineers in their spare time
adjust people's sets to make them more sensitive and to enable
them to minimise the effect of jamming by trying all available
frequencies (*The Times*, 23 May 1985, p. 1). This jamming must
be very costly; it is estimated that the total cost would amount to
$150 million per year, or more than the combined costs of
operating the Voice of America, Radio Free Europe and Radio
Liberty (Schultz and Godson, 1984, p. 31). If one wishes to
prevent foreign broadcasts from being listened to by Russians,
jamming is necessary because the curiosity of Soviet citizens
towards the outside world is far greater than the curiosity of the
outside world towards them. It has been claimed that 15 per cent
of Soviet citizens listen to the Voice of America; clearly the
proportion of Americans, or of citizens of other Western countries, who listen to Radio Moscow is nowhere near this high,
although they have no jamming to contend with. Apparently no
way has yet been found to jam transmitters broadcasting Islamic
propaganda from Iran. (*Sunday Times Magazine*, 10 November
1985, p. 8).

The extent of jamming depends on the current state of international relations: one episode is mentioned below, and may be
compared with others which may occur in the future.

Thus, following the proclamation of martial law in Poland on 13 December 1981, it appeared on 17 December that the Soviet Union had stepped up its jamming of broadcasts to Poland by Radio Free Europe. BBC programmes were not being jammed, but during the previous few days amateur radio enthusiasts were finding it impossible to get through to their Polish contacts. One of the military decrees ordered Poles to hand in transmitters (*D.T.*, 18 December 1981, p. 4). The BBC increased its broadcasts to Poland by 25 per cent on 22 December. BBC broadcasts to Poland were jammed starting from 17.30 on 30 December 1981 for the first time since 1965 (*D.T.*, 31 December 1981, p. 1). Jamming stations in Smolensk and Kaliningrad were used to blot out BBC broadcasts to Poland, with a jammer at Tashkent as back-up, mainly for daytime high-frequency work. Britain protested to the USSR, which countered by denying knowledge or responsibility and attacked the BBC for disseminating 'lies and distortions about the Polish situation and Soviet foreign policy' (*D.T.*, 7 January 1982, p. 32). Clandestine radios were seized, for instance two operated by Solidarity at or near Gdansk (*The Times*, 30 September 1982, p. 5).

INTERRUPTION OF TELEPHONIC AND OTHER CROSS-FRONTIER COMMUNICATIONS

Periodically communications between the Soviet Union and the outside world are interrupted. The second half of 1982 is an illustration. A US newspaper claimed that the USSR was violating an international agreement that guarantees private telephone communications between the USA and USSR (*The Washington Post*, 8 June 1972, p. A32). British Telecom was informed of deep cuts in telephone links between Russia and British as from July 1982. Lines to Britain would be reduced from 46 to 14 while those to Russia would be cut from 42 to 14 until the end of 1984. Lines to Austria were also being cut, it was believed from 24 to 4. This was particularly suggestive as there were thousands of Soviet émigrés in Vienna. Other reports indicated that lines were to be cut with France and West Germany (*D.T.*, 29 June 1982, p. 1). On 15 July 1982, the Soviet government abolished direct dialling from inside the Soviet Union to the West. The Soviet Union then cut automatic telephone links with Western Europe, citing a reorganisation of its internal telephone network and unspecified technical grounds (*The Times*, 4 September 1982, p. 4). It was still possible to dial Moscow directly from West European capitals, but that same week this too ended: all calls had not to be made through an operator and took several hours, or sometimes longer. The USSR had introduced direct dialling for the Olympic Games two years previously (*The Times*, 9 September 1982, p. 4. See also *The Times* leader on the cutting of Soviet telephone links, 13 September 1982, p. 9). Moreover, 'recently, the authorities in Estonia have tried to prevent people watching Finnish TV'. Earlier, the USSR cut Estonia's direct telephone dialling links with Finland and other Western countries. Foreign subscriptions to the more liberal Estonian magazines were stopped and there was a clampdown on Finnish newspapers. Finnish publications brought into Estonia by tourists were censored by customs officials (*The Times*, 13 October 1982, p. 6). Administrative and economic obstacles were placed in the way of book exports, which now required an export licence from the Ministry of Culture and paying a 100 per cent duty. Works on politics, social studies and economics were among those affected (*The Times*, 14 October 1982, p. 5). Was this anticipating Brezhnev's death on 10 November 1982, in the hope of preventing the news from prematurely leaking out, or were there alternative (or additional) reasons?

Specific telephone conversations may also be interrupted; thus, when the attempt was made to inform Sakharov that he was being filmed by hidden cameras, the line was jammed (*The Guardian*, 13 December 1985, p. 6). However, this must be a very special case, and would not justify a deduction that all telephone conversations, even if with some foreign country, are equally closely controlled.

RESTRICTIONS UPON RESIDENCE

Residence in principal cities, including Moscow, Leningrad and Kiev, is permitted only with authorisation; this would normally go with a particular job, but a residence permit for Moscow can reward long service in the BAM project (BBC-2 'The Money Programme', 19 January 1986). Even rail tickets to these cities must be authorised, and anyone who does not possess one will be turned off the train. I was once myself refused permission to purchase a train ticket to Moscow on grounds of not being authorised, and another time heard at first hand of the ejection of someone who presumably had lacked authorisation. (As this latter individual, while I was absent from the compartment, had torn into small pieces the English newspaper I had been reading, I did not at the time feel very sympathetic. He probably vented his wrath on the nearest victim.)

The chief means for controlling movement is the internal passport system. This was introduced by decree of 27 December 1932. All citizens above 16 years of age who resided permanently in towns or workers' settlements or worked in transport under-takings, State Farms or new construction schemes were required to have passports, and these were declared to be the only valid document for identification purposes. Persons arriving in a new place were required to apply for passports. They were not issued to collective farmers. The intention behind this sweeping re-quirement may have been largely to eliminate urban unemploy-ment. The creation of the collective farm system had this among its objectives, and results (see Hutchings, 1967, pp. 29–52). The decree's preamble spoke of securing 'the deportation from those places of persons who are not connected with industry or with work in the offices and schools' (Matthews, 1974, pp. 74–7). However, both this and other provisions would also have had a security motivation; for example, people who are not allowed to reside in Moscow, or to travel there, must experience greater difficulty in making contact with the foreign community in the capital.

The foundation of 'scientific' towns was doubtless decided upon partly in order to preserve confidentiality within informa-tion fortresses, as well as for ideological reasons – more unortho-dox ideas may circulate here than is allowed in a normal community (cf. Medvedev, 1971, pp. 451–2). A similar distinc-tion is found between research establishments, especially those of high standing, on one side and teaching establishments on the other: views somewhat critical of existing institutions or even of Soviet policy more generally may be aired in the former, but not in the latter. This was exemplified in my visit to the USSR under the auspices of the Academy of Sciences in May–June 1971: I then gave much the same lecture in one institution of the former type and in one belonging more nearly to the latter, and in the first place this was well received whereas in the second it apparently caused offence.

The system of passes for gaining entry (or being refused entry) to buildings is, of course, well developed. On one occasion, in May 1971, I mistook my destination and was trying to get into the university skyscraper on the Lenin Hills, in the south-western outskirts of Moscow. However, not having the required pass, I was (quite properly) refused entry. This building is divided into four wings, a different entry pass being required for each.

REDUCING CONTACTS WITH FOREIGNERS

Everything possible is done to reduce unstructured contacts between Soviet citizens and foreigners. Letters from abroad to specific officials may go unanswered. If named Soviet scientists are invited to a foreign congress, the reply is liable to be delayed and that invitee replaced by someone else: the preference usually lighting on elderly specialists who have made foreign trips before, and therefore can be better relied on not to defect. In the other direction, matters tend to work out better: visiting foreign scientists are welcomed and assisted in meeting people who would be likely to be helpful. I am happy to acknowledge assistance of this nature given to myself in May–June 1971, when researching for an earlier book (Hutchings, 1976. Visits of this nature are considered further in Chapter 14).

In general, first meetings between foreign diplomats or other foreigners with Soviet citizens are permitted; in fact, it would be impossible to prevent them. However, subsequent meetings, unless justified by some professional and approved motive, are discouraged – although a determined person can persist, nevertheless. The stationing of a militiaman at the entry to every diplomatic compound has no doubt, as one objective, the diplomats' protection; bearing in mind that diplomats, in the Middle East especially, are sometimes an object of violence, this protection is welcome. Almost certainly, a more active motivation is to hinder contacts between Soviet and non-Soviet citizens; unless specially authorised, the former are prevented by Soviet guards from entering Western embassies. This same motive of hindering contacts is doubtless a principal reason why diplomats must live in *compounds*.

Foreign correspondents who are accredited in Moscow may be expelled because of 'repeated use of impermissible methods of journalism', which was the wording in the expulsion of Andrew Nagorski, Moscow correspondent of the magazine *Newsweek* (*The Times*, 3 August 1983, p. 6). Only officially approved contacts are allowed between Soviet citizens and representatives of foreign media, and the latter's movements and access within the USSR are severely restricted. At a conference about freeing the flow of international news, the Russians (Zamyatin) insisted that the right of foreign correspondents to have access in all countries to members of a political opposition had to be deleted (*Sunday Times*, 30 April 1978, p. 9).

Diplomatic travel is restricted to a 40 km radius from the centre of Moscow unless permission is obtained in advance from the Ministry of Foreign Affairs. A number of areas even within this radius are out of bounds, for example (starting from the centre of Moscow) on the Gorky direction along *Shosse Entuzias-tov*. The Note from the Ministry of Foreign Affairs indicating the zones which, at the time of writing, are still closed to foreigners (No. 1/Pr of 4 January 1978) did not include a map, but one of 1:150 000 scale, based on this Note, has been drawn by the US State Department; there are also three other maps in this series. The map of Moscow shows the 40 km radius as operative only on the southern sector, part of the western sector and a small part of the northern sector; in other segments the forbidden zone either reaches the Moscow ring road (at a radius of about 8 to 12 km from the centre) or comes a long way towards it. The permitted zone forms an island of no easily definable shape, as if the Soviet authorities did not wish any conclusion to be drawn from a very simple shape – which, possibly, was the case. Only about one-tenth of Moscow *oblast'* is within bounds. As regards the entire Soviet Union, the situation is much more complex. The Note of 4 January 1978 took up eight typed pages. There are forbidden zones in ten out of the fifteen republics, only Belorussia, Moldavia, Georgia, Armenia and Tajikistan not containing any, apart from 25-km wide strips along the frontiers of Turkey, Iran and Afghanistan. A number of complete *oblasti* are barred, such as Kamchatka, Sakhalin, Sverdlov, Gorky, Kaliningrad, or complete autonomous republics (Udmurt, Mordvin, Nakhichevan); the three Baltic republics are entirely out of bounds except for named exceptions. Numerous other specific areas, cities or towns are barred. The same regulations apply to all British nationals living in the USSR (as students, etc.); my information does not extend to whether they apply to all non-Soviet citizens, though that would not be surprising.

These regulations are, of course, independent of banned specific sites within areas where no travel restrictions apply. The whole makes up a body of regulations of a complexity which almost certainly is far greater than is applied by any other country. It might be thought that such detailed provisions would be unenforceable. Though complete enforcement is perhaps not attained, travellers recount incidents when even a minor deviation was at once pounced on; it may therefore be supposed that they are enforced to a very large extent.

From time to time, diplomatic travel is restricted further; for example, in 1972, to all areas east of the Volga river. Though this ban did not apply to foreign tourist trips under 'direct control' or to visitors under international exchange agreements, diplomats could not recall when such a wide ban had been issued before (*The Washington* Post, 29 June 1972, p. A24). Also, overflight rights to foreign civil airlines have to be agreed and are not always granted, for example permission to overfly the USSR was denied by the Soviet authorities before a Finnish-Chinese aviation agreement could be concluded (Helsinki home service 21.20 GMT 9 December 1974, SWB 4778).

Deportations from newly occupied territories during the Stalinist period also need to be integrated into this schema. They were on a considerable scale: during the first Soviet occupation of Estonia (May 1940 to August 1941) 58 037 persons were deported (Raud, 1953, p. 31), about 5 per cent of the entire population. Distant destinations were chosen (Brown *et al.*, 1982, p. 313), probably to minimise the possibility of return or of contact with compatriots.

The propensity to confine foreigners within the capital, but to confine Soviet dissidents outside the capital, seems inconsistent unless the objective is that they should not meet. This must have been the intention in the case of Andrey Sakharov, who for almost seven years (until December 1986) was exiled to a city (Gorky) which is out of bounds to foreigners. The latter should remain in Moscow for other reasons too: diplomats must be conceded access to government organs; Moscow has been developed partly with the aim of impressing foreign visitors; also, within the capital visitors can be treated to a more selective exposure than could be managed if they were allowed to roam within a wider compass (cf. Chapter 2).

RESTRICTIONS UPON PHOTOGRAPHY

The range of scope of restrictions upon photography by foreigners is exceptionally wide as it includes not only military supplies and installations but means of communication (bridges, railway junctions, ports) and also industrial areas and scientific research centres, electricity works, signal masts and power stations. All photography and sketching are forbidden in a 25-km wide zone along the frontier. Photography and sketching on the territory of industrial, educational and public establishments is possible if permitted by the administration (Nagel, 1973, pp. 219–20). In practice, restrictions can become still broader in scope, if passers-by take it on themselves to question the right to photograph any object or phenomenon (normally one which in their view does not reflect credit on the regime).

Even amateur photography from Soviet civil planes flying over the USSR is forbidden, and film taken in defiance of the regulations may be compulsorily exposed: a plane will turn back to the airport so that this can be done, or the aircraft's departure is delayed until film has been compulsorily developed (Gaffin, 1975, p. 17). Some restrictions even extend to Soviet property outside the Soviet Union. One of London's newer road signs prohibits photography in the vicinity of the Soviet Embassy at Kensington Palace Gardens (*The Standard*, 28 February 1985, p. 6).

RESTRICTIONS UPON FOREIGN TOURISM BY SOVIET CITIZENS

The same principle of isolation as far as possible from what are seen as undesirable influences is enforced in tourism by Soviet citizens, who mainly visit other socialist countries, including Cuba. They visit only certain 'capitalist' countries and then only in organised groups. Ordinarily, if a Soviet citizen is permitted to visit a Western country, a spouse or other relative must be left behind, so as to curb the temptation to defect. This condition is waived only in the case of very high ranking officials (cf. *The Times*, 21 August 1984). If a foreigner wants to marry a Soviet citizen, the latter's departure from the USSR will be obstructed, perhaps for a number of years, the period being especially prolonged if foreign bride or bridegroom is a specialist on the Soviet Union. The objective is presumably to preserve secrets in this case and to discourage others. Sovietologists also run an enhanced risk of being declared *persona non grata*, a penalty which was imposed on eighteen Britons, academic people and diplomats, including myself, in October 1971 in retaliation for the expulsion from Britain of 105 Soviet diplomats.

There is no legally affirmed right of citizens to go abroad and return – a right which in England was included in Magna Carta (clause 42), granted by King John almost eight centuries ago (in 1215). Soviet citizens may go abroad only if in possession of an exit visa, which is granted only on conditions including political reliability. Any evidence of independent contact with foreigners may have the result that this is refused. Soviet citizens who have permission to live abroad temporarily may visit a third country only with specific permission. For example, Soviet embassies also assert control over Soviet citizens who are temporarily working in one country and wish to lecture in another one, as in the case of Dr Zhores Medvedev (*N.Y.T.*, 7 April 1973, p. C4). Soviet sailors in foreign ports receive only minimal shore leave and spending money, which would severely cramp their style if they decided to jump ship. Visits by Soviet citizens abroad are made to depend on the Soviet state's being able to recover them, against their will, in case they defect. Finland may be visited, since Finland agreed not to grant rights of asylum (Medvedev, 1971, p. 218). The contrary situation in the United States was doubtless one of the main reasons for the decision not to send Soviet athletes to the Los Angeles Olympic Games.

SURVEILLANCE OF FOREIGNERS WITHIN THE USSR

Foreigners within the USSR, whether diplomats or not, are liable to be followed: this may be on foot or by car, or the one after the other. (With train travel, it may be reckoned sufficient to pick up the trail at the final destination.)

In cities, a particular individual is likely to be followed throughout a few days, then attention shifts to someone else. As three people are required to keep track of a single person reliably in an urban environment, the process is liable to become conspicuous; it may therefore be practised as much for the sake of intimidation as with the aim of genuinely finding out where the person is going, especially as that person on detecting that he/she is being followed may prefer to alter the original plan (as much out of devilment as out of calculation).

If the fact of being followed becomes known to the person who is being followed, this is likely to have other results. One will probably feel, in consequence, more important. Later, having returned home, one may miss the excitement; while it continues, the situation appears as a kind of challenge to which one will probably react by enhancing one's own secretiveness. If before, one might have doubted whether one knew anything that anyone else could possibly want to share, those sentiments evaporate. Thus, the fact of being followed actually brings to birth or intensifies the very attitudes of secretiveness which it had been intended to counteract.

Naturally, the 'scientific–technical revolution' has not left this sphere unscathed. According to a US State Department announcement on 21 August 1985, the Soviet Union had been secretly using chemicals in an attempt to track the movements of US diplomats in Moscow. The chemical most extensively used for this purpose was NPPD (nitro phenyl pentadien). It was claimed that the substance had been applied 'indirectly' to embassy personnel. Unofficially it has been suggested that it might be sprayed on steering wheels of cars or door knobs, whence it would rub off on to the hand and on to other things, making it possible to trace which places or people those diplomats had visited. The statement said that these chemicals had been in use 'for a number of years' (*The Times*, 22 August 1985, pp. 1, 4).

Surveillance (bugging) of apartments is no doubt widely practised; technically this is extremely easy, though total listening-in would be laborious, to say the least. But then, there is ample manpower to employ. Consequently, sensitive conversations among diplomats, etc. are often arranged to take place out of doors, or perhaps in special secure rooms.

Sometimes the approach becomes much closer. Traditionally, romance or sex are supposed to be offered to foreigners in return for secrets. This still happens as various cases show, for instance that of Ole Martin Høistad, security officer in the Norwegian Embassy in Moscow (*Time*, 9 April 1973, p. 8), or the black-mailing of Arne Treholt, a former Norwegian minister and diplomat. As in this latter case, a frequent method of pressure is a threat to release compromising pictures taken secretly by the KGB (*The Times*, 26 February 1985, p. 1). Naturally, this method works only when the victim is susceptible to blackmail: it might fail because of his incorruptibility, or because of lack of interest in matters of personal conduct on the part of his associates and employers.

To the extent that diplomats' contact with Soviet citizens is impeded, their contacts with other diplomats are likely to be enhanced. In the same way as a heavenly body, if contracted in diameter but not in mass, spins faster, the social round within the diplomatic corps becomes more frenzied. At these functions, much chitchat of no professional interest is exchanged, but also a modicum which is. The faster the social round, the more quickly and thoroughly this modicum circulates. Consequently, owing to the attempt to isolate diplomats from the citizenry, the flow of information from these latter is contracted, but what does trickle out reaches a larger number of people, and more quickly than it otherwise would. The net result is no doubt to reduce what is harvested, but by not so much as one might at first sight suppose.

RESTRICTIONS ON MOVEMENT OF FOREIGN TOURISTS

A large volume of observations of the Soviet Union must be gathered by foreign tourists, though (as far as I know) this material is not being synthesised in any comprehensive or systematic way. A whole series of regulations nevertheless governs the movements of tourists. Independent motoring is permitted only along certain routes. Motorists may stay only in approved lodging places. Only certain areas of the country may be visited. The ban on putting up foreigners in private houses probably has largely a secretive motivation.

Foreign tourists are naturally barred from sensitive areas, though one's impression is that this is done rather unevenly. Aeroflot aircraft sometimes give the border regions a wide berth or close the blinds, though they did not do so on a flight from Irkutsk to Khabarovsk which afforded a panoramic view stretching away into China. But then, this was a view into *China*. Foreigners who are travelling by train from Khabarovsk to Vladivostok, by a route which runs close to the Chinese border for nearly 300 miles, are transferred in strict security to a special train which covers this stretch at night (Lascelles, 1974, p. 7).

While the number of different places visited by foreign tourists in the USSR is large (in 1984 a total of 147 towns in all the fifteen republics), this reflects the size of the country. Motorists are restricted to specified routes, whose total length exceeded 12 000 km (*Rabotnichesko delo*, 31 December 1984, p. 6). By another account, in 1986 65 cities might be visited independently, though itineraries had to be confirmed by Intourist (Tour Designs Inc., 1986, pp. 4 and 21). Control has been tightened up, so that, for example, Ella Maillart's journey through Turkestan in 1932 would be impossible today. About two-fifths of the area of the Soviet Union remain out of bounds to foreigners (Hutchings, 1982A, p. 8), other large fractions being in practice inaccessible due to lack of communications or of other facilities.

CENSORSHIP IN SOVIET CRUISE LINERS

Soviet cruise liners are, of course, subject to Soviet law. They offer excellent value for money, but one is likely to be largely cut off from world news. On the *Taras Shevchenko* and the *Mikhail Lermontov* the captain does not allow the World Service of the BBC to be made available to passengers (it is called 'propaganda'), although on at least one other Soviet cruise ship it is. (Private source, information provided 1985.)

IMPRISONMENT AND ASSASSINATION

A list of the methods used by the police and judiciary to silence him was contained in the full text of Bukovsky's final speech which was smuggled out of the court. These included that the

KGB had tried to have him certified insane so that there would have been no trial and no publicity (*D.T.*, 8 Jan. 1972, p. 21). In a public trial there would be an opportunity for the defence to make statements possibly disclosing something that the authorities wished to keep secret. The trial of Georgi Dimitrov, who, when arraigned at the Leipzig trial (September to December 1933) by the Nazis, accused of setting fire to the Reichstag, turned the tables on them in court and had finally to be acquitted, must be something that the Soviet authorities would not wish to emulate (see Reed, 1934, pp. 100–4, and Dimitrov, 1934, pp. 1–7). His literary output during this period is catalogued in Savova, 1982, pp. 646–80). In the Soviet Union such trials are therefore held in camera, or still better not at all, via the confinement of dissidents in mental hospitals (*Sunday Times*, 20 May 1984, p. 43).

The keeping of secrets is effected on occasion also via assassination. This was doubtless one of the reasons why Trotsky was killed (1940). Where an extraordinary crime has been committed, extraordinary measures are taken to cover up. Top functionaries of the NKVD in Leningrad were shot to cover the traces of the organisers of Kirov's killing (Rigby, 1968, pp. 39, 97–8).

THE GREAT PURGES

These assassinations have been extremely few by comparison with the numbers killed within the Soviet Union itself. At this point precise numbers are unnecessary: if the number of assassinations outside Soviet territory has reached 100, which might be an overestimate, while the numbers who have perished inside labour camps is 10 million which may be an underestimate, the ratio between deaths inside and outside Soviet territory would be 100 000 to 1. (These numbers exclude people killed at or in the vicinity of the Soviet borders.) Thus whether or not deaths take place in secrecy makes an enormous difference. The fact is that beyond a certain point, mortality ceases to attract attention. One reason has been noticed already in Chapter 2; illustrations are numerous, such as at the present time the Iran–Iraq war which frequently in our press (and also in the East European and Soviet press) fails to gain a mention.

RUTHLESSNESS

Soviet ruthlessness in insisting on safeguarding her secrets merits specific mention. The destruction of the Korean airliner or the shooting of a US liaison officer contrast with the Swedish abstinence from trying seriously to destroy Soviet submarines or other underwater craft which indisputably had penetrated Swedish waters in highly sensitive areas. The Russians are serious about preserving their secrets; other countries frequently appear not to be. This imbalance works insidiously in favour of the Soviet Union.

THE 'SECRET POLICE'

Whenever a totalitarian or quasi-totalitarian state is described from a liberal viewpoint, there is invariably a mention of that country's 'secret police'. The secret police, rather than the regular armed forced, is in such a state the normal instrument of internal repression, because its training and equipment are tailored to combat individuals rather than armed formations. However, the title relates more to what the police are intended to do, that is to safeguard national secrets to the extent that physical force can be used for that purpose, than to a literal description of them. Similarly: 'The secret police differ from regular police, not in their secrecy (for few people knew much about the internal operations of police before the days of television aerials), but in the use of their powers to keep the government secure' (Calvert, 1986, p. 31). As for the existence of such a force, or of a main part of it, 'secret' is often a misnomer, as Mikes illustrates from Hungarian experience: 'in Rakosi's time the adjective "secret" in the name of the Secret Police was a mere convention; there was not much secrecy about its existence which was only too well known. Under Kadar, the very existence of this force is being kept secret' (Mikes, 1959, p. 73). Soviet MVD troops in 1954 were wearing caps with light blue tops, making them rather conspicuous, although these were 'secret police' in some descriptions.

Of course, very much about the Soviet secret police is secret enough, and to a degree which makes writing about them difficult. Individuals who are detailed to follow one will probably be males of working age and be dressed drably and nonde-scriptly. By analogy with Polish secret policemen, they possibly behave and act rather like a Mafia: son following father into the profession, and immunities expected and obtained from ordinary restraints upon behaviour. (Regarding the Polish set-up, as based on the trial of police accused of murdering Father Popie-łuszko, See *The Times*, 17 January 1985, p. 13.) But if, in the special circumstances of Poland, such behaviour can – very occasionally – backfire, in the Soviet Union that result is much more unlikely.

I shall not attempt to tell in detail the history of the Soviet secret police. The OGPU or 'Unified State Political Administra-tion' (a curious title which no doubt was intended to obscure what this body actually did), was set up by decree of 25 Novem-ber 1923 and was immediately entrusted with organising protec-tion of the frontiers and with 'immediate operative work on an all-union scale', *inter alia* (Matthews, 1974, p. 245). Later it assumed wider powers including, in particular, the administra-tion of forced labour camps. While the existence of these latter was not publicised, there are occasional allusions to the GULAG in published material (see Hutchings, 1982A, pp. 104–5). Eventual release, or very occasional escape, from camps would also help to ensure that their existence could not ultimately be hidden.

Labour camps seem at first sight irrelevant to the protection of secrets. From an all-USSR viewpoint their economic value ap-pears highly questionable, when the need for guards and other special requirements are taken into account, as well as the loss of efficiency of employing people not according to their specialisa-tions, and in remote and inhospitable areas scarcely chosen for their economic return (cf. Hutchings, 1982A, pp. 106–7). For the OGPU, on the other hand, the system may have been profitable in the most literal sense, and this is possibly the strongest reason why it developed as it did.

Another reason may have been that the labour camps concen-trated there, and muzzled, in many cases for ever, people who could report more about the Soviet system than its leaders preferred to become known. The hypothesis that concealment of secrets, by means of locking away those privy to them, was one of the motives is supported by the fact that during the purges of the late 1930s intellectuals, officers, Party members, and managerial groups generally were imprisoned in much larger proportions than the population generally, that is to say precisely those groups who knew most about how the system actually worked. As they provided the guards for the forced labour camps, the secret police were in that contorted sense guardians of the nation's secrets.

The purges of the late 1930s showed, however, that the NKVD was not so much an agency for protecting secrets as for generating lies to be put into the mouth of the accused in the form of 'confessions'. In general, where a large organization of this type has been created, it is more readily employable in this way, as an apparatus for oppression is more easily expandable than an apparatus for ferreting out secrets: the former requires only brute strength, whereas the latter requires intelligence. (The condition is, of course, that the judicial system will not hinder the process; in the USSR that condition was satisfied.) Thus a reason for the form taken by the purges may have been the type of organisation which had already been created.

Evidently it would be unjustifiable to maintain a secret-keeping agency which tended to generate more secrets than it was able to conceal. In general, the bigger the organisation, the more difficult it must be to keep its existence or functioning secret, or to express it another way, the larger must be the proportion of its secret-keeping capability which must be devoted to keeping *itself* secret. Conversely, the contraction of such a body would not diminish net secret-keeping capability, if the quantity of secrets generated declined *pari passu*. This helps to explain why the contraction of the Soviet secret police following Stalin's death was not accompanied by any commensurate escape of confidential information. That contraction may even have resulted in an enhancement rather than an impairment of the capacity of the secret police for protecting the nation's more legitimate secrets, those which are really relevant to its security, and on the whole it provides still a formidable protection for them.

Much more recently the harassment, incarceration or exiling of individuals who were active in monitoring Soviet compliance with the Helsinki agreement, or in demonstrating in favour of official compliance with legality, is doubtless intended to serve, and does serve, the same purpose of helping to preserve secrecy about various aspects of the Soviet system.

7 How Secrets Are Kept: II. The Censorship

TYPES OF DECISION RESULTING IN NON-PROVISION OF INFORMATION

Information may fail to be provided as a result of two different sorts of decision. The first decision would be, consciously, to keep secret such-and-such. The second would be absence of a decision to make public such-and-such. Finally – though I think rarely – both sorts might apply in specific cases. Let us call these decisions types *A*, *B* and *C*. Of course, any of these types of decision might be negative rather than positive, for example, a decision *not* to ban something from publication. I believe that each of these types of decision can be found in the Soviet Union, but that they apply in different degrees to different branches of information and at different times. Type *A* applies to military matters in general, most political ones, a large number of sociological and scientific ones, a certain number of economic ones, and a few in other fields. Type *B* applies to virtually no military matters, few sociological and scientific ones, few if any political ones, a certain number of economic ones, and a fairly large number in other fields.

It is clear that type *A* decisions will as a rule apply to matters with a higher classification than type *B* decisions, and that type *C* decisions will apply to matters with a classification not less than that of type *A* decisions.

It must be presumed that spheres of information can be ranged on a sliding scale of sensitivity, which is approximately as follows (most sensitive down to least sensitive): the top leadership, the armed forces, science, economics and sociology, other matters. This presumption in conjuction with the supposition that type *A* decisions should apply to more security-sensitive matters than type *B* decisions is put to work in the previous paragraph but one.

Whereabouts in this schema should one fit self-censorship? There is no doubt in my own mind that this is a form of type *A* decision. Its relationship to a directive not to publish something

114

is much the same as the relationship between deterrence and defence: the same result is achieved but relying on a prophylactic approach. If self-censorship were ineffective, direct prohibition would be substituted.

This, of course, does not mean that self-censorship will be exactly the same in other respects as imposed censorship. Consistency is likely to be less, to the extent that different authors interpret the instructions differently, although it could be greater to the extent that differences among *censors* no longer operate. Collectivity of authorship, which is a common Soviet practice, should tend to make self-censorship more rigorous if, as can be expected, in its approach to censorship any collectively composed piece moves at the pace of the most timorous participant. Nevertheless, it is likely on the whole that self-censorship will be slightly less stringent than directly imposed censorship, as the example of Hungary – where self-censorship is the rule – illustrates. Yet self-censorship may operate effectively with little subsequent need to prosecution, as British experience during the Second World War suggests (see Hutchinson, 1985, p. 39).

The distinction between types *A* and *B* is useful in several respects. First, it helps to explain why the official crackdown on samizdat material has not been more stringent: samizdat material evidently represents a reversal of a type *B* decision; not, or scarcely ever, a reversal of a type *A* decision.

As regards type *C* decisions, either of its elements would bring the result that the item was not publicised; the fact that both elements nevertheless are involved means that the censors had thought that there was a possibility of publication. In effect, the censors say to an official body, 'You must not publish such and such', to which the official body replies, 'We were not going to anyway.'

Also possible is type *D* – where it is desired to keep something secret, but it is also desired to make it public! This is the situation examined earlier, for example in regard to exhibiting military hardware in Red Square: a compromise decision has to be found.

There are obvious advantages about type *B* decisions. Strictly speaking, this is not censorship, so if *only* type *B* decisions occur, it can be truthfully stated that no censorship exists. The cumbersome and potentially faulty mechanism of censorship can then be dispensed with. The disadvantage of type *B* decisions is that they will very possibly be inconsistent, e.g. a particular quantity will be disclosed for certain years but not for others. However, if that puzzles and disorients foreign intelligence, that result would be generally advantageous. The obvious advantages of type *A* decisions are that choices can be consistent, and that there can be a blanket prohibition of publishing various sorts of material. On the other hand, it is then not possible truthfully to say that no censorship exists, and adequate organisational measures have to be taken in this connection. The existence of this organisation may then become known, although that must not be publicised (by a type *A* decision, naturally).

To focus on the Soviet censorship therefore represents conceptually a focus upon only half of the matter. The remainder is type *B* decisions: the fact that no positive decision had been taken to publish.

The fact is that in practice the scope of non-publication exceeds what would result solely from decisions not to permit publication. Furthermore, it is precisely the branches covered by the type *B* decisions which are most characteristic of Soviet secrecy/disclosure policy. Other countries consciously try to guard their secrets, but as a rule there is always somebody who would want to bring to light any given matter, and if one looks in the right place, one will find it illuminated.

The combination of types *A* and *B* decisions creates a 'Heads I win, tails you lose' situation. For example, it is consistent with the Soviet official view of things that Blacks should be oppressed in any 'capitalist' country, so if this really does happen somewhere there is no problem: the item goes straight in. If, on the other hand, in some 'capitalist' country Blacks are specially favoured (as under 'affirmative action' recruitment policies in certain US states), this must not be reported. These are type *A* decisions. If, however, Blacks are neither favoured nor disfavoured, but are treated like anyone else, then this will not count as news so this too will not be reported (a type *B* decision).

Type *B* decisions originate in part owing to the absence of the appropriate sort of media; there is , for example, no *Daily Mail* to bring to light the peccadilloes of prominent personalities. More broadly, however, they result from the entire structure of the Soviet state, in particular its authoritative basis and monolithic and economic structure. In fact, certain sorts of news are not created in the Soviet polity. This applies to news of stocks and shares, and generally to all those phenomena of a market economy which are continually fluctuating. The absence of any legitimate political opposition obliterates a whole fertile newsworthy field.

How large actually are the fractions comprising type A and type B? In principle, one might compare a list of subjects which are presumed to be covered by the censorship (obtained by analogy from the authentic Polish list, to be mentioned shortly) with subjects about which information is not provided. But this is very difficult in practice. Disclosure policy (to be discussed later) may provide a clue. Another approach, precise but limited in application and requiring an initial unrealistic assumption, is to count up the volume of data which is newly revealed in statistical handbooks, with that of data, which are collected there, and which have been published already in previous handbooks. While to calculate this proportion exactly would demand an extremely time-consuming exercise, my studies indicate that in an average all-union statistical handbook, only about one-seventh of the statistical material published in any single year is new (see Hutchings, 1982B, p. 16). Thus, in any given year, in such handbooks, about six-sevenths of the data consist of republished material which by a reversed type B decision is nevertheless judged worthy to reappear, and only one-seventh from a reversed type A decision. (This comparison requires an assumption of a blank slate before any decisions are taken as to what material should be made public in each annual handbook, which probably is not realistic.)

The Russian Revolution obviously altered news priorities and the presentation of news. While in the short run the direct agency for effecting this must have been the censorship, very likely newsworthiness has altered: including such changes among the causes of change, we would need to classify a larger number of decisions as type C, rather than type A, in the terminology proposed above. For comparison: in Britain, over the past sixty to seventy years, there has been a fairly marked change in newsworthiness. Newspapers such as *The Times* (London) on occasion reprint what happened on the same day many years before. Often, what this demonstrates is not merely that the news was different, but that there has been a change in what was regarded as news. For example, detailed descriptions of the dresses worn by named individuals at society functions no longer appear in the daily press (cf. *The Times*, 1 March 1985, p. 17, referring back to sixty-three years earlier). In Russia, which experienced much more violent social upheavals, the changes should have been proportionately greater. If, in some sense – qualifications to this claim cannot be investigated here – the 'working class' has become more numerous and prominent, the greater stress during the Soviet period on economic affairs would be reasonable. However, if social changes animated changes in newsworthiness, it should be expected that this latter would alter continually and not always in the same direction; greater prosperity, for instance, ought to have the result that economic affairs became *less* prominent. In fact, news priorities and newsworthiness have not changed significantly since the early 1930s; in other words, in the Soviet Union social changes have not exerted any close or continuous influence upon news priorities or news presentation. The conclusion must follow that these are not the primary influence, which must therefore be something else – which can only be the official censorship.

HISTORICAL BACKGROUND OF CENSORSHIP

Censorship is of course nothing new, although it cannot be one of the oldest professions, as the prerequisite is some capability to communicate. Over the largest part of human history the problem has been how to communicate, not how to hinder communication. Even in the most dictatorial society of the twentieth century, speech in the most literal sense is only partly censorable: what is meant by 'freedom of speech' comes closer to 'not minding being overheard'.

As for the earliest stages of censorship, not surprisingly knowledge is lacking. As David Tribe (1973, p. 48) remarks, it is impossible to say what was the state of oral censorship in Druidic Britain. In the Greek or Roman worlds ostracism or exile can be regarded as forms of censorship, particularly if applied to *littérateurs* like Ovid. We know little about pre-Christian pagan gods in England because church policy suppressed such information (Laing, 1982, p. 116). Censorship of books by the Christian church followed hard on the invention of printing: a papal bull of 1487 decreed that all books needed ecclesiastical approval before publication (Tribe, 1973, p. 49). In England, pre-censorship of publications disappeared in 1696 (Ibid., p. 55). Censorship is a theme that is rarely mentioned in British historical writing. The invention of the telegraph, not being a medium of mass communication, did not require censorship but radio and cinema were rather quickly placed within its scope. It is unnecessary here to trace the worldwide history of this. In Britain, censorship of the cinema dates from 1912 (following an Act of 1909 which related to structural and safety matters), while radio was brought under control through the requirement that broadcasting stations had to be licensed.

Whatever may become the case in the future, at present censorship refers primarily to printed matter. One reason is that by comparison with most produced objects, written compositions can adopt a much wider variety of form and content, while another is that the process of production encounters a more pronounced bottleneck than is the case with most other processes: namely the moment when a manuscript is accepted or rejected, or is accepted only with enforced alterations. The censorial function thus arises almost naturally from the editorial function. That editors function as censors is well known to everyone who has ever had occasion to submit anything to one of them, as well as to editors themselves – which include the present writer. Of course, censorship arising out of an editorial function is true only up to a point. The censors are not experts in the topics submitted to them, whereas an editor ought to have some expertise at least. The censors do not work with the editors, whereas an editor may work with an author. The censors cannot propose inclusion of material, they can only recommend or insist on its exclusion. The censors are in the most direct sense state employees, whereas editors (in most cases) are not. However, one of the most enlightened Russian censors of the nineteenth century, Aleksandr Nikitenko, also edited newspapers and literary journals (Jackson, 1975, p. xi).

Censorship in Russia is an event of modern history. Though Peter the Great had introduced theological censorship, the first comprehensive law was not passed until 1826, in the aftermath of the Decembrist revolt. Various fluctuations in the scope and intensity of censorship ensued. The years 1865, 1905–6 and February 1917 were moments when censorship was relaxed;

during the 1880s it was strengthened, and the Bolsheviks reintroduced it in 1917 in an especially severe form; its peak was reached under Stalin (Utechin, 1961, p. 90).

The censorship in Tsarist Russia cast its net wide, although it was also noteworthy for various lapses, in particular in allowing the publication of Marx's *Capital*, whereas translations of Hobbes's *Leviathan* or of Spinoza were not allowed (Sumner, 1944, p. 118). Victorian novelists were not exempt from the censors' attention: 'The Legend of St Sophia of Kioff' was to be excised from all copies of Thackeray's *The Great Cossack Epic* which were imported into the Russian Empire. (From the censorship exhibition in New York Public Library, December 1984.) When at Tsushima, in 1905, the Japanese annihilated the Russian naval squadron which had been sent to the Far East, *The Times* (of London) correspondent at St Petersburg with a dateline of 29 May 1905 could write that 'not one Russian in ten thousand' had even a suspicion of the disaster, but later he reported that the news was bound to become quickly known: 'The rigors of the censorship are unavailing against many-tongued rumour' (reported again in *The Times*, 31 May 1985, p. 11). The repressiveness of the Tsarist censorship being limited (Balmuth, 1979, p. 144), ultimately bad news could not be kept away.

The Soviet censorship is of even wider scope, as it includes all printed matter and entertainment, down to the level of circuses and variety shows (Utechin, 1961, p. 89), including of course the cinema, the theatre and music. Posts and telegraphs are censored too. Items may be sent into the USSR by registered mail, but if anything is not received it is incumbent on the proposed recipient to confirm non-receipt of it; this sounds like a Catch-22 situation (see J. Levy, *The Times*, 5 December 1984, p. 13 – something similar was the basis of an 'Irish joke' among British troops in the First World War: P. Lacey, *The Times*, 13 December 1984, p. 15). Yet this might have a much more serious side. It was shown even during the Holocaust that people who were cut off completely from the outside world had less chance of survival than those who were able to maintain contacts. It is believed that books sent from the West to individual addresses in the USSR rarely reach them, though this is likely to depend on who the addressee is, and items sent to prominent officials presumably stand a much better chance. Although under the Universal Postal Union Convention (Article 36) items whose import or circulation is illegal may be confiscated, it appears that these powers are exercised in instances where they could not be applicable (Bethell, 1985, p. 12). Although the privacy of private correspondence is guaranteed by the Constitution, according to one Western view this is frequently violated (Utechin, 1961, pp. 89–90).

THE POLISH MODEL

A more exact basis for describing the Soviet censorship has to be sought where fortune favours, since its priorities and workings are strictly secret. One basis which will be used here is the Polish censorship, about which, fortuitously, more is definitely known. The *Black Book of Polish Censorship* is undoubtedly authentic and cannot fail to shed much light on Soviet practice. Subsequent analysis will attempt to suggest the differences between the Polish and the Soviet situations.

A few extracts will give the flavour of the *Black Book* (page numbers refer to Schöpflin (1983), *Censorship and Political Communication*):

Section III
(o) Material sympathetic to the Eritrean liberation movements in Ethiopia should not be permitted to be published (p. 38).

Section V
8   Criticism of Soviet-produced drilling equipment used in geological exploration in Poland should not be permitted, nor should any proposals concerning the purchase of drilling equipment from other foreign sources be published (p. 42).

Section VI
10   Proposals calling for the sale of new and secondhand tractors to farmers working their land privately should not be permitted publication in the mass media. Material illustrating the farmers' needs for tractors should also be eliminated (p. 46).

Section IX
1   The names of the following persons may not be published and their scientific contribution may not be emphasized

in a positive sense . . . On the other hand, brief information on the work published by them may be permitted as well as all material criticizing their creativity.

Section X

8   Any information on the following illegally operating college or propaganda facilities of the church should be stricken (a list follows) (p. 61).

The Polish censorship focuses especially on matters connected with the Church: in the part reproduced in Schöpflin, almost one-tenth of the total length, 6.0 pages out of 65.5, are devoted to this subject (Section X).

THE SOVIET ANALOGY

How far can the state of affairs as revealed in this remarkable (and nauseating) document be related to Soviet practice?

The starting point must be a likelihood of general congruence. Because of the nature of censorship, uniformity must be presumed to be the general rule among states which comprise such a closely knit bloc as the Soviet bloc in many respects – and above all, surely, in secrecy policy. In addition, individual points evoke echoes. For instance, according to the *Black Book of Polish Censorship*, no information should be published concerning the principles of financing Polish foreign trade (compensatory, surcharges, subsidies, etc.), whereas in scientific and theoretical works explanatory definitions of these terms are permitted, provided that they are not related to Polish foreign trade (Section V, item 4; Schöpflin, 1983, pp. 40–1); this is one line of demarcation between what is not published, and what is published, in Soviet publications.

Looking now in more detail at the Polish situation: the 1970s, to which the document refers (most references are to 1975 and 1976) is regarded as a period of comparative liberalisation in Poland (Schöpflin, 1983, p. 32), so the norm now (1987) for Poland would be stricter regulation.

The Soviet Union, of course, differs from Poland in a number of respects: it is far larger; Communist power has in the USSR a genuine popular base, whereas in Poland it does not; Communist censorship has been in force in the USSR for twenty eight years longer; the internal and external circumstances of the

Soviet Union are different. These differences will be looked at in turn.

The significance of size in secrecy/disclosure policy has already been considered in general terms (see Chapter 2). As regards censorship, it should have the result (other things being equal) that a larger number of items have to be prohibited. However, beyond a certain point, detailed instructions would become very difficult for the censors to observe. One would therefore expect the absolute number of prohibitions to be larger than in Poland, but not in proportion to the much larger size of the USSR.

Since the Soviet regime has to some extent a genuine popular base this should reduce the need for censorship (type *A* decisions), but despite this Communist censorship has been in force in the USSR for a much longer period, enabling the instructions to the Soviet censors to become even more detailed.

The effect of other differences in internal and external circumstances is harder to assess, but the far weaker position of the Church in the Soviet Union would decrease the need for censorship (cf. Ch. 3).

One other consideration should perhaps be ranged on the other side. Soviet thinking habits, by comparison with those typical of a country not subject over generations to Communist censorship, have been warped by that experience, in two respects especially: creative thinking has been impaired, but no less understandably, within a system which is both huge and unitary, attentiveness to including all components of a complicated series has become enhanced. The censors, in other words, come already from a milieu which is habituated to encompassing a multiplicity of concentric details. As Schöpflin (1983, p. 3) notes, 'the extent of censorship is probably greater than most people not living in Eastern Europe recognize. It may, indeed, be difficult for someone in the West to comprehend the full extent of control of information by the state in Eastern Europe'. Underlying this observation may be an evaluation rather similar to that which I have just proposed. If that is even true of Poland, with its shorter experience of Communist rule and quite different historical connections and traditions, it should apply much more to censorship in the Soviet Union.

The general conclusion is that the Soviet censorship would not be stricter than the Polish one, reckoning this strictness by the frequency of type *A* decisions relative to the censors. Owing to the much larger size of the Soviet Union, type *B* decisions should be more numerous in absolute terms but reckoned over a number of years, probably not in relation to the possible volume of news items; moreover, as shown in Chapters 8 and 14, in the USSR type *B* decisions sometimes go the other way, which instigates in individual years a sudden upsurge in the volume published.

One can affirm with more confidence that the instructions to the Soviet censors would differ in emphasis from those to the Polish censors. The religious element would be smaller, so far as the Christian Church is concerned, but larger in so far as other religions, in particular Islam, would have to be brought within the scope of the Soviet censorship. Less attention would be needed to treating emigrants as non-persons, since only since 1960, and especially since 1968, has emigration (mainly of Jews and Germans) been on any significant scale; on the other hand, defections of prominent figures in culture and the arts have caused embarrassment, and Soviet censors are surely having to be issued with a lengthening list of names of dancers, musicians, etc. who may no longer be mentioned in any favourable sense. A noteworthy fraction of items brought to the attention of the Polish censors concerned the Soviet Union itself; for example, Poland's exports of meat to the USSR might not be mentioned, and 'No attempts to charge the Soviet Union with the responsibility for the death of the Polish officers in the Katyn forests should be permitted' (Section IX, item 2 (a), Schöpflin, 1983, p. 56). The Soviet censors would not need to be reminded about either of these, or a number of other, topics regarding which the USSR is cited in the instructions to the Polish censors. On the other hand, certain other topics would loom much larger. These must include the nationality question, Poland being racially and nationally homogenous and the Soviet Union anything but, and probably also relations with foreign countries. Arms spending, arms exports and Afghanistan doubtless take up more of the Soviet censors' attention, and this may be true of economic questions generally; indeed, these last must surely have loomed larger in 1985 in Poland than they did in the 1970s.

The great majority of Polish censors are women. 'The profession in pretty well feminized, because it is a quiet and calm job' (censor K-62, as reported in Schöpflin 1983, p. 103). (This matches the fictional portrayal of the Czech censor in the play *Prague* by John Krizanc.) This is very probably the case in the USSR also. Under Tsarist Russia the censors were, of course, men. This is true of every one of the 131 individuals named in Choldin (1985) Appendix Two, though apparently some women did give assistance. Feminisation of the profession has possibly brought the result that the work is performed even more meticulously, and without the slips which occurred from time to time in the Tsarist censorship.

The present chapter up to this point, and also from page 127 onwards, had been composed before I read the article by Leonid Vladimirov, 'Glavlit: How the Soviet Censor Works' in *Index on Censorship* (autumn/winter 1972, pp. 31–43). As a general rule one is wise to blot out preliminary speculation after having read what is evidently an authentic account, in this case I think it possible to retain what had been written already, as Vladimirov augments rather than denies any of the foregoing.

First, the fact of general congruence is abundantly demonstrated. The Soviet censorship, like the Polish one, works according to detailed instructions. According to Vladimirov, this comprises an 'Index of Information Not to be Published in the Open Press', classified Secret, and known almost officially as the 'Talmud'. Its first section mentions thirteen categories of information which must not be mentioned: natural disasters, man-made disasters, earnings of government and Party people, any comparison between budgets of Soviet citizens and prices, price increases, higher living standards outside the socialist bloc, food shortages in the USSR, any kind of average statistics not from Central Statistical Bureau reports, names of KGB people apart from its 'Chairman, ditto for the former Committee for Cultural Relations with Foreign Countries, aerial photographs of Soviet towns and precise geographic co-ordinates of any populated point on Soviet territory, mention of Glavlit organs or jamming of foreign radio broadcasts, and naming of certain political figures on a special list (Vladimirov, 1972, pp. 38–9). This corresponds quite closely to what has already been deduced. Indeed, by a sufficiently close reading of Soviet materials, one should arrive almost exactly at these instructions.

Other prohibitions are extremely detailed: according to Vladimirov, the 'Talmud' has over 300 pages of rather small print. This doubtless corresponds to the *perechen'*, 'a detailed list of data and information which censors were charged with preventing from appearing in print or in any other publicly assessible communication medium' (Fainsod, 1959, p. 364), as this is disclosed in the Smolensk Archive.

Several other propositions are of great interest. There is apparently no written political evaluation of texts, this being left to the judgement of censors as it has been moulded by frequent internal seminars. This suggests that the censors (except for their contact with editors) inhabit a relatively closed intellectual world. Furthermore, contact is always between a censor and an editor, never between a censor and the author. This, of course, helps to preserve the secrecy of the mechanism of censorship.

The absence of written instructions about ideology permits one to guess that censorship of theories may be less strict than censorship of facts. Previously, I had guessed at the existence of a difference of this general nature. When lacking certain facts, a theory to explain them is much less likely to occur to one; however, to a slight extent one might be less handicapped in theorising than in setting down facts. In my experience, governments are interested in obtaining the latest and most accurate facts and much less interested in theorising about them, whereas in the academic world the bias is the opposite. Of course, this is an oversimplification: there exist academics who are very eager to obtain the latest facts, and on occasion a government may appoint a theoretician to correct the opposite proclivity.

In the USSR certain groups are favoured especially through their access to the facts of the situation. This access must itself be institutionalised: scientists, for example, are supplied with abstracts of articles taken from foreign publications, organised by VINITI (Hutchings, 1976, pp. 16–17, and Lewytzkyj, 1976, pp. 440–1).

Vladimirov notes the existence of several other censorships apart from Glavlit: the Military Censorship of the General Staff of the Armed Forces, the atomic censorship and the Cosmic Space censorship. They are stated to exist for radio electronics, chemistry and State Security – this last being known as the 'KGB censorship'. All this is by no means surprising, given the Soviet preference for specialisation. He estimates that there are at least 70 000 censors; this seems very many if the number handling foreign publications is 500 (see below, p. 128); how-

ever, as by the end of the First World War the number of British
censors handling international correspondence and cables was
4861 (West, 1986, p. 28), in the Soviet case 500 might be an
underestimate. The total of censors should ideally be kept down
to a minimum, as larger numbers must make it harder to enforce
any uniform policy. Furthermore, the censors inevitably become
knowledgeable about approaches or views which are not allowed
to reach the populace; this creates a risk that they may themselves become infected. However, if 70 000 appears high I cannot suggest any other precise number; it must be accepted that
the censors number many thousands, probably in the tens of
thousands. Over time the total must also be growing.

Among auxiliary organs of censorship, the secret or special
departments which have been maintained in each enterprise by
the Ministry of Internal Affairs, and which now may be subordi-
nated to the KGB, may be numbered. The work of these sections
is, or was, of the same character (Peters, 1940, p. 3). But what
was this work? I had previously concluded that this was surveillance of the staff from a security aspect or for transmitting
confidential information (Hutchings, 1984, p. 9). This may not
be incorrect, but according to the Smolensk Archive the work
was to censor any material emerging at plant level (Fainsod,
1959, p. 368). The volume and type of such work would presumably vary a good deal, according to the plant. If these sections
are to be included within the total number of censors, even
70 000 persons would be insufficient.

It cannot, of course, be expected that there will never be any
breaches of security. To judge from the Smolensk Archive, the
authorities even at an early date were fairly satisfied with the
censoring of the central press, but much less so with that of the
local press: it did not prove easy to fill the complements of
censors, and their quality left something to be desired (Fainsod,
1959, p. 79). The restrictions upon travel by foreigners, and more
particularly by diplomats, must help to close this gap, as it is
normally impossible to buy local newspapers except in that locality.
This obstacle also tends to obscure regional idiosyncrasies in
the censorship; for example, one can usually write 'Genghis Khan'
in Moscow but may not do so in Ulan Ude (Belinkov, 1971, p. 24).

The probable organisation of a fraction of the censorship
apparatus is explored by Zhores Medvedev on the basis of the

apparent treatment of his correspondence. His conclusion included the surprising one that censorship of cross-frontier correspondence was total rather than selective, unless that might have been the accidental result of this particular research or there had been some feature identifying his own correspondence which resulted in its censorship being unusually complete. He deduced that about 500 employees were equipped with individual stamps which individually denoted permission or rejection (Medvedev, 1971, pp. 338–47). There must be lower and higher grades of censors, perhaps a 'top censorship team' (Miller, 1977, pp. 590–8).

Censorship is also effected through translation of only selected portions of foreign writings which are published in the USSR in a Russian language edition. For example, the Soviet edition of Senator Fulbright's book, *The Arrogance of Power* (1967 Soviet edition), did not include lines on page fourteen about the American intervention in Korea. (Information from Marianna Tax Choldin.) The Oxford University Press even allowed the publishers of the Soviet edition of the *Oxford Student's Dictionary of Current English* to alter its definitions of political words, including Capitalism, Socialism, Marxism, etc. so that they would conform to Soviet ideology. The effect will be to deceive Soviet readers as to the meanings of those words according to a supposedly reputable English dictionary (see *The Times*, 9 April 1985).

As regards *what* the censorship excludes from foreign-imported material, making the comparison with Tsarist times: in part what is kept out is the same (taking into account differences in chronology, style and fashion), in part it is different. Remarks or judgements denigratory of Russia were excluded by the Tsarist censorship, and as the episode of the *Oxford Student's Dictionary of Current English* mentioned above, tends to show, are excluded now; in view of what has been accomplished, for good or ill, during this long period, the content of such remarks should be very different from what it was. Similarly, what is regarded as pornographic was excluded then, and is excluded now; what the West considers to be pornographic has meanwhile altered, but that is not Russia's fault. Politics and religion are, of course, treated differently. Denigration of the monarchy used to be kept out but now would be let in. Literature in support of Christianity used to be let in but now would be kept out. (In regard to the Tsarist censorship these statements are abundantly illustrated in Choldin, 1985, chapters 6 and 7.)

At a deeper level, however, it could be asserted that there has been no fundamental change. It is a fixed point that no literature is admitted which contradicts, argues against, or offends against, the accepted national ideology. This national ideology is the only thing that has changed. Like an army which fights one day against one enemy, and the next day against another, the censorship has effected a volte-face while in a deeper sense remaining unaltered.

The methods of the Soviet censorship also appear to be scarcely different from methods practised before, with one major exception: lines are no longer covered with black ink ('caviar') or by newsprint. Now, excisions are disguised as far as possible; this tends to bring about bigger deletions, because whole pages are deleted rather than parts of pages. This necessitates renumbering pages, which perhaps involves numbering pages which previously had been left unnumbered. A Soviet version of the American weekly journal *Science*, which was doctored before being reproduced in a Soviet version, exhibited these manipulations (Fishlock, 1975, p. 7). Attempts to disguise the censorship are probably responsible for some fraction of the irrationality of items for censorship which has also been noticed (Zhores Medvedev, as cited by Fishlock).

If a name is to be erased from a standard reference book recipients may be supplied with an appropriate Do-It-Yourself kit. A very telling example is provided by Choldin: following Beria's execution, subscribers to the *Bol'shaya Sovetskaya Entsiklopediya* were instructed to remove the article and portrait of Beria and to replace them with pictures of the Bering Sea! The instruction contrived not to mention Beria by name (Choldin, 1985, pp. 31–2). On the other hand, the naming of manufactured products after some living person – for instance, Molotov, which used to be embossed on the dashboard of 'Pobeda' cars – has sometimes militated against erasing the physical traces of particular individuals. Books published in the USSR rarely have indexes, perhaps because it would add an extra complication to make the index correspond to a text from which items had been omitted, or because the risk that they might not correspond is seen as too great. Moreover, source references are 'a rare virtue in Soviet scholarship' (Keep, 1977, p. 415). The rarity of footnotes to sources may signify that a smaller fraction of the total volume of knowledge belongs in the public domain than is the case in Western societies; certainly it would be consistent with such a conclusion. The information may have originated in some classified institution or branch of science, or perhaps in the source of transmitting this information and releasing it for publication it was decided not to attribute it to the original source.

It is technically easier to cut a film than a book (Tribe 1973, p. 43), which very possibly helps to explain the Soviet official preference for the cinema. Moreover, the cinema, unlike the stage, does not permit ad-libbing or any other unscheduled nuances in performance.

Soviet censorship admits less pictorial than verbal information from the outside world (cf. Hutchings, 1976, p. 17), on the principle that 'one picture is worth a thousand words'. Censorship of TV coverage remains in force. Usually, foreign TV crews are absolutely forbidden, only Soviet technicians being permitted, and Novosti (the Soviet news agency) to which they are answerable refuse to film the elderly (presumably as these do not offer an image of a vigorous young community) or any serious story with political implications (*The Washington Post*, 22 May 1972, p. B1). Yet that report now seems out of date, as a BBC television team was allowed into the USSR to film sequences to be presented in their programme 'Comrades' (December 1985–January 1986), and the persons photographed were of all ages.

Though official censorship exists, it is one blessing that there is no unofficial censorship. Soviet trade unions are impotent in this matter. Likewise, religious or ethnic groups cannot impose their own varieties of censorship, and to that extent – and it is by no means a negligible one – press freedom is upheld in a way that is not possible in more pluralistic societies. In Tsarist Russia, the Orthodox Church had the right to censor anything that touched on theology or faith (Monas, 1984–5, p. 168). Of course, censorship can be imposed by official institutions (schools, prisons, the armed forces, etc.). Within research departments (which is where the great majority of Soviet scientists work) a form of censorship combined with assistance in access to a publication would be exercised by the head of department, who in the vast majority of cases would be a Party member. Within such a set-up, opportunities for independent publication would be very limited, or non-existent. This was my impression from a visit in June 1971 to the Leningrad branch of the Institute of History of

Natural Sciences and Technique. Ernst Neizvestny (1984–5, p. 237) writes that 'in actuality the task of institutions such as the Ministry of Culture, the Academy of Arts, the Union of Artists, and various censorship organs is not to support culture, but to combat any culture that arises spontaneously'. Perhaps this is a little jaundiced, though the reaction from an artist of Neizvestny's stature is understandable.

LINGUISTIC BARRIERS

The Russian language, with its Cyrillic script, has sometimes itself been pressed into service as auxiliary means to promote secrecy. The effect is compounded by the phonetic transcription of names. Put Cyrillic and phonetic transcription together, and (in one instance) Soviet schoolchildren find that their letter addressed to President Reagan never reaches him. Though in this particular case the alphabetic obstacle did nothing to help to preserve secrets, it has happened that the incompatibility of alphabets has been exploited for this purpose more deliberately. Thus, the imperial censorship forbade the publication within the Russian Empire of an item by Bahushevich (1840–1900 – from the Censorship Exhibition mentioned above, 10 December 1984). Analogously, between 1864 and 1904 the Russian authorities forbade printing in the Latin alphabet in Lithuania (from the same Exhibition. Lithuanian is written in the Latin alphabet, Russian in the Cyrillic). All Lithuanian literature and periodicals had to be smuggled in from Germany (*Everyman's Encyclopaedia*, 5th edn. 1967, vol. 7, p. 618). A much more recent illustration of the conscious exploitation of a linguistic barrier was the decision by Finland to close down the Swedish relay television transmitter on the Finnish Åland islands, which have a Swedish-speaking population, at the time when the filmed version of 'One Day in the Life of Ivan Denisovich', by Solzhenitsyn, was being shown on Swedish television (Ellingsen, 1985, p. 6), a decision perhaps taken at Soviet instigation. By itself a trivial incident, it can be seen as a straw in the wind. Occasionally, the Soviet authorities take advantage of linguistic incomprehensibility by refusing to render into an understood language criticisms voiced in one that is not understood, which happened with Swedish criticisms of the Soviet occupation of Afghanistan made at a World Youth Festival in Moscow (*The Times*, 10 August 1985, p. 9).

There is a fine tradition in Russia of excellent translation from foreign languages, for example by Pasternak. However, to offset against this, some foreign terms are not correctly rendered. It is commonly remarked that *demokratiya* is not correctly rendered by 'democracy' in English. Going in the reverse direction, from English into Russian, 'unemployment' is not exactly rendered by *bezrabotitsa*, the literal meaning of which is 'worklessness', a term of wider scope than 'unemployment', as the latter means that one is not employed (although it is presumed, wishing to be): the difference is that 'worklessness', if that word existed (it does not) would mean that one also could not employ oneself. The opportunity to be self-employed is present on a far greater scale in a market economy than in a Soviet-type one, but rendering 'unemployment' as *bezrabotitsa* obscures that, as is perhaps the intention.

It may also be worth dwelling briefly on the fact that the Soviet authorities have not at any time made any move to replace the Cyrillic alphabet of Russian by a Latin one. At first, where no alphabet existed for one of the smaller languages or the Arabic one was used, Latin alphabets were devised; however, the Cyrillic alphabet is now used for all languages in the USSR except the Baltic languages, Armenian and Georgian. That it is possible to replace, for a given language, one alphabet by another is exemplified also by Turkish, which changed to a Latin alphabet from an Arabic one in 1929. Whereas the Latin alphabet was more suitable to Turkish, since the Arabic one did not indicate vowels, a Latin alphabet is not inherently more suitable to Russian. Polish, with its complex clusters of consonants, and Czech with its numerous accents, do not form encouraging precedents, nor can the various systems of transliterating from Russian Cyrillic into a Latin script claim conspicuous success; indeed, their very variety is illustrative of the difficulties. It can also be very reasonably argued that in the midst of so many other preoccupations, to have altered the alphabet would have been a heavy extra burden which could well have been done without. On the other hand, the task of reform would have been simplified by the pre-existence of illiteracy (Bodmer, 1946, p. 416). What was in fact accomplished was a minor simplification of the orthography.

We learn from nineteenth-century Russian literature that among the upper classes at that time a knowledge of French was widespread, and that some individuals preferred speaking French to Russian. The emigration of a large fraction of these classes, in conjunction with the growth of literacy of the Russian population, has actually made of the Cyrillic alphabet a bigger barrier to communication from outside with the Russian people than existed before. This is not to say that the alphabet is a big obstacle in relation to the other considerable difficulties for a non-native of acquiring a fluent knowledge of Russian! However, it certainly does not help. Whether or not with that objective, the Soviet authorities, in promoting literacy in Russian while taking no steps to switch from the Cyrillic to the Latin alphabet, adopted the course which maximised difficulties of communication between Russian on one hand and much of the rest of the world on the other hand.

Inherent inaccessibility is a characteristic of other languages besides Russian, occasionally in an enhanced degree, as witness a remembered conversation in Helsinki which alluded to the 'fortress of the Finnish language'. However – and this is well exemplified in Finland – where a language is scarcely known outside its homeland the natives tend to adopt the practice of writing in a more widely known language – in this case, English. Russians, more commonly, when writing for scientific purposes do not do so in languages other than those of the homeland – it would seem unpatriotic – whereas Indians or Japanese (for example) quite commonly do so. Although Russian has become much more important as a world scientific language (Hutchings, 1976, p. 16), this certainly limits the impact of Soviet science in the world at large. Of course, if the aim is to secure publication in foreign media, the appropriate language is employed.

Great Russian (not including Ukrainian and Belorussian) is the language of only about half the population of the USSR, although it is more widely used as a *lingua franca*. Part of the activity of Soviet philologists has been devoted to assisting the linguistic development of non-Russian peoples of the USSR, including the making up of alphabets where these did not exist already. This aim can be reckoned as laudable, except that it would have bound these languages more closely to Russian, thus facilitating their intellectual and cultural domination; it may also have diverted attention away from keeping Russian up to date with other major world languages. It can be taken for granted that the vocabularies of languages inside the USSR have been developed in directions which conform to Soviet ideology; terms appropriate to non-socialist systems of economy or philosophy would have been deliberately excluded. Even modern Russian lacks terms and expressions for rendering certain non-socialist economic notions, which created many difficulties in the compilation of a trilingual (German–English–Russian) dictionary with explanations of economic terminology. To take another example, on ideological grounds 'design' must on formal occasions be rendered as 'technical aesthetics' (*tekhnicheskaya estetika*– Hutchings, 1976, p. 146).

More generally, there is the whole question of censorship via the use of the jargon and vocabulary of Marxism–Leninism. As Schöpflin (1983, p. 5) well expresses it:

> The continued use of Marxist–Leninist language, even after the genuinely Marxist content of the language has largely declayed, is to be explained by its function of excluding other modes of expression and thought. If everything has to be expressed in a stilted, formalized and alien political vocabulary, it makes criticism and alternatives far more difficult to articulate.

Furthermore, as noted in Chapter 3, the Russian language experiences difficulty in expressing the concept of privacy, so that in effect an initial bias is created against the notion of investigation by an individual of any subject where privacy is essential.

PUBLISHING, PRINTING AND LECTURES

The most spectacular forms of information control, such as book-burning, may not have been practised in the USSR, though according to Medvedev (1971, p. 336) packing waste paper from capitalist countries must be burned. Unapproved literature which is confiscated by Customs is presumably destroyed in the most convenient manner, apart from samples which may be retained for reference and which would be held in closed deposits. A further line of defence against unauthorised consultation is erected in libraries, material here being stratified according to what access to it is permitted. In the enormous Lenin Library in Moscow, even the general alphabetical index is secret and even if one obtains the catalogue number for some items, the library staff may refuse to obtain it (Smith, 1976, p. 438).

Books about the Soviet Union which are published outside the USSR are rarely reviewed in Soviet publications; the prerequisite for any review is that the book should not be regarded as anti-Soviet. In any case, critical books about the Soviet Union, or books written from an independent viewpoint – this one, for example – will not be made available to the public. To the extent that this can be contrived, such books will also be prevented from reaching audiences *outside* the Soviet Union; this is achieved readily in Eastern Europe, but is even attempted outside the Soviet bloc, by making supply of Soviet materials depend on an undertaking not to supply books of the type mentioned above.

Lectures by foreign visitors appear not to be censored, but these are not expected to voice critical views; if they do, it becomes the task of the chairman to intervene with an immediate rebuttal. (This is based on my own experience; cf. Mickiewicz, 1981, p. 127.)

The vast number of Russian émigré publications confirms the tremendous pressure in the USSR to escape from the censorship. The same has been even more true of Poland, to judge only from the large number and wide range of Solidarity publications. 'The socialism that brought us to this crisis – this socialism of police censorship – has been devastating us for 36 years,' was the outburst of Professor Edward Limpinski on the occasion of the disbandment in Poland of KOR (*D.T.*, 29 September 1981, p. 4). What happened during the 'Prague Spring' is also illustrative (cf. for example Campbell, 1985, p. 1). Polish shipyard workers demanded that there should be a law prohibiting censorship, but any country within the Soviet bloc, and especially the Soviet Union itself, is unlikely to be vouchsafed such a liberty.

8 How Secrecy Has Varied over Time

INTRODUCTION

Over time, the censorship *can* become more rigorous or less so. Although, within a period with a given type and rigor of censorship, continuity is of the essence, a *quid pro quo* with a foreign government is possible, if the Soviet government is confident that nothing untoward will result. An example of such a brief and partial intermission was the broadcasting over Soviet television of the same interview as was seen by French viewers, at the press conference given by Gorbachev during his visit to France in October 1985. The questions included mention of dissidents such as Sakharov and Shcharansky, and one about the number of political prisoners in the Soviet Union. Gorbachev dealt with these questions confidently, as had no doubt been expected (*The Times*, 3 October 1985). However, the version printed in *Pravda*, though generally complete, omitted reference to 'anti-Gorbachev posters' in Paris (*Pravda*, 2 October 1985, p. 2 and *Soviet Analyst*, 9 October 1985, p. 3).

Pre-Revolutionary Russia exhibited definite discontinuities over time in its degrees of secrecy. The most abrupt and thoroughgoing was a decree of Tsar Paul in 1797, which prohibited the importing of foreign books and music (Vucinich, 1963, p. 144); this law was repealed in 1801, after Paul's murder. To pick out one or two other noteworthy developments in this chronicle: about 1858, formerly secret naval estimates were published (Violette, 1974, p. 590). Until the 1860s, the Russian budget was a closely guarded secret: annual budgets began to be published only after 1861, following disclosures by émigrés, with detailed estimates being published from 1863 onwards (Pipes, 1974, p. 20; Hutchings, 1983, pp. 4–5). Wide variations in the rigor of the Tsarist censorship at different periods, such as in the percentage of imported German publications which were banned, and in the type of ban – in entirety or less completely – are shown by Choldin (1985, fig. 5–2 and table 5–8). The present chapter attempts to document and describe events and trends in secretiveness over time during the Soviet period, and especially from the First Five-Year Plan onwards.

It is important to establish whether there is any single trend over time in the degrees of secrecy applying to all sectors, or whether different sectors exhibit different trends. This is one focus of the present chapter. I shall not compare volumes of information in one sector with those in another, these quantities being incommensurate.

ECONOMIC AFFAIRS

During the period of NEP (1921–8), published information about both facts and opinions was considerable in volume and the degree of secrecy not very high. The period of the First Five-Year Plan (1 October 1928 to 31 December 1932) showed divergent trends. Factual information of certain sorts, to which the Party desired that attention should be drawn, was fairly abundant; however, as compared with the NEP period published opinions became more uniform, which signifies in the main that less was published about what people were thinking and/or that what was published was less truthful. Moreover, official statistical data about the economy became to a larger extent data relating to industry (or to some extent other favoured sectors), whereas statistics of agricultural output or livestock numbers now left substantial gaps (see Hutchings, 1982B, pp. 9–10). These changes, it later transpired, mirrored the unequal success of economic policies in industry and agriculture. Published data relating to industry were in some directions very detailed: for instance, the Stalin motor vehicle works turned out forty vehicles on 29 June 1932, but only thirty, two days later (Hutchings, 1982A, p. 254). Statistical handbooks covering the years 1933 to 1935 reflected this trend, in that they devoted much more space to industry than to agriculture: the peak ratio in numbers of tables devoted to industry, relative to agriculture (3.63) being reached in the 1934 handbook (Hutchings, 1982B, p. 85).

In 1936–7 the amount of published information about the economy sharply declined, i.e. (assuming, as there is reason to suppose, the gathering of information continued unabated) this information then began to be classified. This may have reflected a decline in the status of the State Planning Commission relative to that of agencies supplying economic information. We know that at this time the personnel of the Commission was almost completely replaced (Zelenovskiy, 1941, p. 17). However, one main reason, perhaps the chief one, for enhanced secretiveness was that the Soviet Union became increasingly apprehensive at the menacing trend of international events in Europe and the Far East.

The period from 1936 to 1956 was much more secretive than either of the flanking periods. During this twenty-year span no statistical handbooks appeared. If a more precise dating is needed, this might be from 15 September 1936 to 19 May 1956 – the dates when the 1935 and 1955 handbooks respectively were signed for the press – or, given operational delays, from a date slightly later than this opening date to one slightly earlier than the closing date. After 1934 the relatively moderate earnings of Party workers were no longer published (Matthews, 1978, p. 127). The last figure for the absolute amount of cash in circulation is for 1 January 1938 (Grossman, 1982, p. 270). There are no data about money turnovers for the post-war period (Birman, 1981, p. 125).

Relating to a year one-quarter through the 1936–56 span, the 1941 Economic Plan, marked *Ne podlezhit oglasheniyu*, eventually became available in the West; however, this was fortuitous and by no means due to release of these data by the Soviet authorities. The Plan has about the same bulk as a statistical annual, from which it could possibly be deduced that compilation and assembly of statistics were, at least at that time, continuing on about the same scale as before. The first handbooks published after the 1936–56 period ended were much smaller than those that appeared in the mid-1930s, which suggests that towards the latter part of the period this effort may have tapered off. This is interesting if it means that publication was to some extent a spur to statistical collection.

During part of this period the Soviet Union was involved in war, at first with Finland and then over a much longer period and far more seriously with Nazi Germany and its allies. Secrecy reached a zenith during this time, yet the difference in regard to reporting of economic affairs, as compared with just before and just after, was less than in the Western democracies. Regarding financial matters, for instance, the periodical *Sovetskiye finansy* appeared, and contained quite informative articles. (See for instance many references in Hutchings, 1984, especially chapters 6 and 7.) Budget totals are available retrospectively for the war years, apart from forecasts for 1942 and 1943. In 1948 (signed for the press on 10 January 1948), there appeared Voznesenskiy's quite informative *Voyennaya ekonomika SSSR* (*The War Economy of the USSR*). Owing to this book and to other material the impact of the war on the economy and then the reconversion to a peacetime economy can be traced in general terms.

We observe a declassification of a substantial volume of economic material about 1956, which possibly reflected a rise at that time in the status of information–user interests relative to that of information gatherers. Here the former can probably be identified with the State Planning Commission, the latter with the Central Statistical Agency, although relative to other government bodies the status of the latter would not have fallen. The declassification must have reflected decisions which were taken a little earlier; most probably the relevant changes took place towards the beginning of 1955, when organisational changes affecting the State Planning Commission (Gosplan) were announced (9 February 1955). The substantial release of data in 1956 suggests a noteworthy advancement of the Gosplan in 1955. Such an advancement did occur as an integral part of the reform of the industrial and planning structure in 1957 (see Hutchings, 1982A, p. 136). It had earlier been intended to combine planning and administration in one body, which was still to be called the Gosplan. Elsewhere, I have demonstrated that the degree of fulfilment of the republic section of the budget offers a kind of preview of forthcoming changes in budget structure (Hutchings, 1983, p. 92); analogously, changes in disclosure policy may preview forthcoming changes in the planning structure.

In the decade before 1964 the whereabouts and nature of industrial plants were revealed in many cases, except as regards defence industry, though precise street addresses in many cases remained unavailable (Flegon, 1964).

Judging by the numbers of tables appearing in successive annual handbooks, secrecy was relaxed successively in: finance and credit (1956); territory and population of the USSR (1960, but a population total had previously been cited applying to April 1956); growth of well-being of the Soviet people (1961); services to the population (1968); science and technical progress

(1971); external economic connections of the USSR (1972: however, foreign trade handbooks were published from 1955 onwards). These titles are taken from the handbooks as stated there. In some cases, such as science and technical progress, it may be more correct to see the addition as arising in part from a new realisation that the subject was of general interest, as well as from a perception of its propaganda value. (Science is considered in more detail below.) This also applies to a considerable extent to growth of well-being of the Soviet population and services to the population, though these can also be seen as illustrations of relaxation of secrecy. The addition of natural resources and protection of the environment (1982 onwards) goes with the conservation tide, while the agro-industrial complex (1983 onwards) reflects enhanced attention to this form of organisation.

From the 1962 handbook onwards, the reporting of every earlier year was discontinued, being replaced by the still continuing practice of reporting mainly past years which end in a 0 or a 5. By reducing unnecessary repetition, this change enabled the annuals henceforth to provide, within a given total space, a larger share of new information.

A lessening of secrecy in the later years of Khrushchev's rule, which was followed by its intensification under Brezhnev, is suggested also by the series included in published quarterly statistics of industrial production. If the list in Hutchings, 1971B, Appendix VI (pp. 286–7) may be taken to be reliable, numbers of items included throughout all the quarters of each year were, in different years, as follows:

1958	43	1961	48	1964	56
1959	42	1962	51	1965	56
1960	42	1964	57	1966	49

A list of items for which seasonality, as measured by log S, can be reckoned over the period 1958–9 to 1974–5 emerges as follows (see below). In this case a peak is reached between 1962–3 and 1967–8 and this is followed by a decline, which confirms the proposition in the first sentence of the previous paragraph. The meaning of log S is defined in Hutchings, 1971B (pp. 259–79). In brief: this is an index of seasonality over the four quarters of the year up to the first quarter of the year following, constructed so as to be distortion-free.

1958–9	35	1964–5	43	1970–1	41
1959–60	34	1965–6	43	1971–2	40
1960–1	35	1966–7	43	1972–3	40
1961–2	38	1967–8	43	1973–4	37
1962–3	43	1968–9	42	1974–5	36
1963–4	43	1969–70	42		

Rather similarly, while secrecy in defence spending is always intense, the published total for defence spending appears to have become slightly less distorted during what was approximately the Khrushchev period. This is reflected in the fact that between 1954–5 and 1963–4 a correlation with certain other movements in budgetary spending which was positive in other post-war sub-periods became negative (see Hutchings, 1977B, pp. 257–83).

The growth of published information about the Soviet economy since 1955 has apparently been due to decisions both of type *A* and of type *B*, in the terminology of Chapter 7. The decision to publish all-union statistical handbooks applying to years from 1955 onwards must have been the result of type *A* decisions, since it revealed genuinely new information of a kind which had not been made public for two decades. On the other hand, the sudden and large augmentation of regional information about the economy, disclosed in statistical handbooks appertaining to republics and lesser territorial divisions, in certain years and especially in 1967 when this addition was unprecedently big, may be ascribed largely or wholly to type *B* decisions. In other words, in those years there may have been little or no relaxation of censorship in the strict sense, but rather an expansion of publication into areas where this was already permitted. A signal, requesting or requiring publication, must have been given, with an appropriate allotment of paper, printing capacity, etc.

As regards reporting of foreign trade, since 1977 the reporting of volumes, as opposed to values, has gone down considerably (Wolf, 1984); this may be connected with the fact that 'in recent years' the unspecified foreign trade residuals were including a larger number of non-strategic items (Smith in Dawisha and Hanson, 1981, p. 118). The percentage of trade which is not itemised is likely to have risen owing also to an increased share of arms in Soviet exports to the Third World (as appears to follow from JEC, 1981, p. 56). Whereas according to the Helsinki Final

Act (1975) the signatories (which included all the East European states except Albania) should have enlarged the volume of their data relating to foreign trade, that volume has actually shrunk (Kaser and Nötel, 1985, p. 8).

Savings indicators have not been included in the handbooks for 1960, 1961 or 1962, and starting with the 1972 statistical annual, publication of expenditures on loans (the 3 per cent loan) stopped (Birman, 1981, p. 143). Starting with the 1976 annual, indicators of national income used for personal consumption ceased to be published (Birman, 1981, p. 254). Following a price reform in 1967 the USSR greatly restricted the circulation of official price-lists (NFAC, 1979, p. 10). However, the 9th Five-Year Plan (1971–5) was the first since the war about which a significant amount of detail was published (Noren and Whitehouse, 1973, pp. 209–10). The potential existed to continue this trend, in that as reported in 1979 the amount of information reaching the Gosplan had almost doubled as compared with the 9th Five-Year Plan (NFAC, 1979, p. 10).

Brezhnev's death in November 1982 and the accession to power of Andropov and then others was followed by much greater attention in the press to negative phenomena, such as corruption and inefficiency. By 1984 the press was in effect showing what economic conditions were like, that is to say how bad they were, although in an unchangingly optimistic manner (*The Observer*, 8 April 1984, p. 7).

SCIENCE

Secrecy in Soviet science has tended to broaden *pari passu* with the increased importance of science in military technology, but has been affected by other influences as well.

One immediate change following the Revolution was a shift towards collective work, which tends to be exercised in, or to result in, greater confidentiality than is normal with individual research. Foreign information was censored and travel abroad became difficult; after 1935 the difficulties in both respects became greater (Bailes, 1986, p. 33). The Great Purge (1936–9) by no means spared Soviet scientists. In 1939–40, many were probably working in defence establishments or imprisoned in camps; the design of military aircraft was apparently conducted mainly within three special prisons (Hutchings, 1976, pp. 38, 149). The intensification of military research during wartime obviously favoured enhanced secrecy (as it did elsewhere). After the war extreme nationalism in the presentation of scientific achievements gained its head in the Soviet Union, and even some non-achievements, such as Academician Lysenko's theory of acquired heritable characteristics, were publicised.

Stalin's last years witnessed an increased secrecy in Soviet science (Klochko, 1964, p. 117), but the post-Stalin period soon saw some relaxation. In 1955, cautious steps were taken to allow research workers freer access to foreign materials which previously had been treated as confidential. A government decree required ministries and republics

> to review with the participation of the Chief Administration for Guarding Military and State Secrets in the Press attached to the Council of Ministers of the USSR, the closed funds of foreign literature within branch scientific literature, and those editions which are kept secret without sufficient grounds to offer for use to scientific and engineer-technical workers.

It also ordered removal of

> incorrect restrictions on the use by readers of foreign scientific-technical literature which is received in State libraries of ministries and departments

and it required

> the Chief Administration for Guarding Military and State Secrets in the Press attached to the Council of Ministers of the USSR to work out a new Institution on the procedure for keeping and using foreign literature in correspondence with point II of the present decree

(i.e. the above quotation). This is from the decree of the Council of Ministers of the USSR of 25 June 1955 (no. 1185), reprinted in Karpov and Severtsev, 1957 (pp. 222–3); my translation from the Russian. The extent of the relaxation, however, remains unclear.

It attracted so much attention that at about this time, during the visit of Khrushchev and Bulganin to Britain (April 1956), Academician I. V. Kurchatov delivered a lecture at Harwell on Soviet experiments on the controlled utilisation of fusion reactions, which impressed his audience profoundly (Hutchings, 1976, p. 99). The USSR became no longer secretive about fusion research since the late 1950s, when it was taken off the secret list in both East and West (Cowen, 1978, p. 15 and Calder, 1969, p. 655). As the detailed preparations to launch an artificial satellite of the Earth had not been announced, Sputnik I (4 October 1957) came as a dramatic surprise; which, for several years afterwards, was also the case with other Soviet satellite launchings. Space spectaculars, which clearly were intended to make the maximum publicity impact more than to make determined progress towards serious scientific objectives – such as the orbital flight of the first woman, Valentina Tereshkova, in June 1963 and that of the first three-man crew in October 1964, also belong to this period of greater openness in Soviet science (Vladimirov, 1971, pp. 113–15, 124–39). In the decade prior to 1973, new forms of scientific collaboration between the Soviet Union and other countries grew up. With the United States, such collaboration occurred successively in the Antarctic, in detecting underground explosions, and in exchanging information about their respective spacecraft bound for Mars (Hutchings, 1976, p. 16); Soviet secrecy had to be appropriately diminished. However, it continued to be claimed that the morale of Soviet astronauts was invariably high, a claim that had been maintained from the beginning. Only in 1983 were extracts published from the personal diary of Valentin Lebedev which described how tedious his space mission had been (*D.T.*, 16 August 1983, p. 3).

As regards more mundane technology, the payment of lump sums for Western licences, which was usually the preferred method up to about the mid-1960s, 'reflected the Socialist predilection for secrecy (not having to disclose the size of output)', *inter alia*. Subsequently, the payment of periodic royalties became more common (Wilczynski, 1974, pp. 303–4).

In the field of copyright, there is extension. For example, a Soviet copyright delegation came to Poland in September 1974, at the invitation of the Poles, in order to reach an agreement on mutual protection of copyright (PAP in English, 18.40 gmt 30 September 1974, SWB 4718). This trend is due directly to decisions taken within the Soviet bloc but under strong influence from the outside world.

POLITICS, SECURITY AND MISCELLANEOUS

The show trials of alleged wreckers (1936–8) did not so much signify any relaxation of secrecy as an exercise in disinformation, which successfully deceived a number of foreign observers (see, for example, Davies, 1942, pp. 179–84). During this period, the results of a population census (that of 1937) were not published: allegedly this had been defective and the work of 'enemies of the people' (Katkoff, 1961, p. 39).

Change can take place in the facts that are reported, but is equally, or more, likely to take place in the angle or tone of reporting. Even subtle changes of this sort may be noticed and interpreted by the politically sophisticated as heralding a major shift in outlook or even in policy. One such development, in April 1941, was Stalin's support for Ilya Erenburg, a strong Francophile, in helping him get his manuscript, *The Fall of Paris*, through the censorship: because of the Nazi–Soviet Non-Aggression Pact, the Moscow censors had refused to allow it even for serial publication. Erenburg understood Stalin's promise of support to mean that the Soviet Union was preparing for war with Germany (Salisbury, 1969, p. 67).

During the Second World War, Soviet secrecy relating to national security did not increase much because it was already so strict; thus variability in this sphere is less than in Western political democracies. Its orientation naturally altered, in that some information could now be given to the Western allies which had to be withheld from enemy or neutral states; however, the Soviet Union remained outside the special relationship now existing between the United States and Britain; the historical and other ties between the two Western partners, in conjunction with their absence between either of these and the USSR, made that result inevitable. The war was soon followed by the Cold War; the Soviet Union withdrew into its shell, and secretiveness increased.

Since Stalin's death, probably the most important single event connected with Soviet secrecy and disclosure policy, in the Soviet bloc as well as within the USSR, was Khrushchev's secret speech to the 20th Party Congress of the USSR in February 1956; a speech which soon came to be more widely known. It not only shed fresh light on the purges but heralded a general liberalisation of attitudes throughout the bloc. For example, most evening papers in the East European countries started to be published after the Congress: these provided some flavour of actual life, as distinct from the propaganda filling the morning papers (Ervin Šoóš). Certain important changes in Soviet policy may be traced to this event; thus, Khrushchev in 1961 ended the censorship of foreign journalists' outgoing despatches (Smith, 1976, p. 30). Probably he was already disposed to do so, although the decision was taken following an approach to himself personally by Edmund Stevens, the veteran American newspaper correspondent (Stevens, 1985, p. 20). Khrushchev also showed 'some readiness to permit a modicum of debate on defence issues to appear in published military journals' (Mackintosh, 1985, p. 175).

Khrushchev was less obsessed than Stalin with secrecy (Medvedev, 1978, p. 74); his ousting (October 1964) and replacement by Brezhnev led to a shift into reverse. It might be said that various trends became less favourable, for example the growth in living standards slowed down. Under Brezhnev, an extension of secrecy made discussion of 'group purging' difficult (Matthews, 1978, p. 153). The fourth volume of the History of the Communist Party of the Soviet Union, published in 1973, considerably toned down criticisms of Stalin. Even the minor criticisms which had survived previous revisions were virtually eliminated, including omission of the sentence 'At the same time, after Kirov's murder, a number of measures were carried out which violated socialist legality'. That is to say, so far as the Establishment was concerned, the Terror never occurred (Murarka, 1974, pp. 69–70). Thus secrecy in this sphere was reinstated, although to the outside world that horse had already bolted. Soviet secrecy practices as reported in 1975 were much stricter than in the 1920s or 1930s (Lee, 1975, p. A-6).

A hardening of the censorship under Brezhnev did not occur at once, but following an escalation of arrest policy against dissenters; this led to the first Constitution Day demonstration by dissenters in Moscow on 5 December 1965, and then to legislation of March and September 1966. In September 1966, Sinyavskiy and Daniel were arrested and eventually received heavy sentences. A gradual tightening of censorship policy continued, and was intensified following the invasion of Czechoslovakia on 21 August 1968. As that invasion provoked condemnation abroad and even to some extent at home, extensive jamming of Russian broadcasts by the BBC, the Voice of America and Deutsche Welle was resumed (based on Rigby, Brown and Reddaway, 1980, pp. 161–9). Similarly, Vladimirov, writing in 1972, considered that 'in recent years, the trend has been towards a greater, rather than lesser, severity in matters of censorship' (Vladimirov, 1972, p. 43). As reported in 1977, the USSR 'in recent years' had steadily reduced the amount of published biographical information about members of the ruling élite. The previous year, 1976, 'for the first time, the Yearbook of the *Large Soviet Encyclopaedia* did not contain biographies of members of the Central Committee elected at the March congress. The official reference work on deputies of the Supreme Soviet is practically unobtainable now' (*The Times*, 31 May 1977, p. 15). Less information was also published about the mass of the population, as reflected in the census results. Whereas the results of the 1959 census were published in sixteen volumes, and those of the 1970 one in six volumes, as reported in 1982 only brief summaries had appeared of the census of January 1979. Murray Feshbach identified four major problems: the USSR had too few men; this shortage was heavily concentrated among Russians; Great Russians would be likely to fall below 50 per cent by the year 2000; and the Russian part of the population was rapidly ageing relative to the Muslim part (Feshbach, 1982, p. 9).

However, more geographical areas were opened to foreigners. Under the latest rules issued by the Ministry of Foreign Affairs, Magnitogorsk, Krasnodar and parts of greater Moscow were opened, though the regions near the Chinese border remained completely closed (*Sunday Times*, 22 January 1978, p. 1. Reference is to the Ministry of Foreign Affairs Note mentioned earlier: see above, Chapter 6). One of the extensions was in the direction of Gorky, beyond Izmaylovskiy Park (own recollection, in conjunction with the US State Department map, mentioned earlier). There had been enlargements earlier in the zones opened to foreigners: some of these occurred during the period 1957–9, and there was some competition among diplomats stationed in Moscow as to who would be first into the newly opened area; following some disappointments in this area of emulation, when on 31 August 1959 I began a brief solo visit to Tallinn, this was the first visit by a Western diplomat to Estonia since its incorporation into the USSR nineteen years before. In Moscow, the

Kremlin was closed to visitors until 1955, then was open to those with a permit, and since then has been open to visitors without any formality: since 1958 up to nightfall through certain entrances, although within the Kremlin itself certain areas remain out of bounds (Nagel, 1973, p. 30). These trends of opening up more territory to visitors are in principle reversible, but do not appear to have been reversed (except temporarily) in practice.

The publication during Brezhnev's rule of Khrushchev's memoirs, which appeared in the West under the title *Khrushchev Remembers* (first published in late December 1970, following the appearance of four articles from the manuscript in November and December 1970), was a more startling exception to the norm of more intense secrecy, but it was not the result of any action taken by the Brezhnev government: on the contrary, Khrushchev was compelled by them to deny that he had passed on material of a memoir nature, which indeed strictly speaking may have been correct, though his denial did not claim that he had not been working on memoirs (Khrushchev, 1977, p. 15). He was in fact working on these during his enforced retirement, which lasted from his dismissal from office in October 1964 until his death in September 1971.

Emigration from the USSR came to be on a significant scale from 1960, and especially from 1968, onwards. The changing attitudes of the authorities between 1972 and 1977 can be seen from three examples. Panov, a ballet dancer, applied to emigrate in March 1972, but was not allowed to do so (*N.Y.T.*, 9 April 1973, p. 37). Since he knew no secrets, the reason must have been the high prestige of ballet in the Soviet Union. Andrey Amalrik declined to emigrate as long as the authorities demanded 4000 roubles on paintings that he was planning to take with him (*D.T.*, 1 July 1976, p. 4). In contrast, Aleksandr Podrabinek was *told* to emigrate, or he would face arrest. He had been the author of a text 'Punitive Medicine', on the subject of abuses of human rights in Soviet mental hospitals (*D.T.*, 3 December 1977, p. 5).

Apparently, about midway through this five-year period there was a change in policy: the new line was expressed by President Brezhnev, who told US congressmen that the number of Jewish applicants for emigration was dropping, and that the Soviet principle was to give permission to all who wanted to leave, with the exception of those who had had access to state secrets (*The*

Times, 16 August 1975). This change may be ascribed at least in part to the Helsinki Agreement (1975). The number of emigrants in fact rose from a low point of 20 000 in 1975 to a peak of 62 300 in 1979, before tapering off thereafter (*Soviet Analyst*, 19 March 1986, p. 5).

One of the significant innovations of the Andropov administration was its disclosure of a little more about the working of the government. While for years it had been known that the Politburo met on Thursdays, the meetings had never been officially announced, nor had any account been given of what happened. Short accounts of these sessions now started to be published, apparently at Andropov's own suggestion (according to *The Observer*, 2 January 1983, p. 12). These reports soon started to become shorter: the first four numbered in words respectively 526 (11 December 1982), 156 (17 December 1982), 436 (8 January 1983) and 247 (15 January 1983. *Pravda* in all cases). A large fraction of the first report consisted of an affirmation of the unanimous support given by workers to the foreign and internal policies of the Central Committee, etc. Subsequent reports of this kind are pithier. Sessions of *oblast'* party executive committees also began to be published. There being so many (over 100) *oblasti* these can be examples only, and the form can be more varied. This started immediately after the start of publication of reports about sessions of the Politburo, which obviously was not accidental. Thus *Pravda* of 5 January 1983 published questions and answers to the Secretary of Chita *oblast'* party executive committee (*obkom*), and *Pravda* of two days later a report of Rostov-on-Don Party *obkom*.

The communiqués on the meetings of the Soviet Politburo are also carried in the Bulgarian press, which has taken to publishing analogous reports about meetings of the Bulgarian Politburo (EIU, 1983, p. 16).

While these measures are in a liberal direction, since 1982 the Soviet authorities strengthened their efforts to isolate the Soviet citizenry from the outside world, using a two-pronged approach: 'propagandistic measures' and 'disciplinary measures of a legal character' (Schmid, 1985, p. 4). As reported in July 1984, it had 'recently' been made illegal to offer a foreigner a night's accommodation, or transport on the way; this measure had been enlarged by rumour. One of its aims was perhaps to hinder marriages with foreigners, by means of putting obstacles in the way of meeting them. A law of January 1984 introduced labour-camp terms of up to eight years for Soviet citizens who passed information about their workplace to non-Soviet citizens (Hatton, 1984, p. 11). According to a law of 1 July 1984, foreigners do not have to be granted consular access unless they are being deported (*D.T.*, 7 August 1984); which could facilitate harassment of them.

On the other hand, accidents were more often reported. *Trud* of 21 April 1984 told of the collapse of a wall in a Moscow underground railway tunnel, which was described in *The Daily Telegraph* as 'the latest example of a new willingness by the Soviet press to report news of some accidents and disasters. For years such items have been suppressed'. The Chernobyl nuclear disaster (26 April 1986), the first news of which came from Sweden where very abnormal levels of radiation were discovered, showed that this 'new willingness' had limits; the contrast with the publicity given to the much less serious Three-Mile Island disaster in the United States was marked. However, Chernobyl is only a moderately strong example of *Soviet* secretiveness, given that in all countries nuclear matters tend to be surrounded with reticence, because of their connection with nuclear explosions and the antipathy to nuclear power generation in some popular (though non-Soviet) circles.

The states of health of the Soviet top leaders continued to be shrouded in secrecy. The deaths of President Brezhnev and of President Andropov were not preceded by any announcements of grave illness, and indeed Zamyatin assured newsmen that Andropov was recovering, just two days before his death in February 1984 (*D.T.*, 12 June 1984, p. 6). President Chernenko's death *was* so preceded, yet just before his death attempts (which were quite unconvincing) were being made to show that he was still in command. His death was followed by a twenty-hour interval until the official announcement; just four hours after that, the obviously predetermined succession was proclaimed to the world: Gorbachev had now stepped into the appointment of General Secretary.

FINAL REMARKS

The three spheres examined above exhibit broadly similar trends over time in secrecy policy, both the directions of change and the turning points being approximately the same. This strongly suggests that secrecy and disclosure policy is a self-contained and specific area of policy which is determined by decisions taken at the highest level. The cut-off points are not equally clear-cut, these being most pronounced in economics and least in military affairs. Moreover, all phenomena are not necessarily heading in the same direction: thus under Khrushchev the system went on a liberal tack, and under Brezhnev on a conservative tack, yet under Brezhnev emigration increased.

The turning points may be affected by various influences, but chief among these appears to be a change in the top leadership. In particular, Stalin's death was soon followed by a decline in secretiveness. The reigns of Stalin, Brezhnev and Chernenko were on the whole secretive or very secretive periods, whereas under Khrushchev and Andropov secrecy was somewhat less. The sequence therefore traces an alternation of more, and less, secretive periods: under Stalin, Khrushchev and Brezhnev these were relatively prolonged, under Andropov and Chernenko very short, but this difference seems to be either solely or very largely due to the accident of longer or shorter tenure of the supreme post.

Gorbachev strongly favours, and has been urging on his colleagues, lesser secrecy and greater openness (in Russian: *glasnost'*), as witness his frank exposition of numerous different shortcomings in Soviet economy and society in his monumental speech at the 27th Party Congress (*Pravda*, 26 February 1986). Other signs of the times have included a speech by the poet Yevtushenko at the RSFSR Writers' Union in December 1985, attacking the censorship. However, the censorship (as well as other manifestations of secrecy) have enormous weight (as previous chapters have shown), and Yevtushenko's outburst may itself have been censored before publication in *Literaturnaya gazeta* (18 December 1985, p. 5).

While all the apparatus of censorship remains in place, it is highly unlikely that it will be left with nothing to do. Similarly, border controls are not going to be relaxed, as indeed Gorbachev has made clear (*Soviet Analyst*, 11 June 1986, pp. 4–5). Those who operate these controls, including the KGB, must be assumed to be entirely in favour of them, and many among the top leadership probably share that view. Fresh data have nevertheless been made available in various spheres, for instance funeral costs (*The Times*, 16 September 1986, p. 1 and cf. Chapter 5), and more importantly and dramatically in the reporting of the sinking in the Black Sea of the Admiral Nakhimov (31 August 1986), in the opening of the nuclear test site for inspection by Western journalists (*The Times*, 29 September 1986, p. 6), and in the extremely detailed explanations eventually provided of the Chernobyl disaster. In October 1986 infant mortality statistics, which for several years had gone missing, reappeared (*Ekonomicheskaya gazeta*, no. 43, 1986, p. 7). One catch is that greater openness to the authorities is meant to apply also to earnings: a blind eye is no longer turned to corruption, the second economy, or drunkenness. While in some directions official secrecy is being curbed, it is less clear whether it is being reduced *relative to individual privacy*.

Besides differing personalities and styles of leadership, might there be other influences? Variation in the international situation are certainly one; in particular the Soviet Union, like other countries, intensified secrecy during wartime. However, it has been noted that the change was less marked in the USSR than in Western countries.

A notion of self-equilibration, as it were harmonising the demand for secrecy and its supply, is not *a priori* absurd. It has been noticed already that one can find reasons both for making secrecy more intense and for making it less intense, and that over time these opposing forces could be expected to alternate. However, such a mechanism can hardly operate as effectively as that of a supply and demand mechanism in economics, where a condition is that sufficient information is available to participating agents; as regards secrecy this is, almost by definition, not the case. Both the defeats and (especially) the victories of counter-espionage must stay very largely unknown not only to the public but to the legislators. The inertia displayed in Britain, where the Official Secrets Act has been under attack for years, if not decades, and yet still remains in force, shows the sluggishness of such a mechanism within a parliamentary democracy, and it is not clear that under the Soviet constitution movement would be any faster; very probably it would be slower. Moreover, the international environment should be either unvarying or neutral, and both circumstances are unlikely. However, perhaps there is a weak force making for self-adjustment.

It has been suggested that samizdat (see next chapter) is tolerated by the authorities – to the extent that it is tolerated by them – because it provides indispensable information to the leadership in regard to what citizens are concerned about (for example ISC, 1980, p. 38). The authorities must indeed learn something from samizdat.

The more relevant issue from our present viewpoint is: might they then be influenced in the direction of making the censorship more (or less) rigorous? It is conceivable that samizdat would provoke a spiteful reaction: let the public be punished for telling each other more by our telling them less! If there *is* any spiteful reaction it would be in that direction (unless it went outside the sphere of disclosure policy). A spiteful reaction is difficult to handle by analytical means; at any rate, it does not seem likely.

As regards rational reactions: the principle of compensation (see Chapter 2) does not apply because samizdat is information supplied by citizens (mainly to each other), not information supplied by the authorities. Thus there should be no reason to expect any *reduction* in the volume of information supplied. Should one expect an *increase*? I noted already that that result could be produced by publication abroad (Chapter 2); the effect of samizdat could well be in the same direction, but weaker in degree because samizdat does not include any important secrets among its revelations (which, as will be noticed, in fact it does not). It seems, therefore, that samizdat could be one of the factors tending to reduce the severity of the censorship, but not a potent influence.

Changes in Soviet society are starting to exert an influence. In recent years, social changes may have been greater than economic ones (Sutherland, 1986). The growing population and its rising level of education inevitably exert pressure, which has been building up over decades and ultimately may prove irresistible. This applies to the main elements of secrecy and disclosure policy. In spheres such as emigration, which are affected by more specific influences, the sequences are harder to predict.

Whatever influences are gradually exerted by evolving circumstances, it is effectively the Soviet top leadership that determines Soviet secrecy and disclosure policy, and therefore also *changes* in these policies. Though the evidence supporting that conclusion is partly impressionistic, it is consistent and there are no contra-indications. During a given rule, concealment tends to be gradually reinforced, as the advantages of hiding what is going wrong under the current administration increasingly overbear any extra advantage from revealing still more about what went wrong under the preceding one.

9 Secrecy and the Soviet Public

How does secrecy affect the Soviet public? First, they take it seriously. It is a fundamental difference between Soviet and British attitudes that the British, in the main – obviously this would not apply to the small minority who handle secret information in the course of their work – find it difficult to take secrecy seriously. Many do not believe that there are any secrets of importance. Different is the Soviet attitude: scarcely anyone doubts that secrets exist.

After that, one would have to draw distinctions. People are not all alike! As has been shown in Poland, public opinion in a Communist country can differ widely from the official Party line. The Soviet Union certainly is not Poland: it is far larger and vastly less homogenous. Poles are mostly religious whereas most Russians are not. Poland has many more historical links with Western Europe, and historically, Russia and Poland have almost always been on opposite sides. But if Soviet opinion is far from being solidly anti-Soviet, it is nevertheless varied. I should guess as varied as in most other countries. In conversations at different times between 1954 and 1971 I found all shades of opinion ranging from complete acceptance of the regime to complete rejection of it. If something like a completely free poll were held, probably a majority would favour some kind of socialism; they have no experience of anything else. There would be a large majority for greater freedom of speech and for unrestricted travel.

However, according to a survey in which Shlapentokh took part, the Soviet public is 4–6 times readier to accept official versions of foreign than of home news. The reasons would include: 'patriotism, fear of the authorities, restrictions on information, and absence of personal involvement' (Shlapentokh, 1984, p. 88). Mickiewicz adds that there is a 'tendency for disagreement to increase as the story comes closer to the personal experience of the reader', and that 'readers are closer to the truth' in regard to local events. It is only via the national mass media that the Soviet public can explore international politics, and furthermore the central press is accorded much more confidence than the local press (Mickiewicz, 1981, pp. 44, 46–7, 63, 66, 135–6). She notes that 'The very lack of alternative sources has inflated the prestige of the central press, and the policy of information restriction has been to that extent successful' (Ibid., p. 47).

It appears that the public has confidence in precisely those areas of reporting where in my view the press provides the most one-sided picture. However, I am not entirely convinced that these two polarities actually are co-existing harmoniously. Mickiewicz points out also the primacy of the demand for international news at the city level, although readers would already have read about them in the central press, which she finds 'almost inexplicable' (Ibid., p. 61). The explanation would possibly be a residual lack of confidence by the public in the truth or completeness of what they are being told.

If there is a large difference, in the direction Shlapentokh indicates, whether the difference is greater in the Soviet Union than elsewhere is not equally clear. Most of us have found that on occasions when the press reports something that is within our personal experience, the report is not accurate. I suspect that the Soviet difference reflects not so much greater confidence by the public in the veracity of foreign news, as less confidence in that of domestic news. On two occasions in the USSR I found myself arguing that it was possible to make use of Soviet statistics if one approached them critically, whereas my Soviet interlocutors denied this: in both cases they argued that no use at all could be made of them, as they were all lies!

It is most unlikely that that is a majority view, but Soviet citizens quite commonly ascribe to foreign countries, indeed precisely to those countries which their publicity depicts in such deprecatory terms, qualities in excess of what they actually enjoy.

In any case, though for many persons this extreme one-sidedness works, for some among the more intelligent, educated and sophisticated groups it does not. The brain may subconsciously recognise what is being done and automatically discover or invent antidotes. Perhaps there is a mechanism whereby if some country is constantly slandered, one cannot fail to recognise that there is something about it which is important enough to attract such considerable attention. Another problem for

Soviet publicists has been that while they are rejecting and criticising the United States, the Soviet Union in several not unimportant departments of life has set out to 'overtake' the United States – an obvious inconsistency.

Foreign exhibitions in Moscow are very well attended, which must have some result in increasing the exposure of Soviet citizens to the outside world. Exhibitions are frequently very large; for example, the second Japanese industrial exhibition in Moscow (1965) was the largest exhibition to be mounted outside Japan itself (Hutchings, 1976, p. 15). In 1985 an exhibition in Moscow of foreign computers, especially as educational aids, attracted excited attendance (*The Times*, 23 January 1985). The information stand at the British Trade Exhibition in Moscow in 1961 displayed pictures of London and other cities, and there were portraits of the Queen and the Duke of Edinburgh. Vast masses came past the stand and many stopped to chat. One might have expected questions about the British economy, foreign policy, public schools, etc. These indeed came but overwhelmingly the most frequent were addressed to the portrait of the Queen and were, first, 'Who is that?' and then followed by 'How old is she?' The reasons presumably included the novelty of seeing any picture of a royal personage, and more prosaically that a comparison of her real age with how she looked would tell one something about how hard or easy life was in that foreign land.

The curiosity shown by Soviet citizens in what has been happening within their *own* country, when in conversation with foreigners – whom they frequently assume to know better themselves – points to how ignorant they think themselves to be. Regrettably, it is probable that the extreme scepticism, exhibited by certain citizens, as to the veracity of official sources contributes towards keeping them in ignorance: one has to believe these in the first place, even if it eventually becomes clear that not all statistics or other sorts of information are worthy of credence. Sceptical examination, in conjunction with other data, is the road to advancement rather than direct disbelief, but Soviet citizens are debarred from attempting the former by the lack of comparative materials or of freedom to examine them at leisure, except in the rare instance when some unusually acute and persistent researcher contrives to overcome those obstacles.

By contrast, the German people under the Nazis are said to have been 'remarkably well-informed about all so-called secrets' (Arendt, 1967, p. vii), but Germany is a smaller country – for instance, most of the Jewish extermination camps in Nazi-occupied Europe were near main railway lines, from which trains entering and leaving the camps could be seen and photographed (Laqueur, 1980, p. 29). That particular horror has never been perpetrated in the Soviet Union, but it would be interesting to know by what means the dead from forced labour camps, or other places where there was heavy mortality, were disposed of. By analogy with the Katyn murders, one would expect inhumation rather than cremation, but this would depend on the season: throughout the long winter, especially in the Russian north – where the winter is longer and mortality is liable to be higher, the ground is frozen solid and cremation would be less laborious. The cremation of enemy dead in wintertime after the battle of Stalingrad is described by Khrushchev (1971, p. 222). In any event, many Soviet citizens must have been aware of, or personally experienced, horrible events but unless that awareness or experience is seen by the authorities as creditable, it is probably made more difficult for these things to be communicated to outsiders. Perhaps this helps to explain the apparent scarcity of disabled people.

Let us now try to put ourselves in the position of intelligent Soviet citizens who know that information is being withheld, and this leaves some of us with a feeling of frustration. What can we do to escape from this?

Though doubtless at present less dangerous than under Stalin, it may be personally risky to attempt any research for the purpose of drawing from officially published material more than its contents allows, or to collect data or documentation with that purpose in mind. Consequently, to be *in* the Soviet Union is not a particularly good qualification for finding out about the country, unless one has some inviolability, for instance as a member of a foreign embassy. Otherwise, almost the sole source of any extra information will be one's own experience, plus what is imparted by relatives or friends.

Where news is not reported in the official media, people usually rely to a greater extent on word of mouth information and other unofficial means. One would expect those means to be more effective in relatively small and compact societies, where the people do a lot of socialising, and where there are mouth-pieces beside the official media. The Roman Catholic Church is such a channel. Fitting these conditions, at Velehrad, in Czecho-slovakia, on 6–7 July 1985 between 200 000 and 250 000 be-lievers gathered for an open-air Mass and celebration, on the occasion of the 1,100th anniversary of the death of St Methodius: this event which is thought to have been the largest religious gathering in the history of Czechoslovakia 'was entirely unpub-licised officially – news of it was spread only by word of mouth and by *samizdat* periodicals and leaflets' (*Religion in Communist Lands*, winter 1985, editorial). By contrast, in the Soviet Union – geographically vast, with a huge multilingual population, and mainly irreligious – word of mouth information should be much less effective, if we are speaking about dissemination over the whole of the Soviet Union. The description 'mainly irreligious' is not meant as denying the large differences in degree of religious feeling among the different nationalities. The Russians are prob-ably the least religious people in the Soviet Union (see Bour-deaux, 1985, pp. 70–5, and Thompson, 1986, p. 11). In fact, no comparable instances have been reported in the USSR of large-scale awareness of events which have not been reported in the media. But rumours can sweep through a city, as witness the hurried exodus from Kiev following the Chernobyl accident.

We can try to tap sources outside censored material, for example by meeting and talking with visiting foreigners. This demands a common language: few foreigners speak Russian, but fortunately the learning of foreign languages, especially English, is widespread in the USSR although most people will have had little conversational practice with a native speaker. As noted above, the authorities deliberately restrict the opportunities available for meeting foreigners; however, such controls cannot be complete, and some unscheduled occasions remain. I myself have had conversations in Russia of surprising length – up to seven hours – about numerous subjects including the Soviet Union itself. I was once asked by a taxi driver in Moscow how living standards in the USSR had changed since 1929. I have never encountered anywhere else a taxi-driver who was so eager to learn from a foreigner about his own country!

We can try hard to listen to news broadcasts from outside, especially the BBC, Voice of America and Radio Liberty/Radio

Free Europe; here knowledge of English is definitely advantageous, and also a seat in the country (see in this connection
Chapter 6). Over a long period this may produce the curious
result that country dwellers are better informed than town
dwellers about the outside world. However, against this rural
people tend to be much less well educated than urban people
(Hutchings, 1982A, p. 97), and so will find it harder to put into
context what they hear. The above mentioned transmitters do
not broadcast anything that has been discovered about the
USSR by confidential means, but they provide an invaluable
fresh perspective and much data about current events which the
Soviet media exclude.

We can try to extract more from censored material than the
censor intends. Whether this is possible depends, of course, on
the type and rigor of the censorship, and on the topic. In many
directions even if the censor has been only semi-competent it will
still be impossible to make any progress. Certainly censorship is
annoying to a writer and on the whole is very harmful to truth,
both in general and in regard to numerous details. The immense
damage resulting from censorship to the breadth and correctness
of the Soviet public's view of the whole must in no way be
minimised. However, the total effects are more complicated and
probably less negative than they appear at first sight. It may be
supposed that to some (albeit perhaps only a slight) degree,
what is censored actually is inaccurate or mistaken. To that
extent, censorship may be helpful. In other words, there is no
law that what is blotted out must have been true and correct.
Secondly, if censorship compels a writer to think more carefully
about what he/she wants to say and how to say it, this must be a
good thing. Thirdly, censorship has an impact on the prospec-
tive audience: to some extent this may be dissuaded from paying
attention, but that effect is often not as strong as might have been
expected, and it is partly or even wholly outweighed by height-
ened attentiveness on the part of those who *do* pay attention to
what the text, even after censorship, may be suspected to have
succeeded in retaining.

An example of this result was to be found in the reactions of
the South African public to the introduction there of censorship.
Some newspapers reported increased sales after severe controls
were placed on what they were allowed to report under the
national state of emergency (*The Times*, 20 June 1986, p. 7). The

fundamental reason for enhanced interest would probably not be censorship as much as anxiety at what was happening; however, blank spaces (which was one immediate effect) at once incite curiosity. In effect, a broad mass of the population becomes involved in ferreting out state secrets, a task normally reserved to journalists and foreign intelligence agencies.

The fact of censorship introduces other important changes into popular attitudes to material which is known to have been censored. First, as has often been noted, fiction is scrutinised for signs that it is really alluding to contemporary life. It therefore becomes necessary for censorship to be extended to fiction, in particular to anything which by some not too subtle transformation (of dates, places, names) might be held to have such an application. An overstimulated imagination may even pick on fictitious or historical material which actually has no such application, in the mistaken belief that it has. For instance in the 1590s, in the reign of Queen Elizabeth I of England, popular imagination found certain parallels with the reign of Richard II. Shakespeare's play of that name was therefore a most popular publication, although incomplete, as the deposition scene was left out. Nowadays, it is less easy to see any parallel between the situations of Richard II and of Queen Elizabeth I (Harrison, 1981, pp. 109–10). But if imagined events, or actual historical events, are mistakenly supposed to have application to the realities of the present day, it is also likely to be supposed that what is given out as being an accurate representation of current events actually is not. Thus, to the extent that fiction is regarded as non-fiction, non-fiction will be regarded as fiction.

Another device is to discuss another country, ostensibly for its own sake but actually (or also) in order to discuss the situation in the Soviet Union. For instance, this may well be an ulterior motive of criticisms by Soviet scholars of China (Rozman, 1986). Other spheres where the purpose is similar have been suggested, but it would seem to be necessary to walk a very difficult tightrope and some degree of scepticism seems in order. At any rate, any coded discussion will reach far fewer people than one that is not coded, and in fact it will normally be confined to a tiny group of specialists in that particular topic. Moreover, with a given strictness of censorship, the clearer the possible application to Soviet circumstances the smaller this group is likely to be.

If it is necessary to join a privileged group to become better informed, many dissatisfied citizens may in effect decide to join a system which they cannot beat. That road would lead towards choice of some specialisation and possible eventual membership of the Communist Party, with the opportunities which that may offer for becoming better informed in certain respects.

Thirdly, we might *play* at penetrating secrets. In British society reading detective novels, or doing crossword puzzles or some other sorts of puzzle, caters for this motivation. For instance, a crossword puzzle can be regarded as a formalised sort of word-secrecy. It seems reasonable that in countries where the opportunities open to individuals of penetrating official secrets are small, a larger provision should be made for working off this desire by playing at secret-solving, that is to say by solving made-up puzzles. These might be puzzles of a linguistic or mathematical nature, or some other kind; they might alternatively or equally consist of games, i.e. intellectual games, such as chess. The more individuals can be diverted into solving chess puzzles, the less energy and time will be left to them for penetrating official secrets. May this not be included among the reasons why chess receives so much official encouragement in the Soviet Union, and is so much more popular there than in the United States?

One may notice also the contrast between the popularity of chess in Russia and of poker in the United States. Chess is 'a game of complete information, with the opponents' forces fully visible unlike poker' (Hartston and Wason, 1983, p. 126); thus a game which lacks secrecy is popular in the secretive Soviet Union, while one which depends on secrecy is popular in the much less secretive United States. This surely is not coincidental; what is apparently desired in each country is a contrast. Note too that Soviet crossword puzzles are invariably 'straight', not including the more oblique and intuitive clues of the English brand.

To some extent curiosity is diverted into scientific channels, and especially into areas of science where blocks to information do not operate, such as the physical and mathematical sciences. To a significant extent these opportunities compensate for other prohibitions. Our imagined Soviet freelance investigator will try to avoid being fobbed off by seductive diversions, including those which exhibit a scientific façade.

In any event, it seems that the better informed group does not transfer much of its knowledge to the worse informed one. How is this? Let us consider this question first in regard to non-secret information. For instance, how does one communicate to fellow citizens about day to day matters? The facilities are not very abundant. Advertising, for example, is on an extremely small scale. Regarding retailed goods, this is partly resolved by asking people in the street where such and such was bought, but a residual inefficiency and loss of satisfaction, as a result of failing to discover what is available or where, must surely remain. In Tirana (Albania) or Cetinje (Yugoslavia) notices of private decease are affixed to trees or poles; in Russia it is often too inclement to linger outside, yet some unofficial notices *are* now seen. Do-it-yourself gatherings include, for apartment exchange, a Sunday market in Moscow (own observation). Many cities have special meeting points for trade in car spares (Demidov *et al.*, 1984, p. 1). To a large extent word of mouth is the answer, and when this is not practicable, the message does not arrive; often (probably) it is never despatched. Notices of the semi-cryptic 'French lessons' type, which flourish in small newsagents in seedier districts of urban Britain, are missing, and as a result various activities, such as prostitution, which find it harder to exist in the absence of advertising, are hampered, although, one can be sure, not entirely prevented. Thus to some extent secrecy is self-fulfilling: pretending that some phenomenon does not exist, may up to a point produce the result that it really does not.

ANONYMOUS LETTER-WRITING

The anonymous letter, which is a common phenomenon in the Soviet Union, can be viewed on one hand as a manifestation of secrecy, in this case on the part of a section of the public, and on the other as an indication of fear or apprehension that the writer, if signing his or her name, would be tracked down and punished; though there should perhaps be added as well a purely criminal or mischief-making element. During the period of the Great Purge, the anonymous denouncer contributed to hotting up its momentum. In the present less murderous circumstances the anonymous writer creates a more mitigated nuisance, besides which the practice still offers a kind of safety-valve to relieve tensions, or to work off a grievance, and even affords an oppor-

Furthermore, there are no institutional channels for effecting the transfer. The Communist Party is, of course, an instrument for preserving distinctions, not for overcoming them. The most prestigious research bodies tend to be sited so as to exclude the public. Elite and foreigners are catered for by special reading rooms. Indeed, all the mechanisms referred to in connection with preserving secrets serve equally well for inhibiting transfer of information as between the better informed and the worse informed groups. To a slight degree, public lectures enable some extra information to be shared with the general public, or more exactly with that fraction of it which is able to and takes the trouble to attend. Finally, foreign broadcasts, information picked up abroad on duty journeys or on holiday, and to a slight extent conversations with visiting foreigners, enable certain breaches to be made in the barriers. However, it must be noted that what is acquired by these means will only with difficulty become diffused more widely. The risk is present that whatever has been discovered will fail to be passed on and, in consequence, will be transformed again into a kind of secret.

Seventhly, there is the question of incentive. The psychology of secret-keeping is not all on one side. Samuel Johnson was doubtless right that 'The vanity of being known to be trusted with a secret is generally one of the chief motives to disclose it' (Frank and Weisband, 1974, p. 68), yet this motive is clearly insufficient to guarantee that all secrets are in fact disclosed. Many people do not fall into the scope of this aphorism: to them, the knowledge of being entrusted with a secret generates a sort of internal glow which seals their lips all the tighter.

The Soviet public in effect, though not necessarily in intention, co-operates with the authorities in that foreigners are rarely invited into their homes, so that these latter are kept away from first-hand knowledge of living conditions and of various other aspects of Soviet life. That these living conditions are usually cramped must be one reason; there are also national differences; for example a foreigner is more likely to receive a home invitation in the United States than in Britain, and more likely in Britain than in France or Belgium.

Finally, many people in the USSR actively co-operate in the processes of maintaining restrictions upon popular knowledge. This includes not only the censors, secret police and frontier guards but many ordinary citizens. No doubt these individuals believe that they are acting in their nation's best interests.

Several times I have been asked by ordinary folk what I was photographing, and whether I had the right to take that picture, even if it was only a building site for a block of flats on a Saturday afternoon. The popular belief in the old-fashioned type of spy is evidently ingrained. The Soviet Union, with its extremely security-conscious population, is also well guarded against infringements of security resulting from careless talk. The security consciousness of citizens is exploited by the authorities when incidents are fabricated which result in foreign military attachés being arrested or roughed up (*D.T.*, 2 July 1979, p. 17). In Leningrad, as witnessed in June 1971, metal receptacles, marked 'For Found Documents' had been fixed to walls at various places in the city centre; evidently they were for the use of the public. If the experiment was successful, it has probably been extended to other Soviet cities, and particularly to those visited by many foreign tourists. The harmless box in a Leningrad street and the lethal wall encircling West Berlin form part of the same system.

10 Cross-Frontier Relationships

EMIGRATION

The previous chapter distinguished between better informed and less well informed groups in the Soviet population. The better informed group clearly includes a part of the intelligentsia, but is not conterminous with the intelligentsia, a substantial fraction of which has no interests outside its specialisation and little knowledge of the outside world. The better informed group also includes some citizens without particular intellectual pretensions, but whose professional experience has made them aware of facts or opinions which are concealed from the mass of the population. These include sailors, airline personnel, minor diplomatic staff and others. The better informed, therefore, do not comprise any coherent body of people, and they are mostly unrecognisable to one another and lacking any common forum. The government and Party doubtless intend that things shall stay that way. Nevertheless, the better informed group comprises a constituency which sets it apart from the mass of the Soviet people. Part of this constituency has already emigrated in spirit, and all Soviet emigrants (as distinguished here, citizens who have applied to emigrate and been granted permission, according to the prescribed procedure) and defectors (citizens who have escaped or failed to return, without having gone through those procedures) come from this constituency.

It is not the case that all who wish to emigrate are free to do so; if that were so, the barriers described in preceding chapters would be pointless. Whoever has had access to secret information (or more exactly is considered to have had access to secret information) is forbidden to emigrate. Those who wish to and are allowed to leave must therefore walk the tightrope of having acquired knowledge about the outside world, which is secret in the sense that it will not have been acquired through the official media, but not of having acquired knowledge of any confidential nature about the Soviet Union itself. This requires an unusual mixture of experience and lack of experience.

167

In practice one has to belong to a sub-group, of experience, intellect, skill or nationality. It helps greatly if compatriots abroad wield influence in national or international affairs. One must be prepared to have one's request turned down and meanwhile to be forced to leave one's job and to vegetate uncertainly in a sort of limbo which may continue for a number of years (see *The Times*, 6 May 1986, p. 5). If permitted to leave, one may never see close friends or relatives again. The psychological barriers to emigration are considerable. The notion of leaving one's country is more strange to Russians than it is to citizens of many other countries, because emigration from Russia has never been on a large scale relative to the size of the country. To an unusual degree, the action of leaving is seen as unpatriotic. Moreover, the self-centredness and bias of disclosure policy brings the result that most people are not well informed about conditions on the other side.

One other consideration is influential: there should not be sufficient possibility of 'internal emigration' to form an effective discouragement to emigration across the Soviet borders. A kind of internal 'brain drain' has in fact occurred among Soviet scientists, who have tended to quit teaching institutions for the more prestigious research bodies where, as already noted, somewhat wider freedom of expression is permitted. The combination of these circumstances tends to produce the result that artistic performers form a larger proportion of emigrants, relative to scientists, than is the case from Western countries. (Regarding the 'internal brain drain' see Hutchings, 1976, pp. 36–7.)

The fairly substantial emigration from the USSR, since 1960 and particularly since 1968, mainly of Jews and Germans (about 250 000 and 60 000 respectively: Hutchings, 1982A, p. 96), must have led to some release of information about the Soviet Union which would not otherwise have occurred. How can this be explained in terms of the hypothesis that the Soviet authorities wish to minimise the uncontrolled release of information?

So far as popular emigration is concerned, this does not comprise people who can provide expert knowledge of the Soviet system; they can report only about their personal lives within a very limited sector. The official reckoning may have been that this group would yield only low-grade sociological or economic data, and even that could probably be obtained only through a very expensive and time-consuming investigation; furthermore, given the special proclivities and ethnic composition of the émigrés, the findings might well be untypical of the mass of the Soviet population. If this was the reasoning, it has not yet been proved incorrect, although specialists may find substantial interest in a survey lately conducted by James R. Millar and others.

The emigration of members of the intelligentsia is a different matter, as these, or many of them, can provide expert knowledge about the system. This is borne out not only from the testimony of such celebrities as Solzhenitsyn but by the analysis of academic luminaries such as Shlapentokh in regard to Soviet public opinion, Birman on the Soviet budget, or Voslensky on the Soviet *nomenklatura* (see below, p. 193). And there are their children who, by the way, may include some interpreters of the future. People who began to be brought up within the USSR are qualified to make the most incisive questioning of it, such as by Solzhenitsyn junior when a Soviet delegation visited his school in Vermont (*D.T.*, 5 May 1984).

Part of the explanation for this apparent boldness may be that emigrants do not necessarily reveal all at once. Even after emigration, some individuals still observe the limitations on freedom of speech and writing which are demanded by an official secrets act. At least for a while, perhaps even for the whole life, of somebody who was once committed, these are likely to exert some restraining influence. Thus, for example, Professor Tokaty-Tokaev after emigration from the USSR 'did not pass on what were regarded, by the Soviets, as secrets. General discussions, yes, but not details' (Daniloff, 1972, p. 228). The explanation may include a tendency to underestimate what can be found out by individual scholars, as opposed to collectives. In Soviet science, the whole emphasis is on team work: the ability of individual scientists to make significant discoveries is discounted.

Moreover, some émigrés wish to leave themselves a loophole for possible return to the Soviet Union, and a few even do. They are therefore reluctant to divulge what they remember, or will do so only when they are confident that the source will not be disclosed.

Also, it does not seem obligatory that we should demand that all policy decisions in the Soviet Union are taken with full consideration of the remotely possible results as well as immediate problems and incentives. We know that other governments do not always take decisions in a completely rational way, or pay due regard to their enlightened self-interest. If such rationality is nevertheless demanded in the Soviet case, the leaking of secrets through the emigration was presumably more than compensated by other advantages, such as getting rid of a disaffected minority, avoiding retribution by an annoyed US Congress, or gathering into the exchequer the sums demanded in compensation for higher education or some other form of emigration tax. Furthermore, it appears that since 1960, and especially since 1968, heavier emphasis has been placed on safeguarding military secrets, as compared with sociological or economic ones.

Another reason, and probably not unimportant, could be not to overload the censorship. In the same way as a government may not wish the number of foreign attachés to exceed what can be conveniently kept under surveillance, a censoring body will not want the number of potentially dissident writers to exceed what can be conveniently censored. Writers who are known to be likely to produce discordant work are best expelled from the scene.

The *sudden* exiling of individuals, for instance of Zhores Medvedev who in January 1973 was allowed to come to Britain to work for a year but was then refused permission by the Soviet authorities to return, must be intended as a punishment and also to have the aim of disrupting that individual's research and personal life. In this case it severed the close partnership between Zhores and his brother Roy, who had to remain in the Soviet Union.

The decisive reason for assenting to emigration may occasionally have been that the émigrés, once they had left, could no longer in person influence others to do likewise. Still another motive would be to leave leaderless the dissidents left behind. As the Soviet leaders may have seen it, the canker would go, leaving the body almost unscathed. The body must, of course, remain: over twenty years, only one in a thousand of the population has been allowed to depart.

Naturally, after emigration the consequences do not end there. One of the consequences of emigration must be an increase in cross-frontier correspondence, as long as any family members or friends remain behind. The total number of letters between the USSR and the United States in 1983 exceeded 12 million in both directions, and also more than 200 000 telephone calls were made that year. Although family matters and economic issues predominate, a substantial volume of other information must be included. This increased flow of information may well be influencing the authorities to permit wider coverage of foreign news and personalities (Shanor, 1986).

Immigration into the USSR has been negligible in modern times, and this too helps to preserve secrecy, through its effect in curtailing correspondence.

To sum up this section, in conjunction with the final section of the previous chapter: in recent years the Soviet public has started to react against information control. Popular sophistication has grown, while popular identification with the regime has been diluted by too much control, maintained over too long. Apparently, this relationship has overborne the cumulative effects of information control. To some extent, this result is a surprise. It can be imagined that in the earlier stages of information control some recollection of freer times will persist, with people being able to form some idea of what they were no longer being told. In the later stages, it used to be thought, that possibility would diminish, unless it could be kept alive by some other stimulus: the usefulness in this connection of foreign broadcasts, or some other information of extraneous origin, appeared evident. It seems that the capability of information controllers had been overrated, and that of folk memory and popular commonsense underrated.

And yet, on the whole it would not be correct to end this section on an optimistic note. The system of information control, of which secrecy is an important part, holds the mass of the Soviet people in thrall to a particular world-picture, which is the one that the authorities wish to project. Only a minority of the population wish to, or can, discover what has been left out.

Various procedures and methods of transferring information across frontiers which do not involve or result from emigration will now be considered.

INTERPRETERSHIP

As a general rule every dialogue between representatives of nations which speak different languages requires interpreters, and their availability can by no means be taken for granted. For example, before and during the Second World War, there were barely half a dozen Britons qualified to interpret from and into Russian at the highest level. On the British side, all top-level contacts were entrusted to this tiny band. Competent Soviet interpreters also were very few. Since the war one of these, known as 'Viktor' (Sukhodrev), normally interpreted for top-level meetings with English-speaking leaders successively for Khrushchev, Brezhnev, Andropov, Chernenko, and most recently Gorbachev. ('Viktor' is depicted in *Time*, 22 April 1985, p. 7.)

The responsibility upon this handful of individuals is formidable, since during a conversation they are the only ones who really know what is going on. Whatever is said by one side is effectively secret until it has been interpreted. The process results in an approximate doubling of the duration of conversations and in a limitation of the possible number of meetings to match available possibilities of providing interpreters. The risk of misinterpretation exists, but is minimised by the persistent re-employment of the same tiny group of experts. Although a substantial reserve of lower grade interpreters exists, in practice these are rarely called on, partly because they cannot be spared from other work and partly in order to contain knowledge of the content of conversations within a very narrow circle. However – looking from the other direction – intimate knowledge must spread throughout that circle.

Soviet practice in the provision of interpreters does not exhibit any obvious peculiarities, with the exception that probably a larger number of individuals has been trained in specialised terminologies, for instance railway terminology: this would be expected on general grounds and also agrees with my own experience.

It is noteworthy that though knowledge of Russian outside the Soviet bloc is rather uncommon (though much more common than it used to be), it is much more widespread than knowledge of any of the very numerous non-Russian languages of the Soviet Union. This has the result that the non-Russian speaking areas of the USSR tend to be less well known and understood in the West than the Russian-speaking areas. To the extent that the Soviet authorities may particularly wish to keep secret events or attitudes in the non-Russian-speaking areas, this circumstance would be of assistance to them. In the next stage of Sovietological studies in the West more attention is likely to be paid to learning the Soviet Union's non-Russian languages.

SHARING OF INFORMATION

However faultless the interpretation from one language to another, it is often the fate of untrue information to be believed, and of true information to be disbelieved, especially when the information is supplied by another country which is not an ally. For example, Stalin's purge of Marshal Tukhachevsky and others, as alleged agents of the German General Staff, resulted from a faked and allegedly secret German document, which fell into the hands of President Benes of Czechoslovakia who forwarded it to Stalin (Rigby *et al.*, 1980, p. 99; Schapiro, 1960, p. 425). In 1941, Churchill warned Stalin about the coming German attack. Soviet military and diplomatic sources also sent warnings, but 'because the leadership was conditioned against such information such data was despatched with fear and assessed with reservation' (Rigby, 1968, p. 53). Therefore, in the upshot, the invasion came as a surprise.

When it is a question of sharing information with an ally, this is much more likely to be believed, but perhaps in part for that very reason the amount of information that is provided tends to be limited. The attempt is often made to lay down guidelines for the kinds of information which are to be shared.

Can scientific knowledge be shared but not technological knowledge? President Truman made it clear in October 1945 that he might share with Russia scientific knowledge about atomic energy but not engineering secrets (Gowing, 1974, p. 67), but it is unclear that any definite demarcation between science and technology can be maintained; also it is necessary to take into account design (the arrangement of the intended completed product, with attention to its convenience, utility, etc.). The British view – regarding whether Britain should co-operate completely with the USA in making the first British atomic bomb – was that 'to be in one set of secrets but not in another would be dangerous'. This appears to mean that 'a little knowledge is a dangerous thing'. (The result of the British lack of publicity was that the Americans did not realise how much the British knew: Gowing, 1974, p. 279.) Only very uncommonly has centrifuge technology been made available by one government to another. (It was once suggested that the Australians might be a recipient of such data from the US Reagan administration – *International Herald Tribune*, 21–22 November 1981, p. 2.) Somewhat similarly, up to the early 1950s the Soviet Union had not been inclined to share her nuclear secrets with the other CMEA countries, but after 1955 she aided other socialist countries 'in various ways best suited to her own interests' (Wilczynski, 1974, p. 65), but apparently without including secrets relating to production of nuclear weapons.

I am not concerned at present with whether the Eastern European countries apart from the USSR share one another's secrets, though on the whole it is probable they do not, except to the extent that this occurs via multinational agencies such as CMEA or transnational ones such as Atominstrument. The more important question is, do they share secrets with the USSR or is it rather the case that this is a situation of dominance, the Soviet Union knowing their secrets but they not knowing Soviet ones?

The answer probably depends to a considerable extent on which secrets we are talking about. A good deal of information about mutual involvement in economic affairs must be disseminated via agencies such as those mentioned above. Some information about economic aspects of defence may be included, but there is reason to believe that one at least of the East European countries would wish to know more about the size of the Soviet defence burden (private source). At a fairly low level of confidentiality there may be a substantial exchange of information between the Soviet Communist Party and other communist parties, though the fact that Khrushchev's secret speech in 1956 was kept secret from most foreign delegates, such as Vittorio Vidali, leader of the delegation from the Communist Party of Trieste (McNeal, 1985, p. 332, reviewing Vidali, 1984) shows that its extent has been limited. Exchanges of this kind are either lacking or almost lacking in relationships between the United States and countries of Western Europe.

Assuming that the East European states learn more about Soviet political and military matters *via official channels* than is learned by the governments of Western countries, against this the latter can, whereas the former cannot, probe Soviet affairs by other means; at any rate, the former cannot do so to anything like the same extent. Sorts and degrees of knowledge of the Soviet Union must differ correspondingly, but it is uncertain whether, on the whole, East European or Western countries are the better informed.

Nevertheless, secret sharing between the Soviet Union and its allies is almost certainly less than that between the United States and its allies. The reasons for so thinking are: the much more intense secretiveness of the Soviet Union generally (see Chapter 13); the fact that the USSR is much larger relative to its allies; its possession of a number of weapons which are quite unavailable to them, whereas (in particular) nuclear weapons are possessed also by Britain and France; and the latent antagonism in most countries of Eastern Europe (especially Poland) to the Soviet Union, which, because its basis is the compulsory inclusion of these countries within the Soviet political and military systems, is more profound, although less visible, than the antagonism in various circles of Western Europe to the United States.

The most dramatic sort of secret sharing is exemplified by Japan's sharing with the United States the secrets of the MiG-25 'Foxbat' fighter, which its pilot had flown to Japan (*D.T.*, 13 September 1976, p. 15). Usually the procedure is less dramatic, though perhaps the results may be not less important.

The legal bases for sharing of information between governments are highly secret, and little has been written about them. Agreements between the USA and Britain must date from the Second World War period or slightly later, and include a secret pact, known as UKUSA, which was signed in 1947 (*The Times*, 27 November 1985, p. 8). Within the Communist world, such agreements must date from the moments when Communist governments were installed in these countries, or later if the necessary technologies did not exist at that time.

EXCHANGES OF UNCLASSIFIED DATA

A large volume of exchanges of unclassified data as between 'socialist' and 'capitalist' countries takes place, but these exchanges are less symmetrical than they appear, and allusions to them are sometimes disingenuous. The 'socialist' countries argue (correctly) that they import many more books, films, etc. from the 'capitalist' countries than is imported by these latter from the 'socialist' countries (e.g. Prague in English for Africa and Asia 1730, gmt 24 May 1974, SWB 4610). The comparison is invalid because the items imported by the 'socialist' countries are carefully selected from the angle of ideological acceptability (a wide range of attitudes being on offer), whereas those imported by the 'capitalist' countries are not – as all material from the USSR expresses essentially only a single attitude. Moreover, Western films do not give a correct impression of the Western way of life; indeed it might be said that they systematically misrepresent it! Because they exaggerate our crime and violence, it is not surprising that the Soviet authorities have no great objection to them.

However, the flow of scientific and technical knowledge is mainly one-way, from the 'capitalist' countries to the USSR. This emerges clearly when a comparison is made of the flows from the US to the USSR and vice-versa. New Russian books are not abstracted or even listed in American publications, and most are not available even in the Library of Congress. Although the average quality of engineering titles published in the USSR is lower than in the USA, many good or exceptionally good engineering books are published. The Russian books usually address more specific problems, as they do not have to exclude specific information of a proprietary nature (Rivin, 1983, pp. 70–1).

SPONSORED TOURS AND FACT-FINDING EXPEDITIONS

The sponsored tour can be seen as a means to convey specific information, or impressions, while not doing away with general secretiveness. This sort of tour is well developed in the USSR and all tourist visits are to some extent within this category. To people who stay a longer time, such as diplomats, sponsored tours do not loom so large, yet these individuals will almost certainly join such a tour several times during their stay. Foreign news correspondents are also treated to tours; for example, a one-month tour of the Soviet Far East was carried out by a group of foreign news correspondents who had been invited to the USSR by the press section of the Soviet Foreign Ministry (MTI in English, 10.21 GMT 11 September 1975, SWB EE/5006/A2/1). No doubt the route of such a tour will be carefully chosen, the main object being to ensure that the participants take away the desired impressions.

It is characteristic of Soviet disclosure policy that short-period visitors to the USSR are allowed to see, or to be told, a little more than is permitted to be seen by, or told to, foreign residents or embassy personnel who are stationed in the USSR for a relatively long period. This selectivity seems to be for several reasons.

First, it may be reckoned that visitors having until now seen less, should be compensated by being shown all the more within the short time at their disposal. Thanks to this, I was enabled in 1971 to visit the panorama of the Battle of Borodino without any long wait. Even diplomats benefit from advantageous treatment in some circumstances, for example when visiting Lenin's Mausoleum in Red Square, which otherwise would require a long period of queueing. To seek the reasons, one may re-use the photographic analogy: exhibits which are exposed for a shorter period must be conceded brighter illumination. This merges with the hospitality aspect. Sponsored foreign visitors are treated to traditional lavish Russian hospitality, and this (within limits) will include showing them what they want to see, whereas envoys are less commonly objects of hospitality, except at official functions. There is also the reciprocity aspect. The visitors, it is hoped, will in return issue invitations to their Soviet opposite numbers, who will be shown things which *they* wish to see, on a subsequent visit to the other country. It might be reckoned also that if embassy staff are shown little by comparison with what visitors are shown, especially considering how long a time they have spent within the USSR, the home country will be less inclined to keep in the USSR a large embassy staff. The object would be to demonstrate that expertise in relation to the USSR is useless, or even counter-productive. Moreover, visitors are often of a higher status than resident representatives (other than the ambassador). Finally, the visitors will be less expert and consequently less able to judge whether what they are shown is typical. It should be easier to imprint on them a particular impression, since they have less experience.

Indeed, sending a fact-finding delegation to the Soviet Union is (and especially, used to be) more common than sending one to most other countries. Apparently this is the preferred way of investigating a Communist country at a fairly early stage in its development. The reasons include linguistic difficulties, and unavailability or presumed unreliability of documentary information. The fact that visits are often commissioned by one's employers, or take place in response to an invitation from a Soviet body, is another principal reason. In general, the Communist states draw a sharp line between tourist visits and scientific or fact-finding visits, because of their desire to pigeonhole people, to simplify surveillance, or because of the insistence in these countries on specialisation in one's profession. The results of fact-finding visits are sometimes published (Sir Walter Citrine's *I Search for Truth in Russia*, London, 1936, being an excellent example of the genre), though many reports of this kind remain in-house, as intra-departmental or company reports. This method usually brings to light much in the way of unpublished detail, useful insights, and closer familiarity with individuals and institutions; there are also risks of being led astray by an unbalanced or at least not perfectly representative choice of institutions or places to visit, and of ascribing too much importance to those institutions or places. To obtain a balanced view, on-the-spot investigations therefore need to be complemented by more general studies.

RELIGIOUS CONTACTS

It was noted earlier that a religious hierarchy could (within limits) ferret out secrets and spread information (see above, p. 47). This may even happen on an international plane. For example, contacts between Swedish and German Lutherans contributed to the fact that the Swedes came to an early realisation of the evils of Nazism (Barman, 1968, p. 25). Contacts between religious groups in the USSR and their counterparts outside may still result in some dissemination of data across frontiers, about matters such as human rights.

DIPLOMATIC RELATIONS

The most important regular contacts are doubtless maintained through diplomatic relations, which thereby comprise the biggest single channel for transmission of information across frontiers. Soviet diplomatic missions typically comprise an exceptionally large number of people. Some of these may duplicate each other's functions, or may have the task of keeping watch on one another from a security angle, or undertake tasks (for instance, photocopying) which are too security-sensitive to be entrusted to outsiders; however, a substantial capability for gathering and transmitting information about the host country remains. Functions are sometimes undertaken which do not correspond to those ostensibly fulfilled by an attaché with that designation. As regards diplomatic protocol (forms of address, titles, security of diplomatic bags etc.) the Soviet Union adheres to international norms.

INTERRELATIONS OF CLASSIFIED AND UNCLASSIFIED DATA

Prior to 1973, the Soviet Union freely translated foreign books, without thinking itself obliged to remunerate their authors (Hutchings, 1976, p. 16), though sometimes making an *ex gratia* payment. This permitted tighter censorship of Soviet achievements, or difficulties, in scientific fields of a non-ideological kind where foreign literature could suffice to inform the public about general principles. Non-Soviet sources, rather than Soviet ones, could be used for presentations to a public about classified themes (Klochko, 1964, p. 187). This possibility still exists, but now (since Soviet adherence to the Universal Convention on Copyright on 27 May 1973) under normal copyright rules. That adherence evoked initial misgivings in the West that the main object was to stifle dissident writings there. Two years later, those misgivings were appearing to be unjustified (*The Financial Times*, 27 June 1975, p. 6).

If country *B* acquires secret information from country *A* and then wishes it to be examined academically, a problem may arise because scholarship is supposed to be based on open sources (otherwise, sources cannot be given, whereas the citation of sources is the hallmark of an academic publication). This had the result that Merle Fainsod refused to study archives of Smolensk under Communist rule, which had been captured by the Germans and later fell into the hands of the US Army, until they had been declassified. (*Boston Evening Globe*, 23 January 1973, p. 12).

The same objection would have less weight in Soviet academic circumstances, if only because it is less usual there to quote sources.

Documents captured during the German invasion of the USSR, which have found their way into the hands of Western Sovietologists, have made a significant contribution to Western knowledge of the Soviet system. This applies to two items in particular, the 1941 Economic plan and the 'Smolensk Archive'; this last has about 200 000 pages (Fainsod, 1959, p. 3). Khrushchev's memoirs also belong to the category of papers which their author has not himself exported; he evidently was not displeased when that happened.

As a rule – for reasons suggested earlier – classified information which crosses frontiers tends to remain classified, and unclassified information to remain unclassified. Occasional exceptions can be seen to this rule. In one case, although the Russians offered co-operation, declassified information and brought it to the United States, the Americans classified it! (Pournelle, 1982, pp. 143, 151). The subject was fusion research. In contrast, details of American plans to lay Captor mines, to stop Soviet submarines entering the Atlantic in wartime, were given in a book published in Moscow (*D.T.*, 18 October 1980, p. 11).

ESPIONAGE

What is the relationship between secrecy and espionage? Both are products of secretive behaviour, and while the object is indeed to spread knowledge, the acquiring agency will normally keep what it finds out no less secret than it was before. Espionage inside an intelligence or security agency tends to be self-perpetuating, due to the 'self-preservation syndrome' (Pincher, 1984, p. 202). Both are founded on a high estimate of knowledge that is available to a tiny circle. It would seem to follow that a secretive society is likely to be more successful than others both in opposing espionage and in conducting it. The first may be correct unconditionally, assuming other things to be equal such as the funds at the disposal of the respective agencies, whereas the second encounters a problem as will be explored further below.

On very numerous occasions Soviet diplomats, or other Soviet functionaries, have been detected as having been involved in espionage. Perhaps as many as 700 Soviet spies have been expelled worldwide since 1970, according to US State Department records (*Sunday Times*, 15 September 1985). Often this is what might be called the old-fashioned type of spying (dead-drops, microdots, the placing of agents in sensitive positions, etc.), but which is very far from being superseded, and which has even taken new life from technical advances and from the enormous enlargement in the number of personnel with some access to secret information, which makes absolutely reliable vetting unachievable. As regards range of activities, it might be added that the Soviet state also undertakes kinds of espionage which in the West may be undertaken by business firms. For example, Soviet snooping on British oil rigs in the North Sea is believed to have been for commercial and technological motives (Mason, 1975, p. 9). The Andropov administration is believed to have intensified spying on Britain for technological purposes. Some allowance must be made for the fact that all such activities are undertaken by the Soviet state, whereas in the West some fraction of them is done by business or other non-governmental bodies.

It is, of course, impossible to report about the espionage community in the Soviet Union or elsewhere from personal knowledge; however, a few propositions must surely be correct. First, given that Soviet citizens are not allowed to travel abroad to the same extent as citizens of Western democracies, the pool of possible spies is much smaller, both in relation to the size of the USSR and in absolute terms. Given that Soviet embassies are relatively large, and that in addition trade missions are maintained in many countries, it becomes extremely probable that a larger proportion of agents are drawn from the personnel of these bodies than is the case with Western countries. Furthermore, among Soviet citizens who are allowed to travel abroad, a much larger proportion is likely to have been entrusted with espionage duties. It is believed that Soviet citizens who do go abroad must report back to the KGB about individuals whom they have contacted, as well as other useful information, and no doubt the extent to which they have co-operated is taken into account when any future application from that person to travel abroad is considered. It seems probable, however, that the return per individual recruited under such arrangements would be small, as they may be resentful of the obligation and would not be professionals. The Soviet Union is the land of specialisation – in scientific work, for example. One would suppose that their spies should also be specialised, yet probably that among non-specialists, a larger proportion is recruited who have no natural aptitude.

There seems, in any case, no escape from the conclusion that restraints upon Soviet citizens, with the aim of limiting their contacts with foreigners and foreign countries, tend to handicap Soviet espionage. It is impossible to pursue simultaneously a policy aimed at keeping foreigners at arm's length and one of maximising espionage into foreign countries.

In one specific case – until October 1986, when all the Soviet employees were abruptly withdrawn in reprisal for US expulsions of Soviet diplomats – the Soviet Union apparently opted for maximising espionage. Whereas the Soviet embassy in Washington employed no US citizens inside its building, the US embassy in Moscow employed 211 Soviet citizens (*Time*, 8 April 1985, p. 28). This immense presence, so completely at variance both with the situation in Washington and with systematic Soviet measures to hinder or reduce contacts between ordinary Soviet citizens and foreigners, seemed to necessitate that all or most of those employed also reported to the KGB. The Soviet authorities presumably reckoned that supervision of their own people could be so strict there was negligible risk of any intelligence contraflow. The employees would also have earned for the state a useful sum in dollars – perhaps $1 million annually. Their withdrawal seemed to cast some doubt on the espionage motive; however, more advanced methods of surveillance may have been eroding the usefulness of employee espionage, as some US opinions had already supposed (*D.T.*, 1 October 1985, p. 5).

Outside the USSR, the limitations imposed by the contradiction mentioned above may be circumvented by other devices. The USSR probably relies on espionage by its own armed forces to a larger extent than the West does; its many AGIs (auxiliary gatherer of intelligence ships), 59 in 1984 (Stuart and Taylor, 1986, p. 7) are an illustration. Espionage tasks can be allotted to other East European countries, especially to the most loyal of them, although the fact that these countries enforce the same sorts of restrictions on contacts (if weaker in degree) must limit the opportunities in that direction. The USSR could also be expected to maximise forms of espionage which do not involve personal contact with foreign citizens, such as the study of documents, satellite imaging, and airwave interception. The USSR launched the first Sputnik, and the lengthy sojourns in Earth orbit of Soviet cosmonauts have doubtless intended some intelligence-gathering. Another element has been the recruitment of individual Westerners as Soviet spies.

On the other hand, the United States has demonstrated its capability, and probably even superiority, in certain types of high technology espionage. The U-2 reconnaissance flights were an example, while another was the tracking down of a Soviet submarine (which the Russians themselves had failed to do) which had sunk in the Pacific, and in recovering some parts of it (*The Economist*, 29 March 1975, pp. 81–2). The Central Intelligence Agency is believed to have recovered about one-third of the wreckage from 17 000 feet down (*The Financial Times*, 21 March 1975. About the CIA's attempt to salvage a Soviet nuclear submarine, see *The Observer*, 20 May 1979, pp. 33–4).

When military hardware is under Third World control, its security is unlikely to be safeguarded as completely as when that hardware is resting within Soviet hands. One example is the Straight Flush radar control unit of the SAM-6 missile, which took a heavy toll of Israeli planes in the October 1973 war: this was photographed for the Paris-based SIPA agency when it took part in President Sadat's anniversary parade in June 1974 of the June 1967 war (Pringle, 1974, p. 9). That so much Soviet equipment has been supplied to Israel's enemies and then lost by them has been of considerable help to US intelligence. Soviet-made mines of novel type, inexpertly laid in the Red Sea probably by the Libyans, are the latest example of this (*D.T.*, 3 June 1985, p. 13). But a transfer in reverse happened following the US retreat from Vietnam.

Whatever the West does find out always seems to surprise the Russians. Khrushchev's banging of his shoe at the United Nations in 1960, following the shooting down of the U-2 plane piloted by Gary Powers, is an illustration. The Russians, it seems, have a supreme belief in their ability to prevent their secrets from being penetrated. It is a triumph of hope over experience – hope that is combined with ruthlessness. So we find them shooting down a Korean airliner which strays into Soviet airspace (1 September 1983), and on the grounds that secrecy was being threatened attempting to justify the destruction of 269 people. Probably there was some secret near the southern tip of Sakhalin, and/or Kamchatka, preservation of which triggered the Soviet reaction. The incident is nevertheless a recognisable example of a recurring pattern of behaviour: violations of the Soviet frontier by Western owned or attributable instrumentalities evoke violent Soviet counter-measures. The fierceness of the response can be explained only as being in defence of secrets, and this is in fact the explanation provided by official spokesmen. Actually, surprise at the sudden discovery that secrets which it was believed were being kept but were not, is a case of overreaction to what is in reality a normal state of affairs, as was argued in Chapter 2.

Where neutral states are involved, more often it is the Soviet Union that is detected in the act of espionage. Especially noteworthy in this connection are the numerous violations of Swedish territorial waters by submarines – which in the circumstances can scarcely be other than Soviet – most notoriously when a Whisky class submarine armed apparently with nuclear weapons ran aground near the Karlskrona naval base in October 1981; because of which, two Soviet admirals were replaced (*D.T.*, 21 January 1982, p. 5). The use of bottom crawling vehicles, which left tracks on the seabed, has been detected. According to the Swedish Chief of Defence, from 1975 to 1982 there were 124 incidents in Swedish waters, and in 1983, not counting 'possible violations', 25; these occurred at points all round the Swedish coastline, from the Finnish border to Halsingborg (Ellingsen, 1985, p. 8). The gathering of intelligence (e.g. coast photography – Crane, 1984, p. 102) could well be a motive for these intrusions; a Swedish parliamentary commission concluded that preparing for possible operations was the main explanation (Rudberg, 1985, pp. 31–2; cf. Oldberg, 1985, pp. 51–60). The USSR perhaps contemplates seizing Sweden for reasons resembling those which induced Hitler to preface his attack on the Western front by invading Norway and Denmark. As Sweden separates two of the largest Soviet naval fleets, the Soviet motive might even be the stronger. Swedish neutrality would hardly offer any bigger deterrent than Norwegian and Danish neutrality did in 1940. The introduction into Sweden of Spetsnaz forces (see section below) could be an objective of these incursions. Any objection that it would not be worthwhile to use covert means to infiltrate agents, when they might much more easily just fly into Bromma airport, overlooks that the Russians would wish the identity and arrival of agents to be kept more secret than could possibly be achieved when they figured in an airline passenger list. (Concerning the subject of the northern countries in a European war see Wallin, 1982.)

Bottom crawling vehicles have left tracks also on the sandy floor of the Tsugaru Strait, dividing the Japanese islands of Hokkaido and Honshu; under the Soya Strait; and under the Tsushima Strait: these being the three main exits from the Sea of Japan, in which two out of the Soviet Union's three main naval bases in the Far East are located (*Sunday Times Magazine*, 20 October 1985, p. 43). The fact that such tracks have been observed at opposite ends of the Soviet land mass can be seen as further evidence of their having been made by Soviet agency.

Although inferior defences or determination would attract that result, it appears rather unlikely that Soviet violations of neutral states would be more numerous than of countries belonging to adversarial alliances, given that these latter pose a far greater military threat. This raises the question whether violations of the latter type are not in reality equally or more numerous, but better concealed? A probable example of the latter would be infiltration of the Western European 'peace' movement by trained agents, for example of the Greenham Common 'peace' women in Britain (see *Jane's Defence Weekly*, cited in *The Times*, 21 January 1986, p. 1).

Soviet special forces, named Spetsnaz, have been set up with the aim of taking the offensive to nuclear-armed countries before or on the outbreak of war. In September 1985, Britain became the first country to test its defences against such an attack. According to the defector Victor Suvarov (literary name) an élite body of Spetsnaz has been formed from among Soviet sportsmen (*The Times*, 18 September 1985, p. 12). Although this has not been confirmed, it is logical: these would be alert and athletic individuals, already with some experience and knowledge of life in the West and of specific countries, and accustomed both to acting on their own and to a form of collective discipline. They are also likely to be very patriotic. At home, they could use various military sports facilities, while their putative wartime role would assure them of a peacetime salary. However, it has been suggested that 'Victor Suvarov' has sometimes gone beyond what the evidence might warrant: his argument that the

Soviet Union may have been intending to attack Germany in the summer of 1941 is put forward in illustration (see Suvarov, 1985, pp. 50–5, and 1986, p. 79; and McMichael, Sasso and Bauman, 1986, pp. 78–9).

Specific daring missions have some part in a secret service, as incidents like the abduction of Eichmann from Argentina illustrate. Their merit is that they avoid an overt breach of the peace, with its possibly incalculable consequences.

Espionage is also a splendid subject for fiction such as a ten-part spy-thriller called 'TASS is authorised to state . . .' with which Soviet television diverted its viewers to offset public dissatisfaction with the TV blackout of the Los Angeles Olympics (*D.T.*, 4 August 1984, p. 11).

Where espionage is the target, retribution takes two forms which are strikingly disproportionate to each other. Espionage by citizens of the country which is itself the target is a most serious crime and is treated with great severity, in some countries, including the USSR but not in peacetime in Britain, by the death penalty. Non-diplomatic spies who are non-citizens are punished similarly or with somewhat greater leniency, though this latter was not markedly in evidence in the Soviet treatment of the British spy Greville Wynne, except that the death penalty was not exacted. In contrast, diplomatic personnel are merely subject to expulsion: an inconvenience to a diplomat, but except in rare cases nothing more. The basis for the disproportion is the Treaty of Vienna (1961) which applies equally to all its signatories. Given this disproportion in the possible penalties, it is obviously humane for espionage to be conducted as far as possible by diplomats. Thus, the frequently heard complaint that diplomats have been engaging in espionage is to that extent misapplied. It is another question whether it *is* possible to combine the two professions, which in several respects are poles apart: diplomats maintaining a high profile, but spies a low one; the former, but not the latter, relying chiefly on their dignity for their defence.

As noted in Chapter 5, international commercial relations are largely conducted from the Soviet side by trade delegations which reside in the countries to which they are assigned. This enables their staffs to form a useful back-up to the Embassy personnel in two respects: in general reporting duties, and if the host country resorts to expulsion on grounds of 'activities incompatible with diplomatic status'. In that event, if one-for-one reprisals are the rule, the Soviet side starts with the built-in advantage that the combined staff of the Embassy and the trade delegation is likely to be considerably larger than that of the host country's Embassy. This advantage was clearly shown in the Soviet response to a British expulsion of twenty-five Soviet personnel (followed by expulsion of another six) in September 1985: the Soviet side in this case could have the last word because further expulsions which also were equal on both sides could have reduced the British representation in Moscow to zero, while still leaving over 150 personnel in the Soviet embassy. Their membership of UN bodies enables Soviet representation in certain countries to be increased, and the presence in both the United States and Switzerland of such bodies may be connected with the dual networks of Soviet espionage in both those countries.

It would be interesting, if it were possible, to state the proportions contributed by classified and non-classified information in the total volume of information reaching the Soviet government. Quite apart from the difficulty of quantifying information, this is obviously not possible.

According to Sir Reginald Hibbert, the British government relies on secret information for less than 10 per cent of the total whereas in the case of the USSR the proportions are approximately the other way round (*The Times*, 21 September 1985). I am sure that he had his reasons for thinking so, although he does not give them. If censorship of printed material exists in the USSR but not in some other country, or not there to the same extent – which clearly is the case – then in relation to that other country one could expect the USSR to rely more on non-classified information. The Soviet authorities may well have a *propensity* to rely relatively more on secret sources; however, it must be remembered that the cost of obtaining secret information is vastly greater than that of acquiring open information and that it would require a proportionately larger number of agents, foreign contacts, etc. If secret information is excessively detailed, micro rather than macro, this too will limit the proportion of useful information that it can supply.

The limitations upon use of secret information owing to the requirement of keeping secret its source must also be remembered. The volume of secret information no doubt exceeds by a substantial margin the volume of *usable* secret information. However, this is probably a less serious obstacle in the USSR than in most Western countries.

On the whole, I would not agree that the Soviet government is likely to rely relatively more on secret information than the British government does (if the discussion relates to the two countries' knowledge of each other); however, it has to be taken into account that the topics regarded as secret are much wider in the Soviet Union than in Britain and knowledge which is acquired of them will tend to be classified accordingly, and therefore (for similar material) unequally.

SIGNALS INTELLIGENCE

The more continuously transmissions are monitored, the greater the probability of detecting changes, possibly of a meaning kind, in their volume or direction. This, in conjunction with the possibility of acquiring intelligence of an otherwise unobtainable sort, is the special province of SIGINT – the interception of radio messages. This must be distinguished from the monitoring of radio *broadcasts* which, of course, are intended for anyone who cares to listen.

Institutional arrangements connected with SIGINT have to be gleaned from unofficial accounts, the reliability of which cannot be guaranteed. Concerning the US National Security Agency, about which in total a good deal has been published, Kahn describes its major buildings at Fort George, Maryland, with an area after enlargement of almost 2 000 000 sq. feet, sufficient to provide working space for at least 12 500 employees (Kahn, 1969, pp. 676–7). Assuming lower labour productivity, the numbers employed in a comparable Soviet facility would be larger. One may speculate that the total numbers employed in SIGINT in the USA might exceed 100 000 (see, for example, Szulc, 1975, p. 70) and on a worldwide basis could be much bigger. Western radio eavesdropping is said to have achieved results such as overhearing radio-telephone chats between Soviet leaders in Moscow travelling in their cars. The period of listening included the period when the Soviet Union invaded Czechoslovakia in 1968 (*The Times*, 6 December, 1973, p. 7), and more than a decade has passed since then. What has been discovered by Soviet SIGINT is unknown, but the far-flung network of communications between NATO allies and between their headquarters and overseas bases and warships would appear to offer broad opportunities. Any NATO naval exercise is accompanied by Soviet warships festooned with listening aerials.

SATELLITE IMAGING

To the Soviet leadership, the fact that the entire territory of the USSR can now be surveyed from orbiting satellites must be one of the most important and ominous circumstances of the contemporary world. It is ironic that this result should have been hastened by their own space research.

Like any other form of espionage, satellite surveillance has its strong and weak points. It naturally focuses on what lies on the earth's surface, or what is on or near the surface of the sea. It can be obstructed by haze or dust, which is why there is no satisfactory Landsat coverage of the Western Sahel. Owing to the Earth's rotation, a satellite (unless in an equatorial or polar orbit) follows a path which is angled south-west to north-east; thus a country whose geographical axis is angled in that direction is covered more quickly (other things being equal) than one which is angled more nearly at right-angles. For example, New Zealand is covered more simply than Italy. The Soviet Union, being situated mainly in high latitudes, requires to be observed from a satellite that is more nearly in a polar orbit than in an equatorial one, which requires more launching power, though this does not now present any insurmountable technical problem (information from Nicholas Hutchings, July 1985). By satellite imaging, a large country can be covered as effectively as a small one, though naturally the larger territory will require longer scrutiny. Such observation can achieve a great deal, but other limitations may remain: for instance, it has been claimed that though satellite control may verify the number of missile silos, it may be insufficient for verifying their type (Duzan Dozet, SWB EE/ 4524/A1/1 – 14,00 gmt 9 February 1974). It is reported that first-generation radar satellites cannot distinguish the vessels under observation; for example, in crowded sea lanes they would not differentiate surface warships from merchant ships (Hodgden, 1985, p. 68).

The possibilities in Soviet conditions of safeguarding secrets either from SIGINT or from satellite imaging appear to be limited. Interception of signals can be prevented by laying landlines, but this is expensive and technically possible in certain cases only, and the resulting network lacks flexibility. The use of coded messages can be extended. Observation from orbiting satellites can be deceived by measures similar to those in use in the Second World War to defeat aerial photography. From a geographical angle, the Soviet Union is rather poorly placed for defeating either form of surveillance: long distances and permafrost (which extends over 47 per cent of the area of the USSR) make landlines more costly, and permafrost also hinders placing installations underground. Smoke-screens would need to envelop vast areas to be effective and would create environmental problems. The centralisation in Moscow of a large fraction of authority in all spheres necessarily entails a huge volume of communications between the capital and outlying centres.

For a country to be invulnerable along its frontiers and tightly censored as regards its press, yet open to satellite observations, appears to make it as vulnerable to investigation as a battleship, which was heavily armed against surface attack but entirely lacked anti-aircraft armament, would be to destruction from the air. Naturally the parallel is not exact as openness to observation from above is never complete. What is underground is not observed (though perhaps it may give itself away by tracks leading to or away from it, or in other similar respects). It is also unlikely that observation can be sufficiently detailed, but no doubt improvements are constantly being made in this direction. In one major aspect, observation is impotent: it cannot uncover intentions, beliefs or attitudes.

11 International Comparisons: I. Spheres of Activity

In the next section of the book secrecy and disclosure policy in countries other than the USSR are examined, making comparisons with Soviet practice, with the aim of placing the Soviet phenomenon in a broader framework. In the present chapter various spheres of activity in relation to secrecy are considered, while in the next chapter the focus is on individual countries.

SECRET SOCIETIES

Very successful examples of preservation of secrecy are offered by Masonic groups and secret societies. These apparently generate in their members a feeling which reinforces the capability of keeping a secret, while not offering such a tempting target to investigate as secrets of national importance.

A western democratic state normally evinces no interest in Masonic societies; apparently it does not mind their withholding information either from the state or from the public. Freemasons' lodges and societies for religious and charitable purposes were specifically excepted from Acts (in Britain) passed in 1799, 1817 and 1846, which made unlawful all societies, the names of whose members and officers are kept secret from the community at large. Certain past or present members of government have belonged to Freemasons' lodges (Knight, 1983, pp. 206–7). That no action follows presumably indicates that these secrets are not seen as nationally significant, but this insouciance is possibly unjustified (see Knight, 1983, pp. 269–303). Of course, the Italian P.2 secret society and especially the Sicilian Mafia have gained international notoriety.

Tsarist Russia's experience of secret societies was limited, being largely confined to post-1815. The activity of the societies which were then formed culminated in the Decembrist plot of

December 1825 (Vernadsky, 1930, pp. 140–1). This was followed by a severe crackdown on all liberal manifestations.

Can the Communist Party of the Soviet Union be regarded as a secret society? Obviously it is not to be placed in the same categories as P.2, the Mafia, or the Freemasons. The CPSU does not need to keep itself secret from the state, and the scale of its membership is also out of all comparison with secret societies of the types mentioned above. It claims to be functioning according to a definite ideology, which also serves to legitimise its status and activities. The Party newspaper is the most important national daily. The General Secretary is constantly in the news, and local Party representatives also maintain a high profile.

Nevertheless, certain similarities can be seen. The Bolsheviks' status in Tsarist Russia was an illegal one, and this is still the status of Communist parties in a number of countries. In writing for *Pravda*, Lenin – itself a pseudonym – made use of no fewer than fifty-one pseudonyms (*Pravda, 1912–14, 1917*, 1962, pp. 80–1), which it is difficult not to see as an example of secretiveness for its own sake. *Konspiratsiya* and *konspirativnost'* were the terms often used (see Tarschys, 1985, p. 525). Though Freemasons or the Mafia may not be imbued by ideologies, they have codes of behaviour. In the nineteenth century the Sicilian Mafia was strongly influential in politics, and in the USA it has meddled in politics; though chiefly at the local level, it may have been implicated in the assassination of President Kennedy. The origin of the Mafia is usually taken to have been the disturbed and corrupt political condition of southern Italy over centuries, a condition which in present-day circumstances would be very likely to give rise to a guerrilla movement and a militant Communist party. It is scarcely difficult to see Stalin as a 'Godfather' figure, and the purges of the 1930s had a similar result, on an infinitely vaster scale, as the St Valentine's Day massacre in Chicago in 1929. Ruthlessness and the intention to dominate at all costs are common to the Mafia and to the Soviet Communist Party. Trotsky's assassination in Mexico City in 1940, long range, remotely controlled and many years after the cause of offence, looks like a typical gangland rubbing-out. In their attitudes to secrecy there is much in common, notably in the intensity of the secrecy enveloping the apex of the power structure, although for understandable reasons secretiveness in the Soviet Communist Party is less all-embracing: in effect, a degree of secrecy has been traded for political power. Above all, membership of the Communist Party confers an opportunity of access to real political power. The Mafia and the Communist Party achieve wealth through power, not – as Marxists view, or claim to view, a Western 'bourgeois' democracy – power through wealth (cf. Voslensky, 1984, pp. 148–50). This conspiratorial style of government continued after the Revolution, reaching its apogee under Stalin. Lenin, Stalin and Molotov continued to use their adopted names, though both the need and the possibility of concealing their identities had passed; only Malenkov and, after him, Khrushchev broke with this anachronism. Among the leadership of other Communist countries, only Marshal Tito revived the practice, and his adopted name had a military rather than a political origin. Even Enver Hoxha, ruler of Albania, used his own name, despite its striking unsuitability in what he has made an atheist state (since in Albanian 'hoxha' means 'priest').

The political thread in the USSR must be pursued further. The Party's role in choosing people to fill all posts of any importance in the Soviet Union (the *nomenklatura*) is secret and quite at variance with what is laid down in the Constitution, yet now firmly established and even routine. For example, whereas according to the Constitution a minister is appointed by the Supreme Soviet of the USSR or by its Presidium, or an ambassador directly by the Presidium of the Supreme Soviet, in fact who fills these posts is decided by the Politburo of the Central Committee of the Communist Party of the Soviet Union (Voslensky, 1984, pp. 159–60). Besides, all political decisions are taken either by the Party or by persons whom the Party has appointed (Ibid., pp. 152–8). In its monopoly of political power, despite what is written in the Constitution, the Soviet Communist Party acts as a secret society might well act which had gained possession of the state.

Historical parallels of some sort may be numerous: the particular combination of monopoly of the reins of power by the Communist Party, but apparent supremacy of the legislative chamber, suggests a similarity with the form of government of the Augustan age of the Roman Empire: 'The masters of the Roman world surrounded their throne with darkness, concealed their irresistible strength, and humbly professed themselves the accountable ministers of the senate, whose supreme decrees they dictated and obeyed' (Gibbon, 1776, p. 68).

By what means do secret societies enforce secret keeping by their members? Certainly fear of retribution is one, while another is the sense of superiority which being privy to a secret confers. Both these inducements apply also to the Soviet Communist Party. It is particularly to be noted that the sense of being privy to a secret cannot be shared by all the citizens of a nation, and more especially not when that nation is extremely large; it is shareable by all the citizens – if that is possible at all – only if the state is very small. The city state of Venice may have come closest to that limiting condition: it was in fact noted for its secrecy, which included keeping secret the names of the members of the Council of Ten, and a method of assassination by a blade of glass which when plunged in up to the hilt would snap off, leaving almost no trace on the outside of the victim's body (AA, 1984, pp. 18–19). In a sense continuing the tradition, Venice is now better known for its masks and carnivals. At the present time, a predisposing factor for the existence of secret societies seems to be that the country within which they flourish should be rather large. The attractiveness of membership of the Communist Party within at any rate the larger Communist states is partly explicable on these grounds.

MAP-MAKING

Cartographical falsification is not confined to the Soviet Union. The first British Land Utilisation Survey 'was not allowed to show airfields, but had to disguise them as farmland'. Apparently the second survey of this kind *was* allowed to show them (Coleman, 1976, p. 412). Still, various areas which on certain maps look uninhabited are not in actuality. Also lacking from the Ordnance Survey has been the Royal Ordnance Factory at Burghfield, in Berkshire (*The Times*, 31 March 1983, p. 2). Maps of Switzerland, even those supplied to officers of Divisionnaire rank in the Swiss Army, do not mark military airstrips in mountain valleys (McPhee, 1984, p. 14). An interesting falsification is reported from Israel. Detailed plans of unnamed but really existing *kibbutzim* and *moshavim* as shown in the *Atlas of Israel* (Tel Aviv, 1970) are mirror images of reality (i.e. left-to-right reversed) as shown in Israeli maps of 1/100,000. The reversed maps of the same villages in the Lakhish region are reproduced in the PLO Atlas of Palestine (Beirut, 1970). If the reversal was (as must be presumed) deliberate, their reproduction in effect falls into the trap. This means that the larger scale maps are false but the smaller scale ones true. Presumably the object was to confuse raiders (private source). However, the Soviet cartographical distortions may have been uniquely widespread.

The making of maps in many countries has a military origin and initially was carried out by military agencies. Britain (the Ordnance Survey) is one illustration; another is Yugoslavia, whose Military Geographical Institute celebrated thirty years of work on 15 November 1974 (SWB 4753, Tanjug 1528 gmt 8 November 1974). The motivation is to supply specially accurate maps to the national armed forces. Obviously, one would not wish a potential invader to be equally well informed, so confidentiality will be preferred. Finland is an illustration: maps showing weight limits of bridges and ferries could endanger national defence, so it was proposed that they should be for official use only (SWB 4911 Helsinki home service 1030 gmt 20 May 1975).

The Soviet Union is especially concerned to preserve secrecy in relation to *where* things are carried on. In Britain, on the other hand, less attention is paid to preserving spatial secrecy, whereas more heed is shown for keeping precise timings secret. One illustration of this is that the date of construction of the British atomic bomb is known less exactly than that of the American or Russian one. More recently, the British government was unwilling to correct an initial misstatement of the date when the Argentine cruiser *General Belgrano* was first sighted: whether this was on 1 May or 2 May 1982. The British are, however, more secretive about locations than the Americans are. Regarding a proposal that the purposes of Aldermaston and Capenhurst within the British atomic weapons programme should be announced, the British intelligence authorities found it irrelevant that the Americans published the location of their production establishments: the American strategic situation was very different (Gowing, 1974, p. 131). The USA occupies an intermediate position, in that while much better situated than Britain for preserving spatial secrets, it in large measure fails to utilise this potentiality.

NUCLEAR WEAPONS

In both Britain and America the initial atomic programmers were determined by the executive branch of government. The US Congress did not know that the cost of creating the atomic bomb was appropriated from a special presidential emergency fund (Kahn, 1969, p. 545). Similarly, the British estimates for expenditure on atomic energy, as on other defence research and development expenditure, were concealed from Parliament by burying them in general subheadings of the Ministry of Supply vote (Gowing, 1974, p. 51). Nearly £100 million was spent without informing Parliament (Ibid., p. 406). Arguably, this expenditure on atomic energy relative to total current spending on goods and services by the central government and local authorities never exceeded 0.6 per cent; it amounted, however, to 23 per cent of total Ministry of Supply spending in 1950–1 (Ibid., p. 87). Stretching a point, it might be seen as relevant that in Britain orders for ammunition are never made public for security reasons (Wettern, 1976, p. 2). This is a striking example of the British government proceeding in secrecy, despite the very large sums of money involved (*The Times*, 22 March 1982, p. 10). The fact that Parliament was not informed is often cited in Soviet or East European propaganda, but it hardly amounts to any behavioural contrast as there is no reason to suppose that legislative chambers in their countries received any prior notification of their analogous programmes.

The importance of secrecy in helping to prevent nuclear proliferation is debatable, but may well be less than is often supposed. According to one view, such proliferation is hindered by cost and by secrecy, but more so by the former than by the latter, except perhaps in the case of uranium enrichment. For the other two 'sensitive technologies', spent fuel reprocessing and heavy water production, have been published, but it is difficult and expensive to reproduce them (*The Financial Times*, 30 June 1975, p. 27).

SECRECY AND THE DETERRENT

The functioning of the deterrent policy exhibits both the importance of secrecy and the importance of setting limits to secrecy.

Secrecy is required, or at least desirable, as regards the precise positions of deterrent elements (the locations at any one moment of Polaris submarines, etc.); where that secrecy is absolute the deterrent effect is greatly enhanced, so the deterrent can be called 'ultimate'. It is required also in relation to the precise mechanisms of command, control and communications (C^3). On the other hand, the general capability of deterrent forces, the fact of their existence, and the intention of using them in response to nuclear attack from the other side (and only in that event) must not be kept secret. If then one wishes to make the nuclear deterrent still more effective, should one make it more secret or less? The answer depends on which aspects one has in mind. Those aspects which need to be secret (location, C^3) should be made more secret, whereas other aspects (existence, capability, intention to use under certain conditions) should be made less secret.

Although there are tactical differences as regards the choice of deterrent methods, the deployment of weapons, etc., there appear to be no differences in principle, as regards secrecy and non-secrecy, in the Soviet and the Western approaches to deterrence.

Among the five powers which admit to possessing nuclear arms, only the USSR and China are relatively well placed for preserving security. The British and French may wish to keep a secret no less securely, but their smaller areas, greater population densities, and relatively uncensored press make that more difficult. US restraints upon systematic secrecy are very strong. Only the Russians and Chinese enjoy a more favourable geographic and institutional environment, though before the Nazi attack in 1941 even Russian activities were not immune from observation by special Heinkels, Dorniers or Junkers (Carell, 1964, pp 59–60). Since the Second World War both countries have been observed by reconnaissance planes, and both, as well as many other countries, are now under continuous observation from orbiting satellites. The Soviet Union practises the latter, but does not appear to have practised the former.

TECHNICAL ADVANCE

On an international plane, orbiting satellites are able to strike a tremendous blow against secrecy, but as the information which they obtain is then, as a rule, kept secret by the country which launched the satellites, the full impact of this development is by no means realised by the general public. It has been suggested that after a few years, with the development of satellite communications, censorship of military operations such as the Falklands War would become impossible (*The Times*, 11 November 1982 p. 1). Recent advances are more capable of revealing secrets in space than in time, which has tended to diminish the particular advantage in preserving secrecy which the Soviet Union has possessed.

Another enemy of secrecy is the typewriter, as is well recognised in Romania where citizens have to register typewriters with the police (*D.T.*, 14 April 1983, p. 8). Among new technical means which are inimical to secrecy is the photocopying machine, which, for example, Sarah Tisdall used to obtain an extra copy of a memorandum by the British Defence Secretary to the Prime Minister which she then supplied to *The Guardian* newspaper. Because of that occurrence, senior British civil servants are reported on occasion to be making photocopies themselves rather than entrusting this to others (*D.T.*, 29 March 1984, p. 2).

The use of copiers has expanded very rapidly in the West in recent years, and they have become an essential tool in all kinds of managerial, literary, educational or research activity. In the Soviet Union, however, copying machines are under close control 'to prevent the distribution of articles by dissidents' (*The Economist*, 17 April 1976, p. 51). Furthermore, the informational revolution of multiplying on-line material is not being approached enthusiastically. The reasons are partly cost – universal education in computer operation must be very costly – but partly also an awareness that this latest development poses serious risks of control being lost, on account of the volume and variety of data which become potentially available to any terminal operator. If data are considered secret, a computer may have to stand idle.

The adoption of word processors evokes similar concerns. In the training of their operators, there is thought to be a risk that the new equipment will be used for undesirable purposes. According to a British team who were allowed in to make a television film, all disks were controlled by the teachers, and Soviet experts refused to be interviewed for the programme (BBC Channel 4, 26 February 1986). On the other hand, the use of word processors should facilitate achieving a 100 per cent (rather than, say 98 per cent) exclusion of forbidden names or topics, so in this direction censorship would be assisted. Video too poses problems of information control: see G. Yordenov, in *Trud* – a Bulgarian newspaper – 20 March 1982. Though with far more limited objectives, analogously in Britain 'video nasties' have been hurriedly outlawed (*D.T.*, 17 March 1984, p. 7), though in May 1985 a high proportion of items on hire was still consisting of horror movies.

In the Soviet Union, the production on a large scale and widespread sale of tape recorders (production rose from 128 000 in 1960 to 2 525 000 in 1975) has been a factor permitting the development of samizdat. The fact that, among the East European states, only Poland implemented a faster increase (from 6700 in 1960 to 735 000 in 1975) doubtless helps to explain the burgeoning of freer expression in that country as well. In the GDR, where there was no development comparable with the emergence of Solidarity, production of tape recorders rose only from 83 800 in 1960 to 134 000 in 1975 (*Statistical Yearbook of Member States of the Council for Mutual Economic Assistance*, 1976, p. 92).

Communist pronouncements profess concern at the possibilities of utilisation of data banks and the classification of data by 'anti-communist centres' for 'propaganda, falsification of Marxism–Leninism, distortion of policies and incitement of nationalistic moods among some groups in the socialist countries' (from a commentary by Jaroslav Kucera, Prague in Czech for Europe 21.00 gmt 10 April 1974, SWB 4575). Extra concern that secrets might be uncovered is underlying this diatribe. Computerisation can also help in uncovering espionage. Fifteen East German spies working in Bonn ministries were unmasked, it is believed, with aid of computers (*D.T.*, 4 June 1976, p. 5). Science also offers means of *defending* secrecy: such devices are commercially available in the USA (bug-detecting, making telephone conversation indecipherable to eavesdroppers, etc.). I would not expect such equipment to be commercially available in the Soviet Union, nor is it as far as my information extends.

Computerisation does offer a possibility of keeping information about individuals which is more comprehensive and readily accessible than ever before, if one has access to it. The Soviet authorities are doubtless aware of this potentiality and taking measures to exploit it. In Western democracies, the phenomenon is seen by most informed public opinion to be undesirable. In Britain, the Younger Committee was charged with examining the need for protection against intrusion into privacy by 'private persons and organisations, or by companies', but not by public authorities (including local authorities and public corporations). According to witnesses who appeared before the committee, 'on balance the view was that privacy was in fact being slowly eroded' (Kaufman, 1972, p. 7; see HMSO, 1972, especially pp. 5–7).

Technical advance also reinforces the *desire* to keep discoveries secret, and this additional impulse is probably stronger in the Western political democracies than in countries like the Soviet Union. This is so for two reasons: in the former group of countries there is a larger possible margin of secrecy to take up, and secrecy is pursued to a greater extent for comparatively rational reasons, rather than for its own sake. The same principle naturally holds good among the Western democracies, according to the degree of secretiveness at any given moment: we would expect to find (and do find) that following a major technical advance, secrecy is reinforced more strongly in the United States than in Great Britain. This was illustrated particularly in the post-war history of legislation relating to nuclear weapons, by which the USA cut off information to her wartime ally, but the remarkably good security still maintained regarding the results of satellite photography is another good illustration. The issue is affected by short-range needs for publicity in order to obtain support for some given project in Congress, or to seek support from America's allies.

One sometimes hears it said, more or less jocularly, especially just after the revelation of some long period of espionage by some well-placed person, that probably there are no national secrets left. The speculation is absurd, for two reasons: new secrets are continually being manufactured, and even if methods for penetrating secrets are invariably effective – though certainly they are not – there is inevitably a time-lag. Moreover, knowledge is irretrievably fragmented. What is 'known' is separated by many divides, between nations and within them; even inside a mutually co-operating group, knowledge is spread amongst many individuals; and it is 'known' with varying degrees of uncertainty.

On a global scale, decolonisation, and the resulting creation since the Second World War of scores of new nations, has multiplied immensely both the number of secrets of the national variety and the efforts devoted to preserving and uncovering them. The divide between East and West has led to the same result. The combination of these two developments has made secret keeping and secret uncovering perhaps the most important single growth industry on a global basis since the war. Therefore, against the hypothesis that perhaps all secrets have now been discovered must be set the reality that the task of uncovering 'all' secrets has become vastly more difficult. On the other hand, it is likely that technical progress during the past quarter-century, satellite observation in particular, has reversed the trend of keeping more and more secrets, or at least has made the upward trend of secrecy far less steep.

At the same time, the gap between secrecy and secretiveness has widened. As knowledge is gained about new sorts of weapons and new technologies, secretiveness is intensified, hardly less by those who have not acquired the new instruments as by those who have, as the former (in the case of nuclear arms) try to compensate for non-possession by not allowing other countries to be certain that they do not possess them. Thus secretiveness spreads, hardly less to nations which have not acquired the weapons than to those which have. However, at present the extent and intensity of secrecy remain markedly different in different countries, as is examined in the next chapter.

12 International Comparisons: II. Country by Country

In this chapter the policies followed in secrecy and disclosure policy by a number of countries other than the USSR will be discussed; the sequence is approximately east to west.

COMMUNIST CHINA

China is an extremely secretive country, a tradition inherited from the days of the Forbidden City. China, which has been first in so many things, has also been outstanding in secret keeping: the death penalty, obligatory by torture for whoever divulged them to a foreign country, preserved for 3000 years Chinese secrets of silk production. Nowadays life in China is criss-crossed by barriers to knowledge, though some 'secrets' get to be common knowledge, as is the case elsewhere. Article 186 of the Criminal Code establishes the punishments for revealing secrets, while the 1951 'State Regulations on Guarding State Secrets' includes in addition to the military police and foreign affairs information about national minorities, culture and the weather. Article 16 of these regulations adds that 'any other State matter not made public is deemed to be secret' (Mirsky, 1982, p. 6). This defines one extreme point in a continuum of degrees of national secretiveness. Subsequently there has been a 'gradual opening of the Chinese press to foreign influence and modern ideas', though certain newspapers, in particular those which illuminate local affairs, are not permitted to be bought by foreigners, who ordinarily also may not visit rural areas.

Repetition is described as the 'worst fault of the Chinese media': this would be evidence either of censorship − which is the most likely − or of poverty of information or imagination (Bonavia, 1985, p. 29). For what it is worth − but this largely amounts to admitting mistakes committed by previous regimes − the Chinese are now reporting with considerable frankness about past mistakes (such as the Cultural Revolution) or current problems. The trend seems also to be towards fuller reporting of the outside world, although 'fine-tuning' is probably not excluded.

EASTERN EUROPE

From China, leaping over the Soviet Union which is covered in the rest of the book, we arrive in Eastern Europe.

There are several fundamental differences between the Soviet Union, on one hand, and the East European countries on the other. In the USSR, the Revolution is at least twenty-eight years older; it was a native growth, not imposed from outside (though, of course, Lenin and many of the other revolutionaries lived abroad during part of their careers), and it took place in a country which was much farther removed from the history and traditions of Western Europe.

The media in all these countries focus overwhelmingly on domestic news, the rest being far behind. Almost solely good news is reported from other Soviet bloc countries, almost solely bad news from capitalist countries. There is one major divide, between Albania and the rest, which can be exemplified by comparing Albania with Bulgaria. As reported in Bulgaria, everything the Americans do is bad, whereas everything the Russians do is good. As reported in Albania, whatever the Americans do is bad – and whatever the Russians do is also bad! Yugoslavia too permits press attacks on Soviet policies or individuals (for instance Milic, 1968, translated Stankovic, 1968), and differs from both Albania and the Soviet bloc countries in not presenting any uniform approach.

None of the East European countries has a tradition of open access to information. Austro-Hungary, for example, maintained censorship, in Transylvania for instance since the *Règlement Organique* of 1831–59 (Oţetea, 1985, p. 313), while South-Eastern Europe long languished under Turkish rule. Yet in these countries, especially the more advanced ones or independent over longer spans, such as Hungary, Soviet secretive practices would be challenged if the international situation allowed; even now there is greater liberality. Czechoslovakia, in 1968, made such a challenge. It is being gradually discovered that truth will out, and that when it does, this engenders the realisation that the press had been leaving its readers in selective ignorance (Ronay, 1983, p. 5). But concealment, with resulting distortion, which is wholly or mainly due to Soviet pressure is still found throughout Eastern Europe. To give only one illustration, there is no memorial in Budapest to Hungarians who died in the Second World War, although the city is dotted with memorials to Soviet troops. This must derive from pressure exerted by the USSR, either directly or indirectly, for it was against the Russians that the Hungarians were fighting. There is, of course, no public reminder of the destruction caused by Soviet forces in crushing the Hungarian uprising of October 1956; the places of burial of Imre Nagy and Pal Maleter, respectively the premier and defence minister of the Hungarian government which took over during the uprising and who were subsequently executed, are likewise concealed.

East European countries deny the existence of censorship, but if censorship exists allusions to its existence would themselves by censored. However, it seems that in Iungary at least self-censorship (cf. above, Chapter 8) is the nurm. In practice, Soviet bloc countries in Eastern Europe observe approximately the same regimes of secrecy and disclosure policy that the Soviet Union itself does. (Indeed, the Polish censorship model was being pressed into service above as a surrogate for the Soviet one.) But there are certain variations in policy or practice between the different countries. Generally, in Eastern Europe (with some qualifications as to Hungary, which tends to express a more independent viewpoint) nothing approaching absolute truth in public expression is to be found in any matter that comes within the sphere of politics or ideology. The most that can be achieved in the pursuit of truth is not to publish untruths, or slanted material, where to do so is not obligatory. Even if sharply expressed, it is not fundamentally incorrect to claim that the Soviet ambassador in Poland decides what history books may be published in that country (ATA in English 1145 gmt 3 June 1974, EE/4617/A2/2).

In specific directions individual East European countries may disclose more than the USSR does. For instance, the volume of money in circulation is not a state secret in Czechoslovakia (Bosák, 1983, p. 4), while the GDR budget is much more informative than the Soviet one (see *Neues Deutschland*, 3–4 July

1982, p. 3). This is also true of Poland, whereas the budgets of Hungary and Romania give away very little in terms of a detailed breakdown of income (Wanless, 1985, pp. 57–60). Yugoslavia publishes fiscal data which the Soviet Union does not; for example, in the USSR rates of Turnover Tax are secret and increases in these rates are never announced, whereas in Yugoslavia they are (for example *Borba*, 25 September 1985, p. 2, cited in ABSEES, item 11782, January 1986). A list is published of names and addresses of firms under the Czech Ministry of Industry (*Hospodarcze noviny*, 11 November 1983, cited in ABSEES, item 09428, May 1984); the USSR does not give such institutional data.

Hungary may occasionally offer an outlet for revelation by Soviet citizens, such as a remark on Budapest radio that research had been conducted into stopping hydrogen bombs by laser strike. Budapest radio, I think, has occasionally disclosed other news about the USSR which Soviet sources have not, such as a huge forest fire in the Urals region, in August 1975 (Gabor Bankuti, Budapest domestic service 1100 gmt 16 August 1975, SWB SU/4986/B/1 20 August 1975).

The ban on mentioning the names of specific individuals applies also in Eastern Europe, as indeed was already noted in regard to Poland. Arturo Sandauer's name is on a black-list for Polish radio which is forbidden to mention or quote him (*Dziennik Polski*, 13 April 1964; an article by him on censorship and literary criticism appeared in *Kultura*, 16 May 1965). Other censored East European writers include Pavel Kohout (Czechoslovakia: Choldin, 1984, p. 13).

The suppression of the 1937 census in the Soviet Union was noticed earlier. Partial suppression or distortion of census results has also occurred in Eastern Europe. A complete set of statistics about the Bulgarian census of 1975 was never published, and what was published caused controversy between Bulgaria and Yugoslavia, as the population of Pirin was treated as Bulgarian by the Bulgarians but as Macedonian by the Yugoslavs. This dispute also aroused questions about the accuracy of the Bulgarian count of other minority groups (*Bulgarian Situation Report/33*, Radio Free Europe Research, 4 December 1975, item 2). Early in 1985 there were numerous reports, which were subsequently confirmed, that members of the Turkish-speaking minority were being compelled to adopt Bulgarian names, apparently so that the census intended for December 1985 should show a reduction in the size of that minority (e.g. *The Guardian*, 18 January 1985), that is to say the intention was that its size should be shrouded in deeper secrecy. There may well have been other motives too, such as to interrupt correspondence between people of Turkish descent in Bulgaria and their relations in Turkey, by refusing to deliver letters which were addressed to their former names; in effect, to make their addresses secret. Enforcement of name-changing is a novel form of oppression.

It was noted that the USSR had sometimes aimed to preserve secrets by assassination. Apparently for similar reasons a Bulgarian, Markov, who broadcast for the BBC, was murdered on Waterloo Bridge, London, in 1978, through injection of a poison pellet. This was almost certainly done by the Bulgarian secret police, not only because the Bulgarians were the obvious beneficiaries from his death (Markov had been reporting about the seamier sides of Bulgarian life and leadership, with which he had acquaintance, and had received many death threats), but because of the specific poison, ricin, which was used; this is known to have been the subject of research in Eastern Europe. Thus, what had been intended as a secret method of killing ended up by pointing to an East European agency. (This exemplifies a point made in Chapter 2; see above, p. 12. See in this connection Markov, 1983.)

Whereas such topics in the USSR have been, and are, strictly secret, Yugoslavia is less secretive about military-oriented research. Dr Milisav Momirski was awarded a prize of 7000 dinars for his PhD thesis 'Direction of guided missiles by impulse emitting apparatus' (SWB EE/4484/B/9 24 December 1973, Tanjug 1416 gmt 20 December 1973). By contrast, in Yugoslavia showing by mistake an old newsreel about a political opponent can land the cameraman in jail. (This relates to a newsreel of Aleksandr Rankovic, as reported by Belgrade REVIJA 92 in Serbo-Croat 8 October 1974, p. 10.) As regards East Germany, no detailed data were made public about 'structure-determining' tasks, products and resource allocation, among priorities for technological change in the ambitious aim launched in 1968, owing to the GDR's 'obsession for secrecy' (Bentley, 1984, p. 135), while science in the GDR in 1973 was still observing a 'high level of secrecy' (Schimanski, 1973, p. 849). In Poland, scientific secrecy appears to be not quite so intense: thus, four 'rationalisers' (innovators) in the Polish Navy had designed an electronic simulator for training purposes, for locating and combating submarines under near-operational conditions (Polish television 1830 gmt 29 May 1974, SWB 4617).

The disclosure of business secrets is also punished in East European countries. This includes Yugoslavia where, however, punishments tend to be lighter. The trial of Juliy Drasinover, accused of leaking business secrets without authority, opened in Belgrade on 23 November 1973 (SWB EE/4461/B/18, Tanjug 0011 gmt 23 November 1973). On 6 March 1974, Drasinover was sentenced to three years rigorous imprisonment for unauthorised disclosure of business secrets: he had forwarded the monthly *Konjunkturni Pregled* (*Market Review*), prepared for the use of federal organs, to foreign embassies and trade missions in Belgrade, and also data on the trade in pharmaceuticals and similar products to the Milan Institute of Statistics; though, for lack of evidence, he was cleared of passing business secrets to Interlogik Institute in the FRG (SWB 8 March 1974). In Poland, Zbigniew Macek, former investment manager of the petrochemical plant in Plock, was charged with betraying commercial and technological secrets to West German firms and accepting US dollars and other gifts in return (SWB 4685, PAP in English 1840 gmt 21 August 1974).

The more liberal Yugoslav policy hardly extends to Yugoslav relations with Albania. Since April 1981 Yugoslavia has not allowed into the country any Albanian book, gramophone record, picture or film, or any Albanian writer (*Zëri i popullit*, 25 July 1985, p. 4), which is something that the Albanians complain of. The sound of pots calling kettles black is commonly heard in protestations in a censored press about some other nation's secrecy or disclosure policy. According to Philip Ward, most Albanian books 'are considered offensive by the Yugoslav authorities and hence confiscated by them' (Ward, 1983, p. 155). Though that did not happen to me in April 1983, the apprehension that such material might be confiscated remained, and in effect created a barrier to bringing into Yugoslavia the Albanian things mentioned above. Moreover, in June 1986 at the frontier crossing of Hani i Hotit the import of literature from Albania into Yugoslavia was indeed prohibited.

Tourist trips abroad for its own citizens from socialist countries show an enormous concentration upon visits to other socialist countries. For example, in 1974 about 5 300 000 Czechoslovak citizens went abroad, including nearly 5 000 000 to the socialist countries. In 1975, Cedok (the Czechoslovak travel bureau) was offering 279 525 places to socialist countries and just 6992 to non-socialist countries (CTK in English 1708 gmt 8 January 1975, SWB 4800). This would give about one Czechoslovak in 2000 a chance to visit a non-socialist country. Albanians may not go abroad except on official business; from their official viewpoint, almost all the rest of the world is non-socialist.

The volume of tourism *into* Communist countries is also a fairly good indicator of the extent of secrecy there. As a rule – if everything else is the same – the fewer the tourists the more secretive the country. Thus, Yugoslavia which is less secretive than other Communist countries receives by far the most tourists, while Albania which is the most secretive receives the fewest. The reasons for this relationship scarcely need elucidation.

It was noted that Soviet citizens have to register changes of address. Similarly, in Hungary under a decree of the Ministry of the Interior changes of address have had to be registered with local councils as from 1 December 1974. From 1 January 1975, the address or any change of address of a child under 14 years of age has had to be registered with the council concerned (Budapest home service 1600 gmt 25 November 1974, SWN SWB 4766). As regards foreigners in Romania private persons are only permitted to accommodate close relatives, such as parents, children, brothers or sisters, or the spouses and children of these; other foreigners may not be accommodated, either as paying or non-paying guests. Infringement of the regulations is punishable by a fine of 5000 to 15 000 lei (SWB 4809, Budapest home service, 2100 gmt 15 January 1975). This ban probably had to a large extent a security motivation (as it would restrict the opportunity to foreigners to mix with ordinary people), though another objective may be to enable the state (rather than private individuals) to earn more foreign exchange. Similar considerations would apply in the Soviet case.

A small country is more vulnerable and therefore more sensitive in matters concerning military secrets and national security, was one of the arguments put forward by the military prosecutor in a trial in Yugoslavia of two British aircraft spotters (*The Times*, 6 December 1973, p. 6). That argument should apply even more to Albania, yet there was no objection raised to my photographing, in 1983, a viaduct, certainly of strategic significance, on the railway route from Elbasan to Pogradec (which is also depicted in *40 Années d'Albanie socialiste*, Tirana, 1984, p. 121), whereas photographing such an object in the Soviet Union would be strictly forbidden; on the other hand, in Albania, even a suspicion of an intention of photographing a market scene provoked immediate intervention. Thus it would seem that in Albania, the desire to publicise achievements of a more modern character (the building of a railway is seen in that light in Albania) outweighs the desire to keep it secret, as being a strategic object, whereas in the Soviet Union the scale of preference is the reverse. Albania also differs from the Soviet Union in providing much more information about natural disasters within the country. Whereas in the USSR I have gone by train across flooded areas the size of English counties, and not a word about the flooding appeared in the Soviet press, the Albanian press even devoted a leading article to heavy rains and depicted 4250 hectares inundated in Lezhë district (*Zëri i popullit*, 20 November 1985, p. 1). It has been claimed that during 1982 a new trend appeared in Albania of releasing information (RFE/RL report of 29 November 1982, p. 7), in contrast to the extra barriers then being put up against leakage of information from the Soviet Union (see Chapter 9; also note Romanian behaviour in 1982 – see next paragraph); if correct, that too would illustrate the fact that Albania in matters of this kind (as indeed in others) had thrown off Soviet domination. However, in reality Albania continued to provide little statistical information about itself.

In Eastern Europe, alongside Albania, state secrecy has been most pervasive in Romania (Matthews, 1978, p. 167); however, Albania makes public a figure for spending on defence, whereas Romania does not. Romania's non-publication of her foreign trade statistics was apparently used to conceal a redirection of her trade towards the West, her trade with the USSR declining from 51.5 per cent in 1958 to 41 per cent in 1961 (Montias, 1964, p. 136). Romania maintained secrecy in foreign trade even longer than the Soviet Union did (Hutchings, 1982A, p. 219). In another sphere, an abrupt decline in the number of Romanian daily newspapers between 1973 and 1974, from fifty-eight to twenty (*Statistical. . .*, 1976, p. 443), must have been due to *force majeure*. In 1982, letters from Romanians to the BBC in London suddenly stopped arriving because they had begun to be systematically intercepted; those who wrote them were called on by the

security police and obliged to promise never to write again
without the authorities' prior approval (*The Times*, 11 January
1983, p. 8). On the other hand, among bloc countries only
Romania took part in the 1984 Olympic Games, and it gave the
Games full TV coverage. Apart from Romania, among the bloc
countries only Poland gave any television coverage at all to the
Games, though transmitters in West Germany, Austria and
Yugoslavia were able to provide coverage for many East Euro-
peans (*D.T.* 4 August 1984, p. 11).

Apart from Albania after its break with the USSR (in December 1961), and apart from episodes (of limited duration, though
very important) such as the Prague Spring and the Polish
Solidarity movement, trends in degree of secretiveness in Eastern Europe tend to run parallel with those of the USSR. This is
not likely to be coincidental: though we do not know the exact
mechanisms, presumably instructions issue from the Soviet
Union. Thus, the 'wave of secrecy which interrupted the flow of
statistical abstracts in Eastern Europe from 1949 to 1956' (Kaser
and Zielinski, 1970, p. 58) – for example, forecast totals in
Albanian state budgets reappeared in 1957 – ended at about the
time the USSR again started to publish statistical handbooks.

It was noted earlier that in the 1970s Soviet reporting of
foreign trade had decreased (see above, Chapter 8). Similarly,
'assessment of the actual role of foreign trade in the development
of the Czechoslovak economy has become increasingly difficult
since the second half of the seventies, because since that the time
less and less of the necessary data are being published' (Havlik,
1985, p. 1). In one respect a difference emerged between the
series for the USSR, the GDR and Czechoslovakia (or of these
plus Poland), on one hand, and the other East European countries on the other. Thus, 'Hungary has recently greatly reduced
its statistical coverage of the budgetary sector and budgetary
income' (Wanless, 1985, p. 57), whereas in the USSR there has
been no comparable trend.

Poland has followed its own tempo, in part at least. Already
during the Gierek period (1970–80) an open-door policy was
pursued, making Poland the most accessible country in Eastern
Europe to Western journalists, and with large numbers of Poles
travelling abroad, uncensored leaflets quoted much detail about
the economy and the *Black Book of the Polish Censorship* (*Czarna
Ksiega Cenzury*) was stolen and published abroad (Hirszowicz,

1986, pp. 172–3, 178–9). In fact, a period of lesser secretiveness arrived earlier in Poland than in the Soviet Union which, no doubt, was one of the signs and origins of Solidarity and later of the proclamation of martial law.

Yugoslavia, being outside the Soviet bloc, is naturally idiosyncratic. Here 1974 is a focal date: in that year legislation was adopted, regulating the work of foreign mass communications media and foreign information activity in Yugoslavia (Tanjug 1411 gmt 20 July 1974 and 1336 gmt 23 July 1974, SWB EE/4660/C/6).

These countries have been systematising their documentary collections. The formation of state archives has, however, occurred later in some countries than one might have expected. As reported in 1974, Bulgaria was intending to constitute state archives, which would include valuable ordinary and secret documents of various Bulgarian establishments, etc. It was admitted that previously there had even been instances when important documents had been destroyed (BTA in English 14.37 gmt 13 June 1974). By contrast, the Albanian State Archives were formed in 1949. The earlier date in Albania may indicate that the ruling group there saw a stronger need to enforce a single consensus.

In Eastern Europe, as in the USSR, if less information is provided this is normally a bad sign; thus, the fact that over the 'last seven or eight' years information about Bulgarian economic co-operation with the USSR has been shrouded in secrecy, whereas formerly the Bulgarian press loved to provide it, was consistent with criticisms of Bulgarian economic performance expressed by the Soviet ambassador to Bulgaria in July 1985 (Nikolaev, 1985, pp. 3–7.)

CMEA (COMECON)

Comparative secretiveness among organs of CMEA can be estimated in several ways, for instance, by the amount of information released concerning names of staff, what proportion of meetings is explicitly reported in relation to those which have taken place according to their serial numbers, and whether titles of subsidiary bodies have been made known. As regards the last measure, fifteen out of twenty standing commissions in existence in June 1975 appear to have had subsidiary bodies, as reported in the press and radio; the only standing commissions for which none were reported being Currency and Finance, Non-Ferrous Metals, Oil and Gas, Posts and Telecommunications, and Statistics. It is possible that these standing commissions actually did not possess any subsidiaries, but much more likely that they did possess them and that their existence was not disclosed.

Could CMEA reveal information which one of the member countries did not want to be disclosed? This would seem to be excluded, since CMEA does not have supranational status; however, Hanson (1981, p. 171) cites production of ammonia from the CMEA statistical handbook, and points out that the Soviet *Narkhoz* series (the annual statistical handbooks) omit this and many other chemicals series. Thus something extra might come out in CMEA statistics, though this would be very exceptional, and the data could not have been classified very highly. Perhaps however, this had been a type *B* decision rather than a type *A* one.

SWITZERLAND

In the East European official view, Switzerland is the secretive country *par excellence*: 'The Empire of Secrecy', according to the Bulgarian newspaper *Rabotnichesko delo* (Shatrov, 1984, p. 6). The focus is on the Swiss facilities for capitalists: 'Capital loves secrecy. That is its nature.' Placing Switzerland at the top of the list of non-Communist countries may be correct. It is true that banking secrecy in Switzerland has come under attack within the country since the 1970s (*The Globe and Mail*, 30 April 1984, p. B8), but an attempt not long before that to change the law failed (Ibid.). However, this sort of secrecy, which is on behalf of others (though the Swiss expect to earn dividends as a result) is rather unusual. Switzerland does not belong to the United Nations, which also is consistent with secretiveness, although the fact that secretive Albania is a member, and according to its foreign minister even an active one (Malile, 1985, p. 4) shows the limits of this argument. The Swiss strategy of military defence is buttressed by a high level of secrecy (see McPhee, 1984), but in the case of a small country which holds aloof from alliances this is entirely natural. Switzerland, in fact, aims both to enlarge its freedom of action (in the economic sphere) and to spring a surprise, or be able to do so (in the military sphere). The pinnacle status assigned by Eastern Europe may help to explain the high level of activity in Switzerland of Soviet espionage (see Chapter 11). Perhaps the recollection of Lenin's sojourn in Switzerland immediately before returning to Russia in 1917 is a contributory reason for this high level.

SPAIN

Spain, under Franco, was strictly censored, both from political and puritanical angles. The original law was adopted in 1938. A law of 1966 suspended the requirement of preliminary presentation of all texts for publication to the censorship, replacing this by a form of 'voluntary consultation'; however, thereafter for several successive years the number of prosecutions of publications climbed steadily (Diéguez, 1973, pp. 93, 97). Though in October 1976 the Ministry of Information, created by Franco, still existed, which according to an evening paper, *Diario 16*, was flagrant proof that censorship, though muted, still survived (Wigg, 1976, p. 6), it is at any rate evident that since Franco's death censorship has been enormously relaxed.

SWEDEN

Extreme strivings towards an 'open society' may jeopardise a nation's military security; thus Sweden found that a range of minor military secrets had become accessible to potential enemies following a court decision to open most of the country's computer registers. Since the court ruling foreign embassies in Stockholm had been 'queueing for information' (*D.T.* 3 July 1984, p. 15). As noted in Chapter 11, Sweden has been the target for numerous submarine incursions, which suggests that whatever Sweden has done to make information available has still not been enough to satisfy those in pursuit of it. The assassination of Olof Palme (28 February 1986) jolted the country but the new prime minister announced that an 'open society' would continue. It takes more than one assassination to change a nation's attitudes towards secrecy and disclosure.

SECRET KEEPING BY THE WEST

Certain military events which at the time would have caused despondency or alarm, or danger to imminent operations, have been kept secret by the Western allies for a long time, in some cases for decades. One such example in the Second World War was the torpedoing by German E-Boats of three landing craft practising for the 1944 D-Day assault, with the loss of at least 749 lives; this was revealed only forty years later (*Pittsburgh Post-Gazette*, 8 May 1985, p. 5).

Certain countries belonging to the Western alliance now came under scrutiny, beginning with not the least secretive of them – Britain.

BRITAIN

Secrecy is not particularly characteristic of any single Soviet institution, though doubtless it is most intense in bodies such as the KGB. In Britain, by contrast, a 'cult of secrecy', less intense, of course, than in the Soviet Ministry of Finance, is ascribed to the Treasury, and to some extent to the Foreign Office – ministries which are concerned with conducting national and international affairs at their highest level (see Lamont, 1975, p. 16). This difference reflects *inter alia* the smaller extent of state involvement in the British economy than in the Soviet one.

However, as regards the Treasury, the contents of the annual budget are kept secret in Britain up to the moment when the Chancellor of the Exchequer delivers his budget speech in the House of Commons, because foreknowledge of its contents (e.g. of rising petrol prices) would enable individuals who had that foreknowledge to make windfall gains. In the Soviet Union, the Minister of Finances' budget speech does not include that sort of announcement, yet still is kept secret up to the moment of delivery. Even in Britain it is thought unfair to spring on people basic changes which would affect, for example, whether they decide to retire (*The Times*, 15 December 1984, p. 7); thus (even if inadvertently) going a little way towards Soviet budget practice. Reciprocally, the procedure whereby the Chancellor informs his Cabinet colleagues about the budget on the morning of Budget Day apparently has a parallel in Soviet procedures (see Hutchings, 1983, p. 55).

According to one of 'Nader's Raiders', 'the rule here seems to be that everything is kept secret unless and until the government decides it wants the public to know what is going on' (Frank and Weisband, 1974, p. 218, cited from Public Interest Research Centre, London, press release of 1 October 1962). There is some truth in this but on the whole it conveys an exaggerated impression. Governmental secrecy has certainly come into question: see for example the leading article 'Right, not Need to Know', *The Times*, 2 June 1983, p. 15. Despite many suggestions over a considerable period that it would be revised or repealed (for example *The Financial Times*, 11 March 1975, p. 9), the Official Secrets Act (adopted in 1911) remains in force, but its enforcement is subject to severe judicial limitations.

On the whole, secretiveness in Britain is far less than in the USSR. For instance, in the armed forces secretiveness is discriminatory. Non-identification of individuals serving in particular units, which is the rule in the Soviet armed forces generally, applies only to the British special forces, such as the Special Air Service (SAS). The British Defence Directory (Brassey's) lists senior service and civilian personnel in the Ministry of Defence Royal Navy, Army, Royal Air Force and NATO Command (Brassey's, 1986, p. 22). The contrast here with Soviet practice is remarkable. The performance of weapons is secret, and sometimes that of the launching platform (e.g. in the Royal Navy, the maximum speed and diving depth of submarines), but training methods are to a large extent non-secret: in 1984–5 substantial information even about training of special forces was provided in BBC television programmes; this required adjustment of traditional policies (e.g. Crane, 1984, p. 4), though some sequences were omitted for security reasons and there were other modifications. However, while in the USSR a secrecy barrier divides defence from non-defence industry, in Britain a barrier divides one firm working in the defence industry from another.

There may also be ministerial censorship. Thus, as reported by Winsor, 1976, p. 15: 'Nothing can be written about Silbury without the permission of the Department of the Environment – it's an ancient monument.' Local government too is often rather secretive, one of the most secretive local authorities in the country being apparently Croydon Council – my home town (*Croydon Comet*, week ending 17 May 1985, p. 1). But opinions differ as to whether local government in Britain is more, or less, secretive than central government (Delbridge and Smith, 1982, p. 19).

A system of information control is not unknown in Britain, but is predominantly confined to wartime, and more exactly to the major and slowly geared-up conflicts that were typified by the two World Wars. The sharp but brief Falklands War consequently caught the arrangements on the hop and only the geographical remoteness of the Falkland Islands made possible strict censorship at the time of the actual military operations, though many details even of these have subsequently become known. One more generally applicable means is available, the 'D notice' system, which is used to notify an editor that publication of a given item of news may violate the Official Secrets Act. The decision then to observe or not observe the warning is voluntary, but cases of non-compliance have been relatively few (Wise and Ross, 1967, pp. 122–3).

The permitted use of information only under certain conditions is a phenomenon which is fairly widespread in Britain. An example is 'Chatham House rules': information given in lectures covered by the rules may be used, but not attributed to the speaker or to the place where it was uttered. This is doubtless based on the system of briefing lobby journalists in Parliament (Kellner, 1983, p. 275).

Confidential documents normally have to wait thirty years before being released for publication, a duration fixed by the Wilson government in 1967 (the Public Records Act), following consultations with the other political parties. Previously the period had been fifty years. It must not be understood that everything is released, either when thirty years expire or indeed at all. A huge proportion – it is said 99 per cent – of documents are not kept permanently, being 'weeded out' in departments. There is much evidence that the non-retained items include substantial numbers of documents which have been destroyed owing to poor records work in departments and lack of adequate supervision (Sir Duncan Wilson, as reported in *The Times*, 22 November 1982, p. 4.) A committee under Sir Duncan's chairmanship recommended that a panel of Privy Councillors and other eminent figures should have access to confidential and sensitive records, but this was turned down by the government (*D.T.* 26 March 1982, p. 8). Sir Duncan strongly criticised sections of a White Paper which replied to his committee's findings.

Certain matters from long ago are still secret. It has been the view of the British government that the cypher-breaking methods of the Second World War were not to be revealed (*The Times*, 1 July 1983, p. 15). Information about the work of 'Ultra' is still totally embargoed (Rusbridger, 1985, p. 13). There is the case of the details of the appearance of Sir Oswald Mosley before the Birkett Tribunal. When pressed on 14 March 1983, the Attorney General would merely concede that a review would take place within twenty years at most (*The Times*, 15 March 1983, p. 4). Documents released under the thirty-year rule now have the cross-indexing – which used to reveal the subjects of the items held – removed (*The Observer*, 2 January 1983, p. 4).

The British thirty-year rule finds some favour among American academics, judging by a seminar (which I attended), 'Declassification of Secret Documents: The British and American Experience Compared', by W. R. Louis, R. A. Divine and H. J. Middleton, which was held in Austin, Texas, on 30 April 1976.

As thirty years is shorter than most careers in the British diplomatic and civil services, memoranda written near the start of a career are liable to be eligible for release before it is over, which conceivably might inhibit giving candid advice; Mr Enoch Powell thinks that the period should therefore again be fifty years (*The Times*, 12 January 1985, p. 2. This is an example of interpenetration of personal privacy and national security, which in principle are distinct concepts). This proposal is unlikely to be adopted.

Within the standard interval, leaks have been relatively rare (though 1984, the year of Tisdall and Ponting – the *General Belgrano* affair – was in part an exception) and usually unimportant, but some have had significant results. During the 1930s, while he was still out of office, information was supplied to Winston Churchill about German rearmament by one person each from the Royal Air Force, the Foreign Office and the Intelligence Service, and Churchill used this for effectively criticising the government of the day. In 1984, Sarah Tisdall passed a confidential document to a newspaper. She was no doubt torn between two loyalties, and thanks to the absence of censorship was able to choose a course of action which in the USSR would have been barred (cf. *D.T.* 26 March 1984, p. 3). Episodes such as the Tisdall and Ponting cases momentarily attract huge attention, but are soon forgotten. They highlight the fact that governments prefer to act in secret, but this is known already. It seems, though, that certain journalists at least part of the time can discern clearly what is happening (see *The Financial Times*, 1 July 1975, p. 25).

In general, whenever an official censorship is lacking, various unofficial bodies are likely to try to substitute their own. Attempts at unofficial censorship have began to rear their head in Britain, such as trade unions' stifling of articles or advertisements which they do not like (*The Times*, 6 September 1984, p. 4). This applies most directly to printers where one union disclosed what must have been intended to be kept secret: the Council of Civil Service Unions issued a comprehensive list of the seven main government intelligence outstations in Britain associated with GCHQ at Cheltenham (*D.T.* 5 February 1984, p. 1). In the USSR nobody in a comparable installation, or any other, would belong to a trade union of British type, and any disclosure of national secrets by the Soviet variety of trade union would be unthinkable.

There are some further elements which might be called quirky. Thus, 'the phone numbers of British Gas showrooms are not listed in public telephone directories and it is impossible for customers to obtain them' (Moore, 1984/5, p. 11). BBC television journalists went on strike on 7 August 1985 against 'censorship' of a programme about Northern Ireland, although at least one ordinary element of censorship, namely that it is kept secret, was not present. The programme was broadcast later. The rules of declassification may be stretched for ex-politicians. Khrushchev, after his deposition, lost access to official papers, so that his memoirs are less accurate than they could have been. In Britain, in similar circumstances, limited access may be granted.

Britain easily comes top in a league table of countries which have expelled the most Soviet attachés for espionage – since 1970 a total of 144, France being in second place with 51 and the United States far down the list with only six (*Sunday Times*, 15 September 1985, p. 15. Provided by the US State Department, this list covers only agents they have positively identified.) The large British total reflects the size of the Soviet espionage effort in Britain, which derives from its geographical position, the stationing here of important deterrent forces, the volume and nature of scientific research, and the international community in London; it also possibly reflects the small area of the country, financial limitations on British counter-intelligence, and the traditional special sensitivity of certain Whitehall departments.

There are also more specific reasons, in particular the determination of the Thatcher government to safeguard security and the information provided by the KGB chief who defected to Britain in 1985, Oleg Gordievsky.

Surveillance is undoubtedly on the increase in Britain, though mainly in regard to the IRA and other terrorist bands. Telephone tapping is the only form of electronic surveillance by the police that needs the approval of the Home Secretary in each case (Walker, 1975, p. 3). Although a Local Government (Access to Information) Act was passed in 1986, on the whole there is little trend here towards greater freedom of information. Anti-racist legislation even tends in the opposite direction.

THE COMMONWEALTH

Wherever a particular system of government is diffused, its characteristics, including secretiveness if that belongs to the original, should be diffused too. However, whereas in the matter of cabinet committees the governments of Canada, Australia and New Zealand make public a list, the British government admits to the existence of only four such committees (Overseas and Defence, Home Affairs, Economic Strategy, and Legislation). The existence of the Overseas and Defence Committee has been acknowledged since the 1920s. No government has admitted to the existence of the Joint Intelligence Committee, some details of whose work are given in *The Times* (29 November 1982, p. 2). The Irish Republic 'stands alone with Britain among the OECD nations in keeping cabinet committees hidden from the electorate' (*The Times*, 15 March 1983, p. 4). Whereas the British rule is that information acquired by an official must not be disclosed, in most of Western Europe as well as in such Commonwealth countries as Canada, Australia and New Zealand the onus of proof is reversed: specific reasons must be shown for preservation of confidentiality (*The Times*, 2 June 1983, p. 15).

AUSTRALIA

Censorship in Australia has been less liberal than in either Britain or the United States: as compared with the former there has been no established procedure for dealing with security reports on individuals, and as compared with the latter, Australians have lacked both statutory and judicial protection against the actions of censors. Moreover, several states have statutes which prevent disclosures of the kind made by *The Washington Post* over Watergate. Queensland, which among Australian states has approximately the (backward and conservative) reputation that Arkansas has in the United States, has (among other states) its Literary Board of Review which banned four times as many works in 1973 as in 1972 (Healy, 1972, pp. 55–7). The fairly widespread Catholic influence, especially in the Australian Labour Party, is a factor which promotes censorship on moral grounds, whereas high living standards, the broad extent of tertiary education and a certain national disrespect for authority are factors which operate against censorship in general. Moreover, in Australia, as in Britain but not (now) in the United States, there is not even nominal protection of privacy (Goldring, 1984, p. 317). The Australian census used to exclude the aboriginal population, but that gratuitous omission has now been corrected. Since 1972 Australia has been moving slowly towards public access legislation (Delbridge and Smith, 1982, p. 35).

SOUTH AFRICA

Owing to South Africa's pariah situation in international relations, secrecy in that country is especially strict and has unusual features, such as the prohibition of publication of details of how the country obtains its oil supplies. However, it was intended to relax the secrecy clauses of the Petroleum Products Act (*The Times*, 14 March 1985, p. 8). South Africa appeared at first to be almost wide open to foreign television reporting communal violence and the state of emergency (August 1985 onwards) but as the emergency wore on the police took action to place foreign correspondents under restraint, which resulted in an immediate reduction by more than 50 per cent in the amount of coverage given to the subject in the British national press (*Sunday Times*, 24 November 1985, p. 1. The number of column-inches devotes to the subject in the eight principal papers declined from 2614 in the twenty-one days just before the ban to 1205 in the twenty-one days just after it). The effectiveness of media controls was therefore demostrated. South Africa is one of the few countries of the world which, like the USSR or Mussolini's Italy, practises internal exile (as applied, for example, to Mrs Winnie Mandela) and it would appear with the same motive as in the Soviet Union – to prevent or hinder contact between the exiled person and the foreign press.

THE THIRD WORLD

The Third World – an imprecise grouping of countries to which South Africa belongs according to the SIPRI schema – is on the whole secretive. As one account put it, nowhere in Africa is there a free press, and nowhere in the world including the Communist countries, does a foreign reporter face so much harassment and so many obstacles (Adamson, *D. T.*, 23 July 1976, p. 14). 'Many Third World governments are even more secretive than the Soviet Union', according to another judgement (Katz, 1986, p. 88). In 1976, following the introduction of censorship in India, it was said that in several respects it was easier for a foreign correspondent to work from Moscow than from New Delhi. Following the June 1975 proclamation of emergency in India, censorship was established overnight; according to Indira Gandhi, it was necessary to protect the nation from an irresponsible and destructive press, although she showed some regret and said that she had always been against press censorship of any sort (*The Times*, 28 June 1975, p. 4). The press and government-controlled All-India Radio and Television presented a picture of India as calm and stable, unified and solving its problems rapidly under a leader who was vigorous and universally popular (*The Washington Post*, 9 November 1976, p. A12).

The Soviet Union is a highly developed country when it comes to censorship. A simpler procedure, more suitable to a Third World country, was suggested by an Ethiopian newspaper. For the time being, African countries should continue to use the foreign news agencies, but replacing certain titles and adjectives. For example 'South African government' would become 'the fascist government of South Africa'; 'extremist regimes' would become 'progressive governments', etc. ('Sirak' writing in the English-language newspaper *Ethiopian Herald Sunday*, cited in *The Washington Post*, 9 November 1976, p. A13).

As has been demostrated at UNESCO, some Third World countries wish to impose Communist-type political controls over information and culture. Both the principle and the operations of the Western media have come under fire (Rosenfeld, 1976; cf. *Sunday Times*, 25 July 1976, p. 12). 'By a resolution agreed recently at New Delhi, 58 developing countries are now committed to replacing the news service of the international press agencies . . . with their own government-controlled news service . . . The governments, in other words, would exchange and circulate each others' propaganda and exclude every other sort of news' (cf. also Ingram, 1976, p. 5, about the Colombo meeting on news. The exchange of news between national news agencies is put into force by Albania which, for example, signed such an agreement with Vietnam – *Zëri i popullit*, 13 April 1986, p. 4). Although supporting the development of national news structures where these helped developing countries against 'colonialist and neo-colonialist domination', the Russians said nothing about Third World proposals that there should be popular participation in communications, or that the 'voice of the Third World' should be heard in industrialised countries through direct contact between their news rooms (*Sunday Times*, 30 April 1978, p. 9).

In the wake of the Falklands War, the Argentine government banned criticism in the state-controlled media of the armed forces' actions in that conflict. Guidelines to state-controlled TV and radio stations also banned discussion of human rights, government corruption, as well as any mention of people who disappeared during the anti-guerrilla campaign of the 1970s. (*The Times*, 27 September 1982, p. 5).

Evidently restriction of information is very widespread and to a large extent occurs independently of Soviet influence, although this is exerted in the direction of controlling information and in the Third World that influence often strikes a responsive chord. However, most Third World lands do not buttress censorship with all the controls which are enforced in the USSR, and as a result their restrictions are less complete. Furthermore, their aim is, of course, to protect their *own* secrets, not necessarily those of another country. It is in fact from Third World sources that an approximate picture can be built up of the pattern of Soviet arms exports to the Third World – about which the USSR publishes nothing. For instance, 'official sources mainly from Iraq, Egypt,

Sudan and Libya sporadically disclosed over the years extremely scarce information about Soviet arms prices' (Efrat, 1985, p. 6).

SAUDI ARABIA

While censorship on moral grounds is always present where an organised religion is influential, in the present age it reaches its peak in the Muslim countries, and especially in Saudi Arabia. Thus, the Saudi censors snipped out the rather revealingly clothed, though only five centimetres high, East German performers from *Time* of 29 April 1985, p. 33 (as well as the entire middle pages, which included a report on the Holocaust), and blacked out the bathing-costumed figure of Monaco's Princess Stephanie (from *Time*, 15 April 1985, p. 43; cf. Mehdi, 1985, p. 13). Sexual puritanism is much in evidence in the USSR, but is not the chief interest of this study. The results of a population census in Saudi Arabia have been kept secret, probably because it would reveal how few Saudis there are by comparison with the number of expatriates working in Saudi Arabia (private source).

CANADA

As reported in November 1982, Canada was about to pass legislation to place limits on media ownership, etc. (*The Globe and Mail*, 6 November 1982, p. 10). The Access to Information Act went into effect on 1 July 1983. Starting the process to obtain information from the government costs $5 (*The Times*, 4 July 1983, p. 4). It has been found to be a difficult task to develop novel rules which limit, or qualify, governmental secrecy so as to achieve a workable reconciliation of different values and interests, while interpreting them requires a very carefully balanced judgement, as well as substantial time in order to enable various conflicting viewpoints to be considered (cf. *The Citizen*, Ottawa, 1 December 1984, p. B1). Canada obviously belongs to that group of countries, regrettably few in number, which try to arrive at a rational disclosure policy, taking into account the general interest. Canada has also become the first country with a constitution of British type to endorse a public right of access to official information (Delbridge and Smith, 1982, p. 38).

THE UNITED STATES

The position in regard to secrecy in the United States is curious and even in part self-contradictory. There being no Official Secrets Act, a radical periodical in Washington could name people who were supposed to be CIA chiefs in 101 cities around the world, and the Agency admitted that there was very little it could do about it, except to neither confirm nor deny (*The Times*, 30 January 1975, p. 6: the magazine was called *Counterspy*. Not surprisingly nobody was listed for Tirana, and there were some other interesting omissions). While the personal privacy of citizens is legally safeguarded, issues asserted to be national secrets are regularly reported in the press. Thus we find that 'The money – the amount is secret – is hidden in an appropriations Bill containing funds for the Energy Research and Development Association. During a rare secret session, Senator Mark Hatfield (Republican, Oregon) urged withholding of the funds until Congress had all the information about the new weapon' (*The Times*, 2 July 1977). Even sums provided by the USA in 'covert' aid (in this case, to the Afghan Mojahedin) may be made public; according to 'US officials' $280 million was earmarked for this purpose in the 1984/85 fiscal year (*The News and Observer*, Raleigh, N. C., 29 November 1984, p. 16A). As one newspaper put it: 'Intended leaks are a commonplace – a form of standard operating procedure' (*The Washington Post*, 19 February 1972, p. A16). It might almost seem that in America everything is open, even after it has been declared a secret!

However, such a conclusion would go too far. A full system exists for classifying information, and classified information in fact exists in enormous volume. Security clearance is required for many posts connected with government, and US citizenship is a prerequisite for applying for them. Any outsider who visits a security-sensitive establishment has to be appropriately badged and escorted. The US record in keeping secrets in certain respects surpasses that of Britain: in recent years there have not been such notorious cases as those of Burgess, Maclean, Philby or Prime, until members of the Walker family were accused of naval espionage (1985). At the very top, there is not only secrecy, albeit punctuated by leaks and indiscretions, not all of which convey information that is at all surprising, but for a considerable period at least genuine obscurity. The extent to which knowledge of the Kennedy administration has been enlarged, a number of years after it has ended, is evidence of that and, of course, the origins of President Kennedy's assassination remain, to this day, by no means fully uncovered.

Without going further into the sensational events, let us consider the normal circumstances affecting the preservation of secrets under American conditions. The range of secrecy is narrower than in Britain; thus in the US financial market decisions are sometimes taken in an informed way, in contrast to Britain's secretiveness (*The Guardian*, 7 February 1984, p. 23). Confidentiality, to the extent that it is achieved, is brought about under a system of appointments which is more flexible than the British one; for example, movement between civil service and academic posts is more frequent. This is undoubtedly one reason why leaks occur: it is acceptable in the United States, whereas it would not be in Britain, for an academic researcher to cite in public the conclusions of a Confidential or Secret document; not indeed its details, if only because to do so would diminish the comparative advantage enjoyed by the researcher who has access to it. Against this, something is thereby done to narrow the gap, which in Britain is noticeable, between the informed but non-communicating official and the academic person who is less informed but who airs his or her opinion nevertheless. However, if flexibility is impossible without sacrificing some vital principle, it is not offered. The Americans, for example – this applies to the British too – are not prepared in any circumstances to divulge whether their warships carry nuclear weapons; the ANZUS (Australia – New Zealand – United States) mutual defence pact may disintegrate first (e.g. Watts, 1985, p. 133; *The Times*, 20 October 1984, p. 4).

When Congressional pressure is considered, the constitutional and traditional role of Congress in legislation and verification of national policies has to be remembered. In 1967, Congress passed the Freedom of Information Act, which was supposed to open up information except for military secrets, the public disclosure of which would help an enemy. In fact – it is alleged – bureaucratic resistance continues to thwart this 'right' even when secrecy is not a factor (*Boston Evening Globe*, 23 January 1973, p. 12).

The sense that the public has a 'right to know' is far stronger in the USA than in Britain, and this puts continuous pressure on the secret-keeping system, pressure which at times results in excesses. Watergate, and the limelight in which for some time afterwards the CIA was compelled to work, is the best illustration of this. Another illustration, more relevant to Soviet studies, is the effort which was made to choke off appropriations for Radio Free Europe and Radio Liberty – the two broadcasting stations in Munich which broadcast to Eastern Europe and the USSR. 'The CIA used to finance these broadcasts covertly, and after this was brought inescapably to light two years ago this government took over the burden openly. (*The Washington Post*, 22 February 1972, p. A16). Shortly after this, in March 1972, President Nixon instituted a new system, designed to restrict the use of 'Top Secret' and 'Secret' stamps on government documents, and to speed up the process whereby classified documents are made public (*The Washington Post*, 9 March 1972, p. 1). No regular time period is enforced for release of US classified documents.

In the aftermath of Watergate, the American people seemed to have gone overboard in their pursuit of freedom of information – for no organisation can operate without confidentiality (cf. Bennis, 1976). Under the Reagan administration, the more extreme pressure to operate openly has been repulsed, and more information is being kept secret. It is claimed that there has not been any central directive to cut back on availability of information, but that various considerations have been involved, including reducing the cost of government and improving national security (*Detroit Free Press*, 15 November 1982, p. 8C). However, at present and for the foreseeable future the United States, at any rate among major powers, stands at a point of minimum secretiveness: on this scale, the USA may be said to stand in roughly the same proportion relative to the United Kingdom, as the United Kingdom stands in relation to the Soviet Union.

JAPAN

We come finally to Japan, which between the two world wars was highly secretive: for example, the policy of building battleships with 18-inch guns 'was to be kept a closely-guarded secret', and indeed this policy 'held out well' (Lengerer, 1983, p. 33). The attack on Pearl Harbor was the culmination of Japan's secret preparedness for war. Since her defeat, Japan has been under strong US influence in matters relating to secrecy. Protection of national secrets has encountered obstacles similar to those which have hindered the post-war building up of the Japanese armed forces. On the other hand, the giant and secretive Soviet Union comes up to Japan's doorstep and even occupies certain former Japanese territories. Thus Japan has been swayed by conflicting pressures. The current trend is towards a considerable strengthening of legislation (David Watts, *The Times*, 9 December 1985, p. 16).

FINAL REMARKS

In this chapter, as far as reasonably possible the countries have been listed in a sequence from east to west – starting with the USSR and ending with Japan. This forms a convenient geographical order, but there is more to it than that. As one travels from east to west, secretiveness diminishes as one passes from more secretive countries to less secretive ones. Thus Eastern Europe is less secretive than the USSR, Britain than Eastern Europe, and the United States than Britain. Even Albania, although often seen as an especially secretive country, does not constitute a clear exception to this rule, especially when its vulnerability and turbulent history are taken into account.

This does not seem to be entirely, or even mainly, a matter of chance; there are reasons. Countries which are adjacent to one another are unlikely to be very different in their degrees of secrecy. As has been noted already, a secretive country is likely to be more resistant to espionage. A country that is adjacent to a very secretive country must take that into account and become rather secretive itself. Secondly, westwards has been the chief direction of individual migration, which requires to be nourished by information about opportunities and prospects. A third reason is the wider scope of political democracy in westerly countries, above all the existence there of an uncensored press. Finally, there is the correlation between openness and living standards: westwards, living standards tend to be higher, so one would expect secretiveness to be less.

In this connection, it may be remarked that more easterly outposts of western countries are much more secretive than the mother country: one thinks of embassies of Western countries in Moscow, or of undersea listening posts for submarines. This is consistent with the rule 'more easterly, more secretive'. Analogously, distance away from an east–west axis which is contained within the northern hemisphere can affect the result. It is noteworthy that the Antarctic, being the continent which is farthest situated from a circuit of the globe which includes both the USA and the USSR, is also the continent where secretiveness is at a minimum, while in comparative proximity to Antarctica is found New Zealand, where the Labour government headed by Mr Lange failed to understand the importance of secrecy in nuclear armament. Where there are clear exceptions to the rule, such as the juxtaposition of the highly secretive Soviet Union and the minimally secretive Sweden, the outcome is likely to be humiliation for the less secretive power until such time as it begins to take the relationship into account.

Of course, the proximity of nations today is not simply geographical, apart from the fact that because the globe is round, Far West and Far East are next door to each other: by their mutual vulnerability to missile strikes and their juxtaposed naval forces the USA and the USSR in some respects are in close contact. In all dimensions where this is so, the normal rule applies: contiguity tends to equalise degrees of secrecy. This can mean not only that the less secretive power becomes more secretive, but the more secretive power becomes less secretive, at any rate in relation to the other superpower and when these two are negotiating with each other.

An illustration of quasi-propinquity is found in the practice whereby some writers in the West on Soviet security matters conceal their authorship under pseudonyms (e.g. Beck and Godin, 1951, publisher's note), in order to protect themselves or their friends from possible reprisals. A global map shows a low degree of secrecy to be correlated also with a high degree of political democracy of liberal–democratic type (See for example 'The Atlas of Freedom: Democratic Elections', by Portik, 1985, pp. 40–1). The relationship is one of mutual stimulus: political democracy demands a wide dissemination of information, which in turn generates pressure to establish political democracy.

The impression had been created that the Soviet Union was particularly secretive. That impression was compounded of the following elements. On an international scale of situations conducive to secretiveness the USSR qualifies on all counts. Its secrecy was highly conspicuous, it being such a big and powerful country. And thirdly, Soviet secrecy was especially systematic and ruthless. However, within three major frameworks – east to west, extent of political democracy, and living standards – the USSR emerges as being about as secretive as one would expect; which must be regarded as an important conclusion, and perhaps a slightly surprising one. This does not mean that the Soviet Union does not generate its own reasons for being secretive, and the thrust of preceding arguments has been that it does generate those reasons; as a result it helps to generate the frameworks already mentioned, and to that extent determines its own situation.

Until recently it has been difficult to imagine that the Soviet Union might become less secretive than the Eastern European countries, and indeed, for a number of reasons, that is most unlikely to become an equilibrium situation; however, it might be a momentary result of reforms carried out by Gorbachev which temporarily outstripped corresponding changes in adjacent states. But Eastern Europe would hasten to follow suit, in the direction of restoring approximately the previous relationship. As regards the Soviet eastern frontier, if the Soviet Union became less secretive, its relationship with China would need to be placed on a friendlier basis, or reciprocally if the *rapprochement* came first, that would facilitate a process of reducing secrecy. Any lasting diminution in Soviet secrecy would also, in all likelihood, be accompanied by a diminution in the secrecy of other countries.

13 Causes of Secrecy

We now tackle the highly important question of *why* the Soviet Union is secretive.

As was shown in Chapter 3, the Soviet state inherited a secretive tradition, several of whose origins could be identified. This tradition would have exerted an important influence, whatever the nature of the Bolshevik Revolution had been. If it had been liberal or bourgeois, various circumstances would have impeded progress towards freedom of information. However, in that event the Soviet Union would not have become such a secretive country as it actually is, although British – or still less, American – standards of openness would not have been reached.

In reality, the Bolshevik Revolution swam with the secretive stream, changing or developing only the specific matters which might or might not be revealed, and perfecting the techniques of concealing or disclosing them. The USSR encountered circumstances of isolation and military threat which made that result in some degree understandable; nevertheless, both Party policy and state structure encouraged the result that secrecy became more intense.

Secretiveness might conceivably be due entirely to how the Soviet state is constructed: there might be no conscious deliberation about reasons, or apparatus for taking appropriate decisions and seeing that they were enforced. In fact, the appropriate decision-making and decision-enforcing bodies exist, and – considering especially the precedent of the Tsarist censorship – it would be unrealistic to suppose them not to be used.

Next, is there evidence to conclude that there is a reason apart from secrecy for its own sake? To anyone brought up in a Western tradition the tendency is to reply automatically 'yes' to such a question. The balance may, however, be different. The evidence strongly suggests that secretiveness has not always served the best interests of the Soviet state (see below, Chapter 15); to that extent, it might appear not to have resulted from rational or well-informed deliberation. I make the assumption that at the very top (at any other level it is clearly impossible) serious deliberation about secrecy and disclosure policy takes place.

It seems likely that such deliberations and decisions, of a major character, occur at rather rare intervals, yet probably not after any *fixed* interval. The accession of a new leader would be the obvious occasion, and this is supported by evidence of changes in disclosure policy following such accessions. Shorter intervals are unlikely, given the relatively long periods over which policy must develop in order to encompass a sequence of plan periods, or to allow time for significant sociological changes.

The successor suddenly acquires the power to make available less, or more, information. He will need to consolidate his authority; one way of doing this is to show himself a superior ruler. But how can that be done, when as yet he has had no time to rule? One thing that can be done at once is to release information which is discreditable to the former ruler, which at least may suggest that the successor would be *likely* to do better. Thus is created the motive to unveil the unworthy actions and events perpetrated under the former administration. (This tendency must not be carried so far as to cast doubt on the successor's intentions or competence.)

How then can one explain the contrary trend, of becoming *more* secretive? Given the less changeable factors in the total scene, secretiveness cannot go on and on being diminished; in fact, a previous reduction in secretiveness is likely to instigate pressure to redress the balance. The new ruler may find it necessary to do unpopular things or make use of unpopular methods, which for the time being need to be hidden; his successor may thank him for providing the leeway which he in turn may eventually use to vary secretiveness in the contrary direction, but for the moment what matters is the immediate necessity.

Furthermore, a change in either direction may be instigated by a difference in style of the new leader, who may intend to rely less, or more, on popular support as generated through the media.

Minor adjustments, resulting from lower level decisions, may take place quite frequently, and there must be sufficient flexibility to enable changes to be made at short notice, if this becomes absolutely necessary. The meeting between President Reagan and General Secretary Gorbachev at Geneva in November 1985 was such an occasion, which necessitated an immediate recasting of the image of Reagan in the Soviet press so that he would appear a suitable person for Gorbachev to shake hands with, or in other words, certain good aspects of Reagan and of his policies had to be suddenly declassified.

The most readily understandable reason for secretiveness is national security, and this is the one that is most clearly shared with other countries. As a Prague commentator put it: 'Military secrets will probably remain for some time to come part of the defence capability of every State' (CTK in English 0944 gmt 9 October 1974, SWB 4725). This applies predominantly to the means of national defence: the size, composition and deployment of the armed forces, the volume and type of arms production, defensive or offensive military plans, training, command and control, morale, etc. Obviously this motive weighs heavily in Soviet disclosure policy, as is exhibited in the exceptional extent and intensity of secrecy relating to the armed forces. We also saw that carefully calibrated exposures are permitted to foreign representatives; in other words, secrecy in this sphere is not allowed to be complete. This, of course, does not mean that secrecy is not an important motive, merely that 100 per cent secrecy is not desirable. The concept of national security may reasonably be extended to the government and Party apparatus in regard to policy-making, systems of control, lines of communication, etc., up to a point.

In Russian eyes, it is a sort of decency not to refer to armaments in the same breath as to civil items. Any reference to armed force is assumed by a Russian to be directly intended to warn or overawe an audience (it is hardly surprising that this was Khrushchev's reaction to a fly-past of Royal Air Force bombers during his visit to Britain in 1956). So that except when that *is* the intention he sees it as in best taste not to advert to the subject. This is one possible reason for reticence though one that would usually be too flattering.

Soviet secrecy is often thought to be swayed primarily by considerations of national defence. This must be an important factor but it is by no means the only one. Indeed, the absence in the Soviet case of the more normal correlation of largeness of size of a country and a low degree of secrecy appears to contradict such a causal relationship. Soviet secretiveness is large relative to the size (area) of the country and relative to its power. That Albania, so much smaller and weaker, is not much more secretive than the USSR (and in a few respects is less secretive) is revealing in this connection. Either this correlation is not a universal relationship or in the Soviet case this is outweighed by something else. It can probably be concluded that Soviet secrecy often is not a compensation for weakness: it may often be in intention, though not always in result, an exploitation of strength.

Zones which foreigners are not permitted to enter doubtless in many cases contain items or installations of military or military–industrial importance. These can occasionally be identified from satellite pictures: for example, Ramenskoye airfield, with its immensely long airstrip, possibly the longest in the world, where the Soviet answer to the US Space Shuttle is tested, lies about 5 km within the exclusion zone, to the south-east of Moscow (Francis and Jones, 1984, pp. 66–7 and the US State Department map mentioned in Chapter 6). It is probable that exclusion zones do not always contain sensitive objects, in order not to define the position of the latter too certainly. Where foreigners are permitted to pass through such a zone along a specified route or to a particular destination, the purpose is often to enable tourists or diplomats to reach touristic or recreational sites.

Another plainly very important motive is to present the Soviet Union in the best possible light. This would be the motive for not revealing information on criminality or forced labour, or the liquidations during forced collectivisation and the purges of the 1930s. One might only comment that 'presentation in the best possible light' rarely seems to include giving a totally frank and unbiased exposition.

A third reason, partly overlapping with the first two, is the desire to present a monolithic view of the Soviet Union: hence erasure of the names of opposition leaders and the refusal of any publicity to dissidents. The concealment of non-officially approved art can be included under the same heading.

It must be made clear that the intention is not merely to present a monolithic view, but actually to create an identity of view. The unanimity invariably exhibited in votes in the Supreme Soviet should extend to the public at large. Secrecy, through its concealment of economic, religious or other sources of discord between the peoples of the Soviet Union or by expressing them only in muted form, makes a definite contribution towards enhancing national solidarity. (Regarding economic aspects of this motivation, see also below in this chapter.) The aim of working towards a unanimity of view extends to nations which are allied with the USSR or are included within the group of economies which are acknowledged to be 'socialist'.

The non-reporting of most accidents is difficult to include under the above headings, apart from serious accidents involving defence personnel or equipment, which may reasonably be concealed for national security motives, or 'accidents' which might have been caused by members of some particular ethnic or economic group. The non-disclosure of most accidents is apparently intended to emphasise control by the authorities over not only persons but the physical world, as is supported by the continued currency of phrases such as 'conquest of nature' or 'conquest of the cosmos' which outside the USSR now appear anachronistic and chauvinistic. In effect, the course of events is supposed to be under official control, to the limit that admitted accidents are rarely allowed to occur. On a vaster scale the same has applied to military casualties, though here (but only up to a point) a national security motive may reasonably be claimed.

It is clearly one of the guiding rules that the public must not be unduly disturbed. This explains the non-reporting of most accidents and the minimum publicity allotted to the death of any Soviet personage who is no longer in favour – Khrushchev for example (Smith in Hoffmann and Laird, 1984, p. 654).

Reticence regarding the ruler's death may also be included under the Soviet attitude to reporting of accidents. In this case the fact of death is kept secret until the succession is assured. The purpose is, of course, to safeguard the state against interference at such a sensitive moment. There was a similar practice in the Ottoman Empire of keeping secret the death of the sultan 'until his successor could reach the capital and forestall any trouble which might break out there' (Bridge, 1983, p. 29).

The treatment of news about the outside world as a state secret cannot be justified on national security grounds, but may help the regime to present itself to *Soviet* citizens in the best possible light, as these are then deprived of the possibility of making various useful comparisons; this then should also tend to uphold in most citizens' minds the officially prescribed views, though in relation to those who have sources of their own it could have the opposite effect.

When access to information is discussed in an East–West context, predictable attitudes are expressed. The West argues in favour of unfettered access to information, freedom of movement, and individual methods of transmitting information such as private correspondence, and stresses the limited usefulness of governmental intervention. The East denies that government restrictions constitute any bar, doubts the usefulness of private contact and of individual choice as to whom to meet, and insists above all on maintaining national sovereignty which it regards as threatened by free movement of information. For instance, the import of hostile information with the aim of undermining the moral and political unity of the socialist countries was an open interference in the internal affairs of other countries, an overt import of counter-revolution which was contrary to the policy of peaceful co-existence (*Bratislava Pravda*, 11 November 1973: CTK in English 09.52 gmt 16 November 1973).

Secrecy in economic affairs may in part be ascribed to the national security motive, but goes well beyond what could be justified under that heading and for the remaining part must be justified under the heading of presenting the USSR in the best possible light, or to some extent for the monolithic motive, e.g. in the non-reporting of domestic service or high incomes. However, non-disclosure of certain facts, for instance of the size of the gold stock, is difficult to ascribe to any of these motives. In this specific case, gold fetishism may be the reason; there are other traces of a mystique of gold in the Soviet financial system (Hutchings, 1982A, pp. 231–2). Other particular reasons may apply to certain other economic quantities.

Gaps and deficiencies in the statistical system must sometimes be the reason why various activities, for instance of a private but legal nature, are not recorded. Of course, all illegal economic activities are as far as possible concealed by those taking part in them (Grossman, 1985B, pp. 2–3).

Secrecy as a defensive screen (when goods are distributed very unevenly, or according to criteria which are not universally accepted) fits the Soviet situation to some extent, as too does a hypothesis that secrecy is connected with goods scarcity. Secrecy should then be intensified when distribution became more un-equal, i.e. directed towards favouring particular groups while conversely an intensification of secrecy might signify a trend of enhanced inequality relative to popular comprehension. In general, the fact that a market system of distribution is not accepted makes it more necessary to conceal whatever principles or practices are being applied in its stead. The purpose of keeping secret high salaries and other privileges of the ruling élite is clearly to prevent any build-up of popular discontent which might endanger those individuals or (if greatly amplified and over a long enough period) even the regime itself. This is not to suggest that such privileges are always unjustified, given the extra heavy workload of Communist Party members (Mickiewicz, 1981, pp. 118–19), and part of this secretive defensiveness might indeed be unnecessary.

Various other partial motives can be suggested. For instance, secrecy in matters of technology may be partly due to a residual sense of inferiority regarding technical skills (as suggested in *Time*, 21 July 1975, p. 37).

Various data are kept secret not directly for any of the above reasons, but because they would tend to cast doubt on, or argue against, the ruling national ideology. This is, for example, reflected in the characterisation of states in the popular media as either socialist or capitalist, as if there was nothing in between and no overlapping, which is a gross oversimplification since in reality all economies are mixed. The aim must be to hide the many socialist elements within modern capitalist systems, so as not to dilute opposition to them, while also hiding the elements of a capitalist system within socialist economies, so as not to appear to lose face in the 'struggle between two systems – socialist and capitalist', but above all the aim is to win that 'struggle'.

Historical evolution, especially the fact that such and such has traditionally been kept secret, is highly influential. Russia, and Eastern Europe generally, inherited inefficient and bureaucratic forms of administration; the abacus is symbolic of this. Similarly, Bulgaria inherited the administrative system which existed at the time of the Liberation from the Turks; President Zhivkov in 1973 was seeking to modernise this system (RFE paper, 2 March 1973). At any one moment, non-reporting of particular items may be attributable primarily to the fact that they have not been reported before. Up to a point, the longer the time that has elapsed since the last disclosure, the stronger the pressure to continue non-reporting is likely to be, as with the passage of time (until the reverse trend sets in, the news becoming eventually quite obsolete) disclosure will offer a bigger and bigger gift to foreign intelligence.

One of the major conclusions of *Chronological Patterns . . .* (Hutchings, 1982B) was that in a specific case secrecy may not be due to deliberate intent but to adherence to a certain generalised pattern of disclosure. This has been true of certain economic statistics in particular years.

Another highly important motive is to achieve conformity between the disclosure of information and current Soviet policies, either at home or in international affairs. Furthermore, consistency in presentation, so as to avoid internal contradictions, must be a major objective.

Another general reason for secrecy may be summed up as 'interconnections between facts or events'. Most of the data which are kept secret about the economy can be subsumed under this heading: in themselves they would convey little or nothing of importance, but they might be combined with other data to create a meaningful picture. How far secrecy which is derived from this cause would extend, would depend on the estimate of how practicable it was to make such combinations. Attentiveness to interconnections explains in particular the reticence concerning quantities on the margin of two spheres, for example economics and defence. The fact that in the USSR everything is interconnected, so that data about one part sheds light automatically on the whole, is a powerful motive for secretiveness to the extent that the authorities believe in that interconnection, and the facts suggest that to a large extent they do.

Secrecy legislation enshrines the deductions from these principles, or of certain of them, but also casting them in a more permanent and inflexible form which, in turn, must affect what precisely is included in the secret list. Propensities such as the tendency to overclassify also exert some influence.

Throughout its lifetime a secret is in danger of being uncovered, and a proportion of secrets will indeed be exposed; hence a continual natural selection takes place, eliminating the less viable secrets while preserving the more viable ones. At any moment, the catalogue of secrets incorporates the results of this process. Although what has to be kept secret can be defined in general terms to apply over a fairly long period, its precise cataloguing and definition has to be redone at more frequent intervals, and more exactly whenever the need arises. This will be the consequence of technical progress, the development of new prototypes, etc. The censorship must therefore keep constant watch on what lies immediately ahead.

In regard to the wider world, including Eastern Europe, the previous chapter already concluded that this, through various levers, made its contribution to the causation of secrecy in the Soviet Union. Among states within the Soviet bloc, the influence would be almost entirely one way, that is from the Soviet Union in the direction of enforcing secretiveness, though perhaps to a slight extent the contrary influence is exerted *from* Eastern Europe towards the Soviet Union.

Similarly, the existence of a buffer ring of socialist states around the USSR should have the result that the Soviet censorship can become less rigorous, if the alternative would be a ring of independent states generally hostile to Bolshevism, as during the inter-war period. This, however, is under the condition that the buffer states are themselves subject in some large degree to Soviet censorship, which clearly is the case. Thus the censorship would be diluted, but growing in radius. In actual fact, the formation of the ring of buffer states was not accompanied by any relaxation of the Soviet censorship; indeed, this immediate post-war period witnessed the peak intensity of Soviet secrecy. This was probably due to other contemporary circumstances, especially the conditions of the Cold War, not to any error in the above argument.

Does the existence of a world outside the USSR, and not subject to Soviet control, tend to bring about the result that the Soviet censorship is more rigorous or less rigorous? If censorship is reactive, if there is nothing to react against, the censorship will surely become less rigorous. It has to be inferred that the existence of the world outside normally makes the censorship more rigorous. However, changing patterns in international relations may sometimes favour a relaxation of the censorship, or its momentary intermission in some specific dimension; the Gorbachev interview in Paris in 1985 exemplified this (see Chapter 8). Hence, the existence of the non-socialist world makes the censorship more variable.

International agreements must exert a certain influence, though less than some people in the West had expected, or claimed to expect; in particular the Helsinki agreements appear to have had little effect in promoting disclosure of information from the Soviet side.

While these reasons are presented above as if they were quite distinct, in practice several may operate together in a specific case; reasons for travel restrictions, or for lifting them, are never given, and often a mixture of considerations may be involved. For example, the Baltic republics, especially Estonia, as it forms the southern littoral of the Gulf of Finland which leads up to Leningrad, have great strategic importance. However, it seems likely that another reason why these republics remained so long closed to foreign visitors was that the Soviet authorities did not wish visitors to learn at first hand of their inhabitants' true opinions.

14 Consequences of Secrecy: I. Disclosure Policy

Presenting Soviet disclosure policy as one of the consequences of Soviet secrecy does not mean that the latter has been its sole determinant but is one among a number of factors. There is no doubt that what must not be disclosed has a profound and wide-ranging influence upon the presentation of information and news of various kinds.

Soviet disclosure policy is considered in this chapter solely from the angle of the influence upon it of secrecy; and from the angle of its influence upon secrecy. The description does not reflect the somewhat wider freedom of expression and more varied topics which are emerging during the Gorbachev period.

In a narrow and banal sense, having eliminated what is not disclosed one arrives at what is. The Soviet Union discloses a very great deal, both about itself and about other lands and subjects; however, one of the distinguishing features about Soviet disclosure policy is the large volume of information which is non-secret outside the USSR but is in effect classified on crossing the frontier. As compared with Tsarist practice, the principal change is that although still relying heavily on keeping secret what it does not want disclosed, the Soviet state actively manipulates opinion through its monopoly of the media (cf. Sumner, 1944, p. 119).

Reference was made earlier to a 'principle of compensation'. This is continually illustrated in the interaction of secrecy and disclosure policy: if more is kept secret about one subject, more will be revealed about another, and vice-versa. In the discussion that follows, this must constantly be borne in mind, and frequently it supplies the guiding thread.

Given the relatively small reliance of the system on published information, one might wonder why anything is published. This may be for political, ideological, sociological, economic or other reasons. The political one is highly important; even if printed primarily for a propagandistic purpose, the press will not achieve that result unless it supplies some hard and relevant facts at least from time to time. The publication of information is

240

a characteristic of a modern state, which enables informed presentation and discussion of its performance. From this angle the USSR publishes more than the necessary minimum, although much less than could be desired.

Information about the Soviet economy may be said to be especially abundant. This is provided both at the national level and at republic and lower levels, and includes a considerable volume of information about what goes on within business organisations. The geography and geology of the USSR are written about at length. Cultural matters are illuminated along a wide front and in much detail. Political arrangements, especially names of appointees, are stated, although not the reality of the methods used by the Party to enforce its control. Scientific organisation is reported to a fairly big extent. Just a little is reported about present-day military matters, much more about military history. Non-fiction is supplemented by a large volume of fiction, much of which must reflect reality at least in some degree, though 'socialist realism' influences fiction in directions – biased rather than realistic – chosen by the authorities. Nevertheless, fiction often contains scenes from ordinary daily life, which shed light on or supplement whatever can be gathered from non-fiction.

It has long ceased to be possible for any single individual to absorb or even be aware of this vast mass of information, though collective authorship can offer an idea of how much is known to a group of specialists who pool their information, such as *The Cambridge Encyclopedia of Russia and the Soviet Union* (Cambridge, 1982). Even such a compilation as this supplies only an outline of the collective knowledge of the contributors, much of which has been obtained directly from Soviet sources, not to speak of everything that is reported about other topics.

The information publishing network is organised around the government. TASS (founded in 1925 and supplying both domestic and foreign news) is one very important mouthpiece. The Party publishes on a large scale but in the main it gathers information for its own use, while also inspiring national policy relating to disclosure and secrecy. It being very time-consuming to follow everything that is happening, foreign observers of the Soviet scene may be among those who are best informed about it. However, the May Day slogans (which are published two weeks before 1 May) reflect some of the leadership's priorities, problems and preoccupations in a form that can be presented to the public (cf. *The Times*, 16 April 1980). These are publicised not only in the press but as red and white banners to be slung across streets or under factory ceilings. At the regular Party congresses (the 27th, held in February 1986, being the latest) a full-throated effort is made to achieve that result on a more intellectual level.

It is easily arguable that because the Soviet Union is so large, a greater part of the information about itself must be expressed statistically. Soviet practice being to put into effect a given decision at all administrative levels, a wide range of regional authorities, indeed across the entire country, are consequently affected. If it is decided to release information about the whole USSR, this is liable to instigate its simultaneous and subsequent release in regard to lesser territorial divisions. The front across which information has been released has been broader than titles of the books in which information is included would suggest; these titles are sometimes misunderstood to be narrower in scope than they really are. Thus, the annual statistical handbooks are often regarded as economic handbooks in the West, but they contain some data also about science, population, cadres and culture.

Although very large, Soviet printing capacity is not unlimited and in fact appears to constitute a significant bottle-neck. Some capacity is utilised in other socialist countries (Walker, 1978, p. 41) though not usually outside the bloc, or if so, not in substantial amounts. Some specialised printing is performed in the USSR on behalf of foreign firms, including that of *The Modern Russian Dictionary for English Speakers* for the Pergamon Press. That printing outside the bloc is not used to a larger extent can probably be seen as a result of secrecy, or at least this must be one of the considerations. Shortage of domestic printing capacity is clearly suggested by gaps in certain years in the series of statistical handbooks, due apparently to an overload of capacity in adjacent years. Thus, the lack of a full-scale all-union statistical annual for 1966 was due apparently to the unusually large numbers of handbooks put out in 1967, to celebrate the fiftieth anniversary of the Revolution. (Hutchings, 1982B, p. 6). The lack of a full-scale statistical annual for 1981, owing probably to a specially big effort in 1982, the Revolution's sixty-fifth anniversary, which pre-empted printing capacity, is the latest example of this relationship.

Published material comprises only a fraction of all written material. Although this must be the case in all countries, it seems certain that in the Soviet Union the fraction is unusually small. The censorship and the lack of outlet for various sorts of critical, philosophical or frivolous writings lead to this conclusion. Indeed, samizdat probably had among its causes a lowering of this fraction, which was not due to any diminution in the amount published but to a larger amount seeking outlets.

As a substitute for information, what can be used apart from repetition? One may go into still greater detail, in matters which would have been treated more broadly, or may introduce subjects that otherwise would not have been introduced.

The authority will seek to multiply radio sets and to enlarge access to them: naturally, the programmes will be devised by the authority, others being, if possible, prohibited or physically excluded. Likewise with television. Whether an information-controlling country adopts the tactic of multiplying sets but monopolising production of the programme, or alternatively of prohibiting and excluding programmes, will depend on whether the country is able to generate its own programmes. The USSR, being a very large country, adopted the former tactic; South Africa, being much smaller, adopted (until recently) the latter. As reported in 1974 about 50 million TV sets, more than 60 million radio receivers and a similar number of wired radio points were receiving the programmes of Soviet Central Television and All-Union Radio, and more than a hundred towns were receiving colour television services from Moscow, Leningrad, Kiev, Tashkent, Baku, Yerevan, Tallinn and Riga. (Information provided on Radio Day – May 7 – by Radio Moscow and regional stations: BBC World Broadcasting Information, no. 20, 16 May 1974.)

Some information can be a substitute for other information, provided that the former is (while the latter is not) the kind that the government wishes to be disseminated. Such information, or the fact of its being disseminated, is likely to be given the maximum publicity in order to counter any suspicion that the government is actually trying to limit the volume of information. Thus any favourable statistics of book production and publication will be emphasised, and in the Soviet Union they are (see for example *Book Publishing in the USSR*, brochure, 1986). Indeed Soviet book output *is* very large. This is due to the large number of people writing, not to high productivity on the part of individual writers (other than the Marxist classics). Collectivity of authorship almost certainly tends to reduce output, as opportunities for individual authorship are thereby constricted.

Moreover, wherever a political angle can be discerned, the content of books, relative to their length, is diminished by obligatory references to the Marxist classics. This raises the proportion of references to years before 1900 (these are to Marx and Engels) and to 1900–24 (to Lenin). There tend to be fewer references per year to the period 1925–49 (except of course that books published during the Stalinist period included many allusions to Stalin's works). Not surprisingly, there is a focus on sources in the year immediately preceding the book's year of publication; this is perhaps more marked than in Western books about the USSR, for which one can imagine two reasons: there is no (or less) time-lag in obtaining the latest materials, and collective authorship (which is common) enables a more rapid scanning of recent material. (This is based on my own counts of references, but it was not practicable to undertake any thorough enumeration, so the conclusion is impressionistic.) The 1925–49 period began with Lenin's death, which is one reason for the comparative paucity of references; another may be relative non-availability of archive materials of those years, while a supplementary reason may be not to spotlight opinions which differ from those expressed today. Finally, the latter half of the 1925–49 period coincides with a time of exceptionally intense secrecy.

In Communist bloc countries, many meetings of a semi-political kind take place – of workers in a factory, trade union members, a Party *aktiv* or otherwise – under officially approved arrangements. Besides political exhortation, some information is aired at these and can include self-criticism among one's peers, especially during more idealistic periods. To the extent that information is provided, this usually repeats word for word the published media such as voluminous speeches, declarations, etc. which ordinary folk would not have found the time to read for themselves. However, information of a more local or specific nature helps to fill certain gaps in the media and consequently enables the latter to provide less information.

Only certain sorts of news appear in *Pravda* or *Izvestiya* or the other national dailies. There are no scandals, romance or sex, crime (except very occasionally in retrospect), or information about private lives; not much on human problems, fashions or household hints; nothing in colour except a headline (and that only in pillar-box red), no competitions or crosswords (though some journals do carry them) or advertisements unless severely factual or cultural, no humour except for cartoons (mainly of a political nature) or sardonic *feuilletons*, and nothing frivolous. Accidents and disasters, which come first in interest value for both men and women in the United States (and most probably in other Western countries too), either are not reported or are reported without graphic details or pictures (see above, Chapter 5). International news, to the (quite large) extent that it is reported, finds an attentive audience (Mickiewicz, 1981, pp. 58, 60–1). The national dailies periodically report some important domestic news, such as the economic plan results. There are many special days for particular professions or services, such as Geologists' Day, Inventors' Day, Border Guards' Day, etc. On these occasions there are usually press articles and talks on television (*D.T.*, 13 August 1983, p. 5). Readers' letters have become an important part of press coverage and sometimes result in action. For example, the railway newspaper *Gudok* in 1984 received about 40 000 letters, 6000 of which were sent on for further action, and over 8000 official responses were obtained (*Gudok*, 30 December 1984, p. 2, cited in ABSEES, May 1985, item 10616).

News space is largely taken up by material of restricted appeal to readers, such as full pages devoted to speeches by the Soviet leaders: these are even reproduced in the newspapers of other East European states, such as Chernenko's speech on 15 November 1984 at the Politburo, which was reproduced (in Bulgarian, so the text must have been transmitted beforehand) in the Bulgarian Party daily *Rabotnichesko delo* of 16 November 1984.

Any event or circumstance which is unfavourable to the Soviet official view of things or casts doubt on Soviet *amour propre* is reported (if it is reported at all) only once, whereas any very favourable event is reported again and again, echoes subsequent to the original announcement being normally orchestrated on the anniversary of the event in question. A large amount of space is given up in the press to the commemoration of Communist anniversaries – sometimes even each one, not merely each decade or two; these are occasions for lengthy panegyrics which rehearse bygone events. This *penchant* is perhaps not quite so marked as in Bulgaria, and in general it appears that the briefer a country's history since independence or revolution, the more time it devotes to national anniversaries. For example, a meeting in Albania celebrated the forty-first anniversary of the 2nd Shock Brigade (*Zëri i popullit*, 8 November 1984, pp. 1, 3). Where there is no independence, so *no* time has elapsed, the reminder may become perpetual, like the 'Je me souviens' on vehicle number-plates in Quebec.

One seems to have met before the practice of giving enormous attention to anniversaries and it is similar to the practice of churches (in particular, the Christian Church) in reproducing every year the same calendar of events. That Marxism–Leninism resembles a religion has often been remarked: here is another illustration. Even the Soviet mixing up of anniversaries and news is found in religious practice, for example the 'Good News' circulars which are pushed through our letter-boxes at Easter time. If one celebrates enough anniversaries, and/or reports them at sufficient length, one can never be at a loss for 'news'.

Verbosity in Soviet texts sometimes turns reader off, so that a text fails to convey what had been intended. Uninformative headings, and absence or rarity of subheadings, contribute to the same result. One origin of verbosity is the system of paying authors mainly according to the length of their writings (Walker, 1978, p. 75). Another reason is the invariable inclusion of a preamble which relates, or purports to relate, the main part of the text to Marxism–Leninism. Similarly, the peroration is obligatorily couched in ideological terms. Anything that may be factually original must be looked for in the ample torso of the text, and probably will be discovered only after a close examination, although a habitual reader may acquire a kind of sixth sense for anything novel. Appointments and international news are found on the back page. Reading the papers back to front has become second nature to Soviet citizens.

The significance of news can be evaluated only if one already has some knowledge of the circumstances. For example, Soviet newspapers list signatories of obituary notices, and it is the business of Kremlinology to discover and interpret them; however, most Soviet citizens could not have to hand the necessary analytical records.

While *Pravda* and other newspapers can be bought freely (although normally it is the practice to obtain newpapers and periodicals by regular subscription, rather than by buying them at news stands), it is possible that they are written in a way that discovers a certain information only to the initiated. This is not because they address themselves explicitly to particular groups, although 80 per cent of the subscribers to *Pravda* speak Russian while almost half are Party members (Mickiewicz, 1981, pp. 54, 120). Rather, the specific language used on some strategic occasions may convey more than is apparent to the uninitiated reader. The Finance Minister's speech when introducing the annual budget may be an example. It has been noted that how the Minister phrases his characterisation of the United States and 'imperialism' on this occasion is one of three clues on which a prediction of Soviet defence spending can be based (Zimmerman and Palmer, 1983, pp. 358–67). This could not have been recognised by anyone who had not made a deep study of the budget.

Pravda mentions radio and TV programmes, sport (briefly) and chess, and there are short notices of the theatre and the weather. Some other papers, such as *Literaturnaya gazeta* or the Moscow evening paper *Vechernaya Moskva* are much more readable, although because of the exclusions mentioned earlier there is nothing approaching the sensational.

Disclosures are strictly controlled not only in nature and scope but as regards *when* they are made; this would tend to fall in with general trends of secretiveness over time (see Chapter 11). For instance, during the first two months of 1983 the Soviet press carried a flood of carefully controlled revelations about the Afghan war (*The Times*, 3 March 1983, p. 12), whereas previously it had largely gone unreported. To a large extent the Soviet press does not report sudden events, but gradual achievements. Virtually all news of a positive kind in economic affairs is of this nature, so there is an affinity between the reporting of economic developments and Soviet disclosure policy. This allows, and indeed requires, a high proportion of the contents of a daily paper to be written well in advance (see Mickiewicz, 1981, p. 53).

The formula that might seem ideal for combining secrecy and propaganda, that is never to report anything discreditable about the USSR, conceals three pitfalls. The first is that there might really be a need to inform the population about some noxious circumstances or impending peril. The second is that official news will soon offer nothing worth listening to. Most news is bad news, because news is mainly about sudden events and it is easier for things to go suddenly wrong than suddenly right. Also a constant diet of good news soon becomes insipid. Without shade as well as light we cannot make an interesting picture. There are two conceivable ways out of this dilemma: to report only good things about one's own country or its allies, but only bad things about an adversary or potential adversary. Both these solutions are in large part adopted.

In Soviet publicity, the West is 'racist'. This means blacks are depicted only in situations of being under arrest or physical attack. They are invariably presented as underprivileged, and no allusion is made to any manifestion of racial harmony, except when both black and white 'workers' are shown battling against their common oppressors. Cartoons which include blacks depict them with idealised facial features. Since the majority of Soviet citizens have probably never seen a Negro, the idealisation may go unremarked. Blacks are often shown in the act of bursting fetters, or liberating themselves in some other directly physical manner. The true variety of racial composition of Western societies, as well as the fact that gradations of colour and feature exist, are not illustrated. Cartoon faces are either quite white, quite black, or Mongoloid (again idealised), and they suggest strength and determination, rather than intelligence.

Social phenomena in 'capitalist' countries are depicted from the angle of an idealised class war between 'capitalists' and 'workers'. The latter have all the right on their side but are oppressed by the former, who deploy against them a brutal police force, paramilitary, army, etc. The 'workers' are normally shown being struck or arrested, particularly when demonstrating in the streets and carrying banners, but what precisely is being attempted on these occasions by security forces, or why, is never explained. A strike is likely to be presented as if all workers in that branch were involved solidly. No work process is shown, nor any street scene unless dominated by a demonstration, so that what a typical street looks like is also concealed. The distinction between 'capitalist' and 'socialist' (countries, for example) receives heavy emphasis. The fact that in reality there are wide differences within these groups is either ignored or played down.

Despite their own secretiveness, the Russians are not shy of accusing the West of the same. For example, secrecy of economic planning there is decried (Lebedinskiy, 1971, p. 13). While Communist sources present Western intelligence as constantly prying into their secrets, they pour scorn on any suggestion that they are doing likewise. For instance, while *The Secret Front*, by S. K. Tsvigun, warned the Soviet public about the nefarious activities of foreign spies, saboteurs and tourists (Stevens, 1974, p. 6), Polish radio asserted that it 'cannot be feared that Communists may gain access to secret documents' (PAP in English 02:30 gmt 9 November 1974, SWB 4752); the allusion was to reservations of other NATO countries towards discussions with Portugal, reservations which led to postponement of a meeting of the NATO Nuclear Planning Group scheduled for 7–8 November, because the Portuguese government contained Communists. The Soviet interpretation of secrecy that is practised by others is almost invariably unfavourable: for example, their interpretation of secrecy of a space satellite launched by China: 'The top secret atmosphere surrounding China's programme of space research merely reaffirms that it serves military aims' ('Radio Peace and Progress' in English 3 August 1975, SWB 4973). Soviet commentators are conditioned to expect from their own society a greater degree of secrecy than they claim to be legitimate for others.

The 'warmongering' of the Western powers, and especially of the United States, is a permanent theme, somewhat intensified between 1980 and 1984: 'Since 1980, official Soviet domestic information media have conveyed a new, alarming assessment of the dangers of nuclear war and of the possibility of the Soviet Union's involvement in such a destructive conflict' (Shlapentokh, 1984, p. 88). On the other hand, among the events not reported are terrorist acts carried out by or on behalf of Third World countries, unless these are represented as having been carried out by 'patriots' or 'freedom fighters'. Any riposte by Israel or any other Western state which is the target for such attacks is reported prominently and fiercely denounced as 'imperialist' or 'playing with fire', and no facts or arguments which offer support for such a riposte are allowed to appear. This extreme partiality is not, however, entirely without its draw-backs. Because the Soviet (and East European) press continually cries wolf about allegedly aggressive plans or intentions of the Western powers, it is harder for it to arouse alarm if any genuine disaster or threat occurs, particularly as space is pre-empted in the media for covering routine economic reports or political anniversaries. If it becomes unavoidable to admit that some-thing has gone wrong in the Soviet Union, the admission will be balanced by accusations of similar evils in capitalist states, and of sensationalism in reporting by the Western media.

However, the Soviet leadership is not above exploiting that sensationalism when it is to their advantage. One of the propen-sities of the Soviet leaders is to respond to approaches from children in Western countries, not only because of the greater naïveté of children but because this must guarantee heavier press coverage in the West. Such was the case with Samantha Smith, an American schoolgirl who was invited to Moscow after writing to the Kremlin about her fears of war. She gave inter-views, in one of which she described America and the Soviet Union as looking much the same. Samantha died in an aircrash in August 1985 and a Siberian diamond 'of rare beauty' has been named after her (*The Times*, 9 September 1985, p. 8). Another 12-year-old girl, this time Aiko Fukuda of Japan, has received various gifts from Mr Gorbachev, including a life of Lenin and photo albums of Moscow (*The Times*, 11 January 1986, p. 5). Next, an 11-year-old Soviet girl, Katerina Lycheva, toured the United States; she too appeared on television and was photo-graphed holding peace doves signed by pupils during a visit to a school in Washington (*The Times*, 28 March 1986, p. 14). This might seem at first just a human interest story, but this is only the icing on the cake. Yet even the cake is not what it seems. It is not the main purpose of such visits to promote peace: the Soviet leaders are aware that this does not depend on public opinion. Rather, the aim is to convey that it is the United States that is the warmonger. (Colonel Gaddafi has begun to act in the same way: in this case an 8-year-old London schoolgirl received his reply: *The Sunday Times*, 18 May 1986, pp. 1, 3).

It would be possible to continue to describe Soviet disclosure policy, but at the cost of getting further away from the theme of secrecy. As far as we have gone, the 'principle of compensation' supplies the link: what is not reported must be compensated by one means or another. It emerges clearly that the Soviet media are required to report certain sorts of information but not other sorts. The objective appears to be dual: to report what is to the credit of the Soviet Union (and the Soviet bloc) – this includes reporting what is to the discredit of imagined adversaries – and in so doing to compensate for the absence of news of an opposite tendency which is left out. If we were to continue the description, we would find it necessary to devote more space to the methods and motives of presenting a particular view of the Soviet Union and of the world.

Disclosure policy as practised in the East European countries is essentially the same as in the Soviet Union. Co-ordination is doubtless effected at many levels and in considerable detail, but in general the mechanics of co-ordination are not disclosed. Occasional glimpses are possible. For example, between 2 and 5 December 1986 there was held in Sofia a 'consultation' of press sections of the ministries of foreign affairs of Bulgaria and the GDR, during which there 'was an exchange of experience about the role and place of the means for mass information of the People's Republic of Bulgaria and the German Democratic Republic in the spirit of the recent peaceful initiatives of the Soviet Union and of the fraternal socialist countries' (BTA, as reported in *Rabotnichesko delo*, 6 December 1986, p. 2).

The effect is that Soviet propaganda issues from many more outlets. Public opinion in the East European countries must be influenced, though probably not to a degree that is commensurate with the prominence of the items. The extra impact upon Western governments or public opinion is relatively slight, it being understood that the East European presses are relaying Soviet views at secondhand.

Except that the cue is taken from Soviet behaviour, the *modus operandi* of achieving *glasnost'* will also be the same in Eastern Europe as in the USSR: this will result from a top-level decision, not from any structural change in society. Thus, a decision of the Bulgarian Council of Ministers required the Bulgarian media 'henceforth to give broad openness to the work of restoration in the aftermath of the earthquake' (of 7 December 1986) and in this connection 'to examples of friendship and mutual help' (*Rabotnichesko delo*, 17 December 1986, p. 1).

15 Consequences of Secrecy: II. Other Consequences

POLITICS AND PUBLIC OPINION

As a result of secrecy and disclosure policy, for a long period, perhaps indefinitely, policies can be pursued which might not be supported by most of the population – if they were allowed to see them. For example, the Soviet public is unaware of the true burden of defence spending and of various Soviet actions in defence and international affairs, or is fed a distorted picture about those actions. While that is the case the authorities are shielded from domestic criticisms, or it might be more accurate to say that secrecy interposes an *additional* shield, as the one-party system plus all the other apparatus of repression already erects one obstacle.

In the running of the state, a huge inertia is created, or again it might be more accurate to say that inertia caused by the one-party state is considerably reinforced. The two ingredients are intermingled and mutually reinforcing. At the centre, reinforcement against criticism can become so great that in effect it bends the other way, so that negative criticism, to the point of adulation, is generated. This, perhaps, is one of the origins of a 'cult of personality', which then itself generates an inertial momentum. Thus under Stalin the true condition of Soviet agriculture was not conveyed to him, which brought the result that agriculture constantly languished. This inertia can be overcome, but as long as it persists it swamps any calculation of marginal advantage through small policy adjustments. Any objective, once set, is therefore pursued long past the point where diversion would have been judicious, probably indeed until its author dies or is replaced.

Among the effects of inertia is an inordinately long tenure of appointments, for example of the Minister of Finance (V.F. Garbuzov), the Minister of Foreign Affairs (A.A. Gromyko) or the Commander-in-Chief of the Soviet Navy (S. Gorshkov) – to mention three of the most notable examples. This is clearly both cause and consequence of the intensity of secretiveness; while secrecy protects against failure or defamation, the concentration of knowledge into fewer heads, if those are not unreliable or scatterbrained, inhibits revelation. Hence some trends are due to inertia, as much as or more than to malignancy; for instance, these might include the immense expansion of the Soviet Navy.

Similarly, the exclusion of all data and comment which might shed an unfavourable light on official policies ensures that the governing circles always obtain an adequate measure of popular support. Soviet individuals express in private conversation very diverse opinions, but dissent never presents any political threat because it is confined to independently thinking individuals, who in any society are a tiny minority. Consequently, the government and Party perpetuate their supremacy.

Information control dampens down potential discord and encourages a consensus view, and in these respects it promotes solidarity. However, it is divisive as between those who are in the know and those who are not. This creates a gulf between the intellectuals, and in particular certain of them, and the rest; and a further gulf (overlapping with that just mentioned, to the extent that the intellectuals travel abroad) between Soviet citizens who can travel outside the Soviet Union (especially outside the Soviet bloc) and those who cannot. The result is to encourage defection of the groups who realise the most clearly that their knowledge is deliberately limited. Consequently, a limited and gradual deintellectualisation and deculturalisation of the Soviet Union are taking place.

The Soviet state is interested in stifling this outflow. Measures such as the requirement that close relatives must remain within the USSR slow down the outflow, without halting it altogether. Other punishments play their part, but the only complete solution would be a further extension of the Soviet frontiers, which have in effect already been extended to encompass the rest of Eastern Europe.

Secrecy holds the mass of the Soviet people within their own country, without direct experience of the world outside: thus confining them in the prison of their prejudices and, in certain politically or ideologically influenced directions, nurtured misconceptions.

ECONOMICS

It has been noticed already that secrecy generates inertia in the formulation of policies: in the Soviet economy this has been exhibited in the stubborn continuation of industrialisation based primarily on ferrous metals, rather than on non-ferrous metals or plastics (Hutchings, 1982A, pp. 84–5), while in agricultural policy it contributed to holding up essential moves in the direction of privatisation.

Obstacles to informing the public comprise another aspect, though it sometimes seems that despite the paucity of advertising Soviet shoppers are better informed about what is available than one might expect. As regards traditional items some enterprising person may fill the gap, though unofficially and at considerable personal risk. For example if, in Latvia, caramels shaped like cockerels are not made by state industry, such sweets have been produced privately and are on sale, although this is illegal (Kaleja, 1984, p. 3). Yet by disguising the divergence of plans from demand, secrecy makes it more difficult for the retail trade to satisfy consumers more fully (cf. Asselain, 1981, pp. 74–5). Less obvious gaps, which one would become aware of only through advertisement of foreign-made things, are even less likely to be filled. Secrecy also obstructs discussion or comparison of inequality in earnings, and a misleading impression about these can be the result.

The discomforts resulting from secrecy in the Soviet economy are reduced by the narrower range of decisions which can be taken by Soviet citizens, relative to their own lives, which would be influenced by unexpected news. For example, the annual budget does not announce changes in taxation rates (Hutchings, 1983, pp. 24–5). On the positive side, the regular reporting of quarterly and annual plan results for a wide range of items and territorial divisions assures a considerable availability of knowledge about economic trends (in particular, relating to the domestic economy), for whoever has the time, expertise and facilities for analysis of these results: however, that combination would ordinarily be found only within an institution which was dedicated to that purpose.

The importance of published information in running the Soviet economy must rise as attempts are made to loosen it up and to allow wider scope for the initiative and self-interest of individuals and institutions, as instanced in various economic experiments. Similarly, the introduction of mathematical–economic models requires the collection of key indicators, instead of 'masses of useless data' which clog up the system (Fedorenko, 1985, p. 14).

The effects of censorship in reducing or distorting knowledge about the economic scene outside the USSR are serious, especially in regard to understanding the mechanism of 'capitalist' economic systems, and this constitutes a far from unimportant obstacle to the introduction into Soviet practice of modern managerial methods.

Admittedly, business secrecy is typical of a market economy, though rarely remarked because it is so familiar. Glimpses into the internal workings of a capitalist firm or corporation are rare, and normally stem from court decisions. In the USA, the antitrust laws sometimes compel disclosure, for example, in 1974 by IBM of its plans for a new generation of computers (*The Financial Times*, 29 October 1974).

Secrecy tends to have the result that incoming ministers have no conception of the problems they may face; in Britain this applies to Chancellors of the Exchequer in particular (Bracy, 1975, p. 2). This would have various negative results, but once an incoming minister had mastered his brief there would be a stronger reason for keeping him there. In the Soviet situation this may contribute to longevity of appointments, unless preliminary discussion within the Central Committee of the Party, or otherwise within Party channels, might enable some preparation.

Secrecy has very serious effects at the interfaces of economics with defence or with international affairs, as the Soviet public is left in ignorance of the costs of particular policies and of how these change over time. Similarly, the absence of credible statistics of administrative expenses conceals the true cost of the chosen forms of economic structure, thereby starving discussion of possible alternatives – discussion which would immediately acquire political resonance. Concealment of the third interface of the triangle – expenditures on administration in relation to expenditures on defence – has the effect that the existence of any 'military–industrial complex' is obscured, with the result that it is not merely the case that official statistics do not show how military spending has evolved; there is also no body of theory which might suggest how it should have evolved. In turn, obscuring the financial relationships between government and defence industry brings weighty dividends in Soviet propaganda, given that in Western countries these relationships are not obscured, or at any rate not to anything like the same extent.

SCIENCE AND TECHNOLOGY

The 'no interface illumination' syndrome also affects Soviet policy in the provision of information about science and technology, which has various consequences. In spheres such as cartography, it has a directly distorting effect.

Research within the USSR must be hindered by secrecy; this effect cannot be quantified but is surely important (cf. Klochko, 1964, p. 117). The frequency of dissertations on classified themes might be roughly proportionate to the frequency of higher educational institutions which are empowered to grant higher degrees secretly. In August 1956 these latter seem to have numbered altogether 64 out of 528 (12.1 per cent), not including any institutions under the control of the Committee of State Security. (Based on lists nos. 1 and 2 attached to a decree confirmed by the Central Committee of the CPSU and the Council of Ministers of the USSR of 20 August 1956, no. 1174 (Karpov and Severtsev, 1957, pp. 310–19).) However, a larger proportion is suggested by the fact that according to Medvedev (1971, p. 129) 80 000 scientific workers would constitute 'about one-fifth of the total number of scientific workers in open scientific establishments'; the total of all scientific workers in 1967 (the year he was probably referring to) being then about 700 000, workers in closed establishments would have comprised about 43 per cent of the total. One cannot at present decide between ways of reconciling these results. These might include a lower proportion of persons with higher degrees at work in closed establishments, and a rise in the proportion employed in such establishments between 1956 and 1967.

Not surprisingly, there is a tendency to overclassify: 'There are serious shortcomings in the defence of dissertations of classified themes. In a number of cases works are kept secret without sufficient necessity, which leads to a diminution of control over the quality of the work from the side of the scientific community' (from an instruction of the Ministry of Higher Education of the USSR no. 692 of 30 April 1956, quoting decree no. 1174, above-mentioned; see Karpov and Severtsev, 1957, p. 285).

Secrecy engenders an excessively narrow profile in the qualifications of individual scientists, and consequently an unduly narrow specialisation. Secrecy in research conveys an impression of incomplete groundwork. If discoveries are being kept secret, this hinders research but may also stimulate it. Research is so difficult anyway that the extra hindrance may suffice to prevent it from succeeding. Moreover, where secrecy comes to be regarded as normal and as usually impenetrable, people may become accustomed to having information withheld from them, and if they are lazy they may take this as an excuse to make no particular efforts to discover the information. In effect, it becomes normal for them to seek to absorb only a small proportion of the total information which is available and which would be relevant to their work. A kind of resistance to being informed may then develop (Meetham, 1968, p. 74; cf. pp. 76, 78). On the other hand, mutual exchange of draft papers within a group of researchers will quickly clog up the works, and the more quickly, the more productive the group. In a large scientific community, and so (other things being equal) a large country, this will happen more quickly than in a smaller community. To prevent it happening, a mild degree of secretiveness is not necessarily unhelpful.

Collaboration between Soviet and foreign scientists is diminished. Soviet bloc countries are probably not in a very different position here, as the Russians would fear that any important disclosure might be leaked to the West. This may be illustrated in an extreme case by the fact that the Russians – like other nations – have not passed on the know-how of nuclear weapons manufacture, although here other considerations too have been involved. As Soviet experience showed, secrecy would hinder co-operation with allies (Daniloff, 1972, pp. 213–14). Recognition to certain groups of Soviet scientists within the world scientific community is denied.

Scientific espionage by foreign powers is stimulated, i.e. these powers divert scientific effort into discovering new means of espionage or perfecting existing ones; moreover, at the next stage, the secretive power will acquire an incentive to strengthen research into *defeating* espionage. Whatever these powers find out must itself be kept secret by them, lest the Russians find and block the leak; consequently a barrier of secrecy is erected between their government scientists, on the one side, and non-government scientists and the general public on the other side. Thus, secrecy begets secrecy.

Scientific research in the foreign power is thus also impaired by comparison with a situation when the results achieved by all are freely published, though stimulated as compared with a situation when that power had not spied itself. Secrecy on the part of that power now stimulates espionage by the USSR; so the cycle is repeated in reverse order, and so on.

Consequently, no published account of Soviet science can be complete. The probable limits of error are reduced by such considerations as the following:

(a) There is the 'logic of scientific discovery'. Knowledge progresses along a broad front, and any very deep penetration cannot be achieved without corresponding advances in adjacent sciences, all of which are unlikely to remain hidden.

(b) Phenomena have a way of coming to light, carefully as one may try to conceal them: for instance, rockets emit heat and reflect radar or nuclear explosions generate radioactivity. The extent of leakage depends primarily on the efforts that other nations devote to scientific espionage, and some – though obviously by no means all – of what is then detected is later published.

(c) There is a large interchange of scientific information and experience between the USSR and other countries on a basis of mutual benefit. As Soviet scientists can, on the whole, expect to gain more from this interchange the more they themselves contribute, here is a built-in incentive to set limits to secrecy, though this does not prevent secrecy from being much more pervasive and insistent than in the freer society.

(d) National prestige demands that Soviet scientists participate to the fullest permissible extent in the affairs of the international scientific community. For example, they – or some of them at least – should be eligible to win Nobel prizes.

Although these considerations limit the extent of secrecy, they do not encourage reporting *unsuccessful* experiments, or accidents;

or at least, any incentive to do so in order to warn others within the USSR or other socialist countries at work in the same field is susceptible to being outweighed by the possible damage to Soviet *amour propre*. As an unsuccessful experiment may still have been useful, as it warns against repetition, the objection applies even more forcefully to the reporting of accidents, any causes of which can be evaluated only following an expert enquiry.

Because secrecy results in a stifling or stunting of public discussion, or in its taking place within too rigid time-limits (perhaps, to fit within a plan timetable) or along too specialised lines, then, particularly if the subject is a complex one, extending across boundaries of scientific disciplines (relating for example to ecological matters), there is an enhanced risk that it will not cover adequately all aspects. Decisions are consequently liable to be taken which are based on oversimplification. The results can potentially be serious both for the USSR itself and for other countries. Among non-specialists, the results may include complacency in the face of potential or actual hazards. On the other hand, programmes which might be rejected by public opinion, but which specialists endorse, can be planned and implemented.

INTERNATIONAL RELATIONS

Secrecy and disclosure policy exert extemely important influences on Soviet foreign policy.

One of these, in conjunction with the setting up of the buffer ring of socialist states in Eastern Europe, is that censorship corresponding to the Soviet model has been established in these states as well. The aim must be to reinforce the censorship provisions to the populations of the buffer ring. The comparative weight of these two considerations in the minds of the Soviet leaders is debatable; the former must be the more weighty, the more commonly Soviet citizens visit the other East European countries. At any rate, Czechoslovakia was invaded in August 1968 by the forces of the USSR and of some of its vassals in part because, in the Soviet view, the Czechoslovak government and Party were no longer completely in control of the nation's information output. Romania was not invaded, probably because the Romanian leaders *were* considered to be in control. Soviet relations with France have been relatively good, one reason perhaps being French censorship of radio and television. Relations with Britain have been relatively bad, and the British government does not censor radio and television. Similarly, it was no accident that Soviet relations with India became closer after India introduced political censorship. Certainly, for this relationship to hold, news has to be regulated so that it does not conflict with Soviet preferences. In China, news is controlled by the Chinese authorities but from the Soviet viewpoint this fact – in itself propitious – is offset by an anti-Soviet Chinese position. Whenever there is any whiff of *détente* in the air, the Soviet Union loses no time in requesting from the nation with which *détente* is envisaged a cancellation of anti-Soviet publicity.

From the standpoint of whoever is trying to penetrate it, secrecy has two principal and general effects: it creates ignorance, with all the results (insecurity, misjudgement) which may follow from that; and it stimulates efforts to overcome it, and thereby to mitigate those effects. The stronger the second effect, the weaker is likely to be the first.

In confrontational relationships, where forces have to be created and massed to meet a perceived threat, uncertainty will have the result that in some directions the forces massed will be too strong, and in others too weak; on the whole, probably excessively strong forces will be massed, so as to make doubly sure. This, however, is not certain, and will be affected by many other circumstances. Secrecy which is not overcome through superior intelligence therefore has the consequence that a random element is introduced; instead of a balance being achieved, there is more likely to be imbalance (either positive or negative). If – as seems incontrovertible – imbalance is more likely than balance to provoke an outbreak of hostilities, to be secretive and to be peaceloving must in some sense be a contradiction. If one is loving peace, one may not be going the right way about achieving it.

One example, but a strong one, may illustrate the point. It is now reported that production of the Soviet defence industry was 47 per cent higher in 1939 than in 1937 (*Sotsialisticheskoye . . .* 1963, pp. 260–1). Although the growth of spending on defence in the budget was not concealed and was noticed (for example) in a despatch dated 6 June 1938 from the American ambassador (Davies, 1942, p. 256), little other information was provided about defence preparations. It is now known that total defence output rose by 286 per cent between 1933 and 1938, whereas total industrial output rose over the same period by only 120 per cent (*Sotsialisticheskoye* . . ., 1963, p. 610). If the growth of Soviet arms production had not been so well hidden, Hitler might have been deterred from launching the 1941 invasion.

Currently, Soviet secrecy fuels the arms race. The analogy with the 1930s is again instructive. Nazi secrecy then encouraged a British deduction that German rearmament was proceeding at a tremendous pace which Britain had to match: this was Winston Churchill's advocacy. Only after the war, when documentary evidence became accessible, was it found that that pace had not actually been quite so fast. The same thing can happen now with Soviet arms production, the more so as Soviet secretiveness is even more intense than Germany's. As the Stockholm International Peace Research Institute has recognised, 'if exaggerated estimates of Soviet military expenditure are propagated in the Western media, the Soviet Union has only itself to blame' (SIPRI, 1979, p. 32, cited in Leitenberg, 1979, p. 265).

Not only is it natural for Western defence bodies to expect the worst: it is otherwise hard to find a logical reason why secretiveness is so intense. If to a fairly large extent secretiveness is a hangover from previous attitudes, this is impossible to prove in specific instances. The stumbling block is not merely that volumes of arms production and the full amount of defence spending are kept secret, but that the USSR fails to conceal that it is behaving secretively. Hence there must be something of importance to hide, surely that arms production or arms spending are larger than one had guessed. If, in the present state of international relations, secrecy in national security matters cannot be abolished, one might wonder why the Soviet Union does not try to *appear* less secretive when to do so would not only promote *détente* but even enhance secrecy.

The secrecy of intelligence agencies, when these are unbridled, leads to adventurism, such as the repeated violations of territorial waters right up to the Swedish coast.

Soviet membership of various international bodies is inhibited by the requirement to supply information about itself. For instance, the Soviet Union is not a member of the FAO. Soviet absence from the World Food Conference in Rome was ascribed to their not being overanxious to supply facts about their domestic situation (*The Times*, 7 November 1974). If the USSR joined the IMF, this would have revolutionary implications for Soviet secrecy. The USSR though represented at Bretton Woods (1944) did not undertake membership (Kaser and Nötel, 1985, p. 8). It is not a member of the Institute of Nuclear Power Operations (*The Times*, 30 April 1986, p. 13). Non-membership must, in turn, entail further consequences.

International negotiation is profoundly affected by secrecy but, on the other hand, it is a factor which results in its diminution. The greater the secretiveness of one or both parties to the negotiation, the larger the impact on the negotiations but also the larger the possible diminution.

Negotiations with the Soviet Union encounter the problem of Soviet secrecy at the outset in all situations where a common agreed basis is required as the starting point, as this must include a common factual basis and the facts as regards the USSR must normally be supplied by the USSR itself. Naturally, in negotiations relating to the military balance the problem is at its most acute. This has been the chief stumbling block in Mutual Balanced Force Reduction (MBFR) negotiations, which have made little progress since they were commenced in 1973. However, to the extent that a serious effort is made by both sides to overcome the problem, such negotiations must also tend to bring about a diminution in secrecy. It is perfectly possible that this process can bring about the result that the two parties to the negotiation learn more about the other party than either party is willing to disclose to its own public. The condition for this to happen is either a tacit or an explicit agreement that the exchanged information will not be given wider distribution.

Such negotiation therefore emerges as an important limitation on secretiveness, the assumption being that the possible gains from the negotiation matter more to the participating parties than those to be anticipated from secretiveness. A decision about that aspect must have been taken at a very high level. If the decision is negative, or if it is positive yet the disclosed information is not believed by the other side, the progress of the negotiations can be held up indefinitely.

The governments of both superpowers have become vastly better informed than their respective publics, or even (in much less degree) than those among their own specialists who lack access to the latest findings. Whereas in Russia the existence of these wide gaps is normal, in the Western democracies it is not;

consequently, there the clash in views is sharpest. There is the possibility of a certain degree of accord between governments, but – as in the case of the non-ratification of the SALT II agreement in the United States – there is a greater danger that public opinion will not be carried along, or that if public opinion *is* carried along, that opinion will not be based on adequate knowledge.

This imbalance in Western knowledge of the USSR – which combines precise and definite knowledge of certain aspects of economics, or of defence capability, with considerable ignorance in many directions of intentions and attitudes – profoundly affects international relations. *Détente* which is based on an appreciation of intentions is liable to be constantly undermined by more definite and exact knowledge of capabilities.

For foreign observers and policy-makers, the consequences of Soviet secrecy must include: disbelief in any assessment of Soviet affairs which fails to take into account that important news is perhaps not revealed from Soviet sources; awareness that this is probably concealing events or incidents which would reflect on the Soviet system unfavourably; and alertness to the possibility of noxious occurrences which are kept secret for as long as possible.

16 Final Remarks

Soviet secrecy belongs within a theoretical framework appertaining to secrecy generally; it is definable; the subject has philosophical aspects, and arouses a moral dilemma; is enfolded within a cognisable historical, intellectual and geographical setting; arises from identifiable multiple origins; is upheld by physical and legal systems and by censorship; is opposed by various forces and subject to certain limitations; its intensity varies over time; it applies to specific topics, and to some more than to others; its causes and consequences, in a variety of spheres, can be deduced or at least imagined. In an international context the degree of Soviet secrecy is near to the high end of the range, although not outlandish; moreover, an unusually large fraction can aim at springing a surprise, as opposed to enlarging freedom of action. Its impact is increased also in proportion to the country's size and power.

The presence of so many harmonious, converging and mutually reinforcing elements proves that Soviet secrecy is no accident, and indicates that it is really intended to achieve its purpose – in some directions, whatever the cost. Given that such enormous trouble, in so many dimensions and at such expense, is taken to preserve secrecy, what is kept secret must be considered to be of great importance.

To a considerable and increasing extent the apparatus of secret-keeping is aimed not at keeping secrets from the world outside and in particular not from the Western alliance, but from the Soviet people themselves. This conclusion must be drawn from the complicated barriers for keeping Soviet citizens apart from foreigners, or for censoring what they are permitted to be told, when so much can nevertheless be learned from satellite photographs or airwave interceptions. However, preserving secrecy is not an absolute goal: it is combined with no less elaborate and purposeful methods of controlling what is disclosed, and of varying the manner of disclosure to produce the desired impression.

Secret-keeping in the USSR is more systematic than in most countries, because it partakes of the more systematic character of disclosure of information. What is kept secret falls between or

264

outside the branching systems of information which are characteristic of a hierarchical society. The more systematic pattern of secrecy does not altogether tend towards keeping secrets if equally determined attempts are made to uncover them. Although the various dark areas lend each other some support, as a blacking-out of knowledge in one area conceals possible clues to investigating another, against this it may be inferred that the various areas of secrecy have something in common. To modify the area of secrecy becomes an especially delicate operation in the USSR, owing to its more systematic character.

The specifics of what is kept secret can only be inferred, but they must be congruent with what is disclosed. In the broadest terms, secrecy and disclosure policy must be intended to bring advantage to the Soviet state. In defence, for example, the chief aim appears to be to conceal the country's military potential, but with exceptions so that its deterrent ability is not missed.

Given the nature of the subject, it is not surprising that it resists investigation; however, further study will result in clarification of some at least of the many aspects which still remain rather obscure. For instance, it should become possible to define the following more precisely: the particular topics which are regarded as secret; the degree of classification, and how this has altered over time; or the timings of decisions to alter the regime of secrecy. Its origins – how far these must be traced back to structural or other features, ante-dating the current regime – demand more painstaking investigation. The degree to which the Soviet Union has benefited, or on the contrary has suffered, from its secretive policies could be the subject of prolonged researches. Closer study of the policies and circumstances of other countries would enable a more exact placing of the Soviet Union in regard to secrecy and non-secrecy within an international setting.

This is not the moment to attempt any assessment of the changes, in regard to secrecy or non-secrecy, intended or carried out under Gorbachev; but obviously changes are taking place. In this field, subsequent studies are likely to notice other novel developments to which attention will need to be devoted.

Bibliography

This lists books and articles where references in the text are indicated in the form: author's name, year, page number. If other details are indicated in the text, that item is not mentioned again. Titles of articles are not given.

AA (The Automobile Association (1984) *Baedeker's Venice* (Norwich: Jarrold).

ABOUCHAR, A. (1981) *Osteuropa-Wirtschaft*, June.

ADAMSON, D. (1976) *The Daily Telegraph*, 28 July.

AKADEMIYA NAUK SSSR, INSTITUT EKONOMIKI (1963) *Sotsialisticheskoye narodnoye khozyaystvo SSSR v 1933–1940 gg.* (Moscow: Izdatel'stvo Akademii Nauk SSSR).

ALEKSANDROV, A. M. (ed.) (1961) *Gosudarstvennyy byudzhet SSSR* (Moscow: Gosfinizdat).

AMANN, R., J. COOPER, R. W. DAVIES (eds) (1977) *The Technological Level of Soviet Industry* (New Haven: Yale University Press).

ANDREW, C. (1986) *The Listener*, 2 January.

ANNENKOV, Y. (1966) *Dnevnik moikh vstrech, Tsikl tragedii*, vol. II (New York: Inter-Language Literary Associates).

ARENDT, H. (1967) *The Origins of Totalitarianism*, 3rd edn (New York: Harcourt Brace and World).

ASSELAIN, J.-C. (1981) *Plan et Profit en Economie socialiste* (Paris: Presses de la Fondation Nationale des Sciences Politiques).

BAILES, K. E. (1986) *Slavic Review*, Spring.

BAKULE, V. (1983) *Politická ekonomie*, September, cited in *ABSEES*, item 10257, January 1985.

BALMUTH, D. (1979) *Censorship in Russia, 1865–1905* (Washington D.C.: University Press of America).

BARMAN, T. (1968) *Diplomatic Correspondent* (London: Hamish Hamilton).

BECK, F. and W. GODIN (1951) *Russian Purge* (London: Hurst & Blackett).

BEERMANN, J. R. (1971) *Studies on the Soviet Union*, vol. XI, no. 2.

BELINKOV, A. (1971) *Studies on the Soviet Union*, vol. XI, no. 2.

BENNIS, W. (1976) *Saturday Review*, 6 March.

BENTLEY, R. (1984) *Technological Change in the German Democratic Republic* (Boulder, Col.: Praeger).

BERG, G. P. VAN DEN (1985) *The Soviet System of Justice: Figures and Policy* (Dordrecht: Martinus Nijhoff).

BERNAL, J. D. (1969) *Science in History*, vol. 3. *The Natural Sciences in our Time*, 3rd edn (Harmondsworth: Penguin Books).

BETHELL, N. (1985) *The Times*, 5 June.

BIRMAN, I. (1980) *Soviet Studies*, January.

BIRMAN, I. (1981) *Secret Incomes of the Soviet State Budget* (London: Martinus Nijhoff).

BIRMAN, I. (1984) *Russia*, no. 10.

BODMER, F. (1946) *The Loom of Language* (Woking: Unwin Brothers).

BONAVIA, D. (1985) *The Times*, 3 June.

BOSÁK, B. (1983) *Hospodarske noviny*, 7 January 1983, cited in *ABSEES* item 08574, September 1983.

BOURDEAUX, M. (ed) (1976) *An Early Soviet Saint: the Life of Father Zachariah*, trans. J. Ellis (London: Mowbrays).

BOURDEAUX, M. (1985) *Policy Review*, Fall.

BRACY, J. (1975) *Sunday Times*, 27 July.

BRASSEY'S (1986) *Defence Yearbook 1986* (London: Royal United Services Institute and Brassey's).

BRIDGE, A. (1983) *Suleiman the Magnificent* (London: Granada).

BROWN, A. *et al.* (eds) (1982) *The Cambridge Encyclopedia of Russia and the Soviet Union* (Cambridge: Cambridge University Press).

BROWN, R. (1968) *Lasers* (London: Aldus Books).

BROWNING, R. (1980) *The Byzantine Empire* (London: Book Club Associates).

CALDER, N. (1969) *New Statesman*, 7 November.

CALVERT, P. (1986) in N. O'Sullivan (ed.) *Terrorism, Ideology and Revolution* (Brighton: Wheatsheaf Books).

CAMPBELL, F. G. (1985) *Slavic Review*, Spring.

CAMPBELL, R. W. (1972) *Soviet Studies*, April.

CARELL, P. (1964) *Hitler's War in Russia* (London: George Harrap).

CHOLDIN, M. T. (1984) *Censorship in the Slavic World* (?New York: New York Public Library, Astor, Lenox and Tilden Foundations).

CHOLDIN, M. T. (1985) *A Fence around the Empire* (Durham N.C.: Duke University Press).

CITRINE, W. (1936) *I Search for Truth in Russia* (London: George Routledge).

COLEMAN, A. (1976) *The Geographical Journal*, November.

COLEMAN, A. (1984) *The Geographical Journal*, January.

COWEN, R. C. (1978) *The Christian Science Monitor*, 1 November.

CRANE, J. (1984) *Submarine* (London: British Broadcasting Corporation).

DANILOFF, F. (1972) *The Kremlin and the Cosmos* (New York: Alfred A. Knopf).

DAVIES, J. E. (1942) *Mission to Moscow* (London: Victor Gollancz).

DEACON, R. (1974) *A History of the Chinese Secret Service* (London: Frederick Muller).

DELBRIDGE, R. and M. SMITH (1982) *Consuming Secrets* (London: Burnett Books).

DEMIDOV, N. *et al.* (1984) *Komsomol'skaya pravda*, 30 June, cited in ABSEES, item 10174, January 1985.

DEUTSCHER, I. (1949) *Stalin, A Political Biography* (London: Oxford University Press).

DIÉGUEZ, D. (1973) *Index on Censorship*, no. 1.

DIMITROV, G. (1934) *The Reichstag Fire Trial* (London: John Lane, The Bodley Head).

DIVINE, R. A. (1976) See entry for LOUIS, W. R. *et al.*

DURHAM, E. (1909) *High Albania*, 1st edn, repr. 1985 (London: Virago).

THE ECONOMIST INTELLIGENCE UNIT (1983) *Quarterly Economic Review of Rumania, Bulgaria, Albania*, no. 1.

EFRAT, M. (1985) in P. WILES and M. EFRAT (1985) *The Economics of Soviet Arms* (London: Suntory-Toyota International Centre for Economics and Related Disciplines).

ELLINGSEN, E. (1985) Paper 'Soviet–Scandinavian Relations' (at Cambridge – NASEES).

ERENBURG, I. (1945) *The Fall of Paris* (London: Hutchinson).

FAINSOD, M. (1959) *Smolensk under Soviet Rule* (London: Macmillan).

FEDORENKO, Acad. N. P. (1985) *Ekonomicheskaya gazeta*, no. 1 (cited in *ABSEES*, item 10558, May 1985).

FESHBACH, M. (1982) *Sunday Times*, 19 September.

FISCHER, G. (ed.) (1967) *Science and Ideology in Soviet Society* (New York: Atherton Press).

FISHLOCK, D. (1975) *The Financial Times*, 28 August.

FLEGON, A. (ed.) (1964) *Soviet Trade Directory* (London: Flegon Press).

FRANCIS, P. and P. JONES (1984) *Images of Earth* (London: George Philip).

FRANK, T. F. and E. WEISBAND (eds) (1974) *Secrecy and Foreign Policy* (New York: Oxford University Press).

FRENCH, R. A. (1961) *The Geographical Journal*, June.

FRIEDMAN, N. (1985) *Naval Forces*, no. 1.

GAFFIN, J. (1975) *The Times*, 16 April.

GARDINER, L. (1976) *Curtain Calls: Travels in Albania, Romania and Bulgaria* (Newton Abbot: Gerald Duckworth for Readers Union).

GARMASHEV, A. F. (1962) *Izobretatel'stvo i ratsionalizatsiya v SSSR* (?Moscow: VTsSPS Profizdat).

GIBBON, E. (1980: 1st edn 1776) *Decline and Fall of the Roman Empire*, vol. 1 (London: J. M. Dent).

GLAZOV, Y. (1985) *The Russian Mind since Stalin* (Dordrecht: Reidel).

GLEZER, A. (1975) *Index on Censorship*, vol. 4, no. 4.

GOLDMAN, M. (1972) Address at the Russian Research Center, Harvard University, 29 November.

GOLDRING, J. (1984) *The Australian Quarterly*, Summer.

GOTTINGER, H. W. (1968) *Osteuropa-Wirtschaft*, no. 2.

GOWING, M. M. (1974) *Independence and Deterrence: Britain and Atomic Energy 1945–1952*, vol. 2 (London: Macmillan).

GREGORY, P. R. and R. C. STUART (1974) *Soviet Economic Structure and Performance* (New York: Harper & Row).

GROSSMAN, G. (1982) in *Soviet Economy in the 1980s: Problems and Prospects*, part I (Joint Economic Committee of the US Congress; Washington: US Government Printing Office).

GROSSMAN, G. (1985A) *Inflationary, Political and Social Implications of the Current Economic Slowdown* (Berkeley-Duke Occasional Papers on the Second Economy of the USSR, Paper no. 2, September).

GROSSMAN, G. (1985B) *A Tonsorial View of the Soviet Second Economy* (Berkeley-Duke Occasional Papers on the Second Economy of the USSR, Paper no. 4, December).

GUNTHER, J. (1957) *Inside Russia Today* (London: The Reprint Society by arrangement with Hamish Hamilton).

HANSON, P. (1981) *Trade and Technology in Soviet–Western Relations* (London: Macmillan).

HARRINGTON, R. (1982) *500 Inside Tips for the Long Haul Traveller* (London: Wexas International).

HARRISON, G. B. (1981) *Introducing Shakespeare* (Harmondsworth: Penguin Books).

HARTSTON, W. R. and P. C. WASON (1983) *The Psychology of Chess* (London: Batsford).

HATTON, D. (1984) *Sunday Times*, 28 July.

HAVLIK, P. (1985) *Comparative Economic Studies*, Spring.

HEALY, A. (1974) *Index on Censorship*, no. 2 (Summer).

HEIKAL, M. (1975) *Sunday Times*, 27 April.

HEWETT, E. A. (1974) *Foreign Trade Prices in the Council for Mutual Economic Assistance* (Cambridge: Cambridge University Press).

HEYMANN Jr, H. (1972) *The US–Soviet Civil Air Agreement from Inception to Inauguration: A Case Study* (Santa Monica: RAND).

HILTON, R. P. (1985) *Naval Forces*, no. 1.

HINGLEY, R. (1977) *The Russian Mind* (London: The Bodley Head).

HIRSZOWICZ, M. (1986) *Coercion and Control in Communist Society* (Brighton: Wheatsheaf Books).

HMSO (1972) *Report of the Committee on Privacy*, July (London, Cmnd. 5012).

HODGDEN, L. (1985) *Naval Forces*, no. V.

HOFFMANN, E. P. (1975) *Soviet Union*, vol. II, part 1.

HOFFMANN, E. P. and F. J. FLERON Jr (eds) (1971) *The Conduct of Soviet Foreign Policy* (London: Butterworths).

HOFFMANN, E. P. and R. F. LAIRD (eds) (1984) *The Soviet Polity in the Modern Era* (New York: Aldine Publishing).

HOLLOWAY, D. (1982) in R. AMANN and J. M. COOPER (eds),

Industrial Innovation in the Soviet Union (New Haven: Yale University Press).

HOPKINS, M. (1983) *Russia's Underground Press: The Chronicle of Current Events*, foreword by Andrei Sakharov (New York: Praeger).

HOPKIRK, P. (1971) *The Times*, 26 February.

HUTCHINGS, R. (1966) *Soviet Studies*, July.

HUTCHINGS, R. (1967) *Soviet Studies*, July.

HUTCHINGS, R. (1969) *Survey*, Autumn.

HUTCHINGS, R. (1971A) *Soviet Economic Development*, 1st edn (Oxford: Blackwell).

HUTCHINGS, R. (1971B) *Seasonal Influences in Soviet Industry* (London: Oxford University Press).

HUTCHINGS, R. (1976) *Soviet Science, Technology, Design* (London: Oxford University Press).

HUTCHINGS, R. (1977A) *Soviet Design and its Influence on Soviet Naval Design* (unpublished).

HUTCHINGS, R. (1977B) in F.-L. ALTMANN (ed.), *Jahrbuch der Wirtschaft Osteuropas, Band 7* (Munich: Osteuropa-Institut München).

HUTCHINGS, R. (1978A) *Osteuropa-Wirtschaft*, June.

HUTCHINGS, R. (1978B) *The World Today*, October.

HUTCHINGS, R. (1982A) *Soviet Economic Development*, 2nd edn (Oxford: Blackwell).

HUTCHINGS, R. (1982B) *Chronological Patterns in the Presentation of Soviet Economic Statistics* (Cologne: Berichte des Bundesinstituts für ostwissenschaftliche und internationale Studien, no. 20).

HUTCHINGS, R. (1983) *The Soviet Budget* (London: Macmillan).

HUTCHINGS, R. (1984) *The Structural Origins of Soviet Industrial Expansion* (London: Macmillan).

HUTCHINGS, R. (1985) *Osteuropa-Wirtschaft*, December.

HUTCHINSON, R. (1985) *RUSI Journal for Defence Studies*, March.

INGRAM, D. (1976) *The Sunday Times*, 15 August.

IOFFE, Ya. A. (1935) *Planovoye khozyaystvo*, no. 5

ISC (1980) *The Soviet Empire: Pressures and Strains* (London: Institute for the Study of Conflict).

JACKSON, H. S. (1975) *The Diary of a Censor: Aleksandr Nikitenko* (Amherst: University of Massachusetts Press).

JEC (1977) *Allocation of Resources in the Soviet Union and China* (Hearings before the Subcommittee on Priorities and Economy in Government of the Joint Economic Committee, Congress of the United States, Ninety-Fifth Congress, First Session) (Washington: US Government Printing Office).

KAHN, D. (1969) *The Codebreakers* (Toronto: The Macmillan Company. Collier-Macmillan Canada).

KALEJA S. (1984) *Cīna*, 5 May, cited in *ABSEES*, item 09760, September 1984.

KARPOV, L. I. and V. A. SEVERTSEV (eds) (1957) *Vysshaya shkola: osnovnyye postanovleniya, prikazy i instruktsii* (Moscow: 'Sovetskaya Nauka').

KASER, M. (1970) *Soviet Economics* (London: Weidenfeld & Nicolson).

KASER, M. and R. NÖTEL (1985) *East European Economies in Two World Crises*, Papers in East European Economies, no. 71 (NASEES Conference at Cambridge, England).

KASER, M. and J. ZIELINSKI (1970) *Planning in East Europe* (London: The Bodley Head).

KATKOFF, V. (1961) *Soviet Economy 1940–1965* (Baltimore: Dangary Publishing Co.).

KATZ, M. N. (1986) *Problems of Communism*, July–August.

KAUFMAN, W. (1972) *The Daily Telegraph Magazine*.

KEEP, J. (1977) *The Russian Review*, October.

KELLEY, D. R. (1978) in K. R. Ryavec (ed.) *Soviet Society and the Communist Party* (Amherst: University of Massachusetts Press).

KELLNER, P. (1983) *Parliamentary Affairs*, Summer.

KENEALLY, T. (1982) *Schindler's Ark* (London: Hodder & Stoughton).

KHRUSHCHEV, N. S. (1961) *Mezhdunarodnaya zhizn'*, no. 12.

KHRUSHCHEV, N. S. (1971) *Khrushchev Remembers*, vol. 1 (Harmondsworth: Penguin Books).

KHRUSHCHEV, N. S. (1977) *Khrushchev Remembers*, vol. 2 (Harmondsworth: Penguin Books).

KIRKMAN, W. (1972) *The Daily Telegraph Magazine*.

KLOCHKO, M. A. (1964) *Soviet Scientist in China* (London: Hollis & Carter).

KNIGHT, S. (1983) *The Brotherhood* (London: Grafton).

KNIGHTLEY, P. (1982) *The First Casualty* (London: Quartet Books).

KOMAROV, B. (1978) *The Destruction of Nature in the Soviet Union* (London: Pluto Press).

KOROL, A. G. (1965) *Soviet Research and Development: Its Organization, Personnel, and Funds* (Cambridge, Mass.: MIT Press).

KOSMODEM'YANSKIY, A. A. and Vs. I. OSTOL'SKIY (1969) in Nesteruk, F. Ya. and Vs. I. Ostol'skiy, eds. *Energeticheskaya, atomnaya, transportnaya i aviatsionnaya tekhnika. Kosmonavtika* (Moscow: Izdatel'stvo 'Nauka').

KOSTA, J. (1973) in W. Gumpel & D. Keese (eds), *Probleme des Industrialismus in Ost und West* (Munich: Günter Olzog Verlag).

KOTELEVSKIY, Y. and E. GOLUB (1971) *Zhurnalist*, no. 12.

KRAYUSHKIN, V. et al. (1983) *Vodnyy transport*, 17 December.

LAING, L. and J. LAING (1982) *Anglo-Saxon England* (Frogmore: Paladin).

LAMONT, N. (1975) *Sunday Times*, 7 December.

LAQUEUR, W. (1980) *The Terrible Secret* (Harmondsworth: Penguin Books).

LAQUEUR, W. (1985) *A World of Secrets: the Uses and Limits of Intelligence* (London: Weidenfeld and Nicolson).

LASCELLES, D. (1974) *The Financial Times*, 23 October.

LASCELLES, D. (1975) *The Financial Times*, 27 June.

LAWTON, Lord Justice (1975), giving the Ninth Riddell Lecture, *The Financial Times*, 5 June.

LEBEDINSKIY, N. (1971) *Literaturnaya gazeta*, 17 February.

LEE, W. T. (1975) *The Credibility of the Reported 'Science' Expenditures* (Santa Barbara: General Electric – TEMPO).

LEITENBERG, M. (1979) *Journal of Peace Research*, no. 3.

LENGERER, H. (1983) *Warship*, January.

LEWIS, G. (1974) *Modern Turkey* (London and Tonbridge: Ernest Benn).

LEWYTZKYJ, B. (1976) *Osteuropa*, June.

LOUIS, W. R. *et al.* 'Declassification of Secret Documents: The British and American Experience Compared', seminar at the Lyndon Baines Johnson Library, Austin, Texas, 30 April 1976.

MACKIE, J. L. in P. H. NIDDITCH (ed.) (1968) *The Philosophy of Science* (London: Oxford University Press).

MACKINTOSH, M. (1985) in C. KEEBLE (ed.) *The Soviet State* (Aldershot: Gower for the Royal Institute of International Affairs).

McMICHAEL, S., C. SASSO and R. BAUMAN (1986) *RUSI Journal for Defence Studies*, March.

McNEAL, R. H. (1985) *Slavic Review*, Summer.

McPHEE, J. (1984) *The Swiss Army: La Place de la Concorde Suisse* (London: Faber & Faber).

MAILLART, E. (1985) Lecture at the Royal Geographical Society, London, 22 April.

MALILE, R. (1985) *Zëri i popullit*, 1 October.

MANGO, C. (1980) *Byzantium: The Empire of A New Rome* (London: Weidenfeld & Nicolson).

MARKOV, G. (1983), trans. Liliana Brisby, *The Truth That Killed* (London: Weidenfeld & Nicolson).

MASON, R. (1975) *The Times*, 25 June.

MATTHEWS, M. (1974) *Soviet Government, A Selection of Official Documents on Internal Affairs* (London: Jonathan Cape).

MATTHEWS, M. (1978) *Privilege in the Soviet Union* (London: Allen & Unwin).

MEDVEDEV, Z. (1971) *The Medvedev Papers* (London: Macmillan).

MEDVEDEV, Z. (1978) *Soviet Science* (Oxford: Oxford University Press).

MEETHAM, R. (1969) *Information Retrieval* (London: Aldus Books).

MEHDI, M. (1985) *The Times*, 28 May.

MELLOR, R. E. H. (1966) *Geography of the USSR* (London: Macmillan).

MICKIEWICZ, E. P. (1981) *Media and the Russian Public* (New York: Praeger).

MIKES, G. (1959) *A Study in Infamy* (London: Andre Deutsch).

MILLAR, J. R. (1981) *The ABCs of Soviet Socialism* (Urbana: University of Illinois Press).

MILLER, J. H. (1977) *Soviet Studies*, October.

MILSOM, J. (1970) *Russian Tanks 1900–1970* (London: Arms and Armour Press).

MIRSKY, J. (1982) *The Observer*, 22 August.

MONAS, S. (1984–5) *Studies in Comparative Communism*, Fall/Winter.

MONTIAS, J. M. (1964) *Soviet Studies*, October.

MOORE, J. (1984/5) *Crossbow*, Winter.

MORTON, H. V. (1964) *A Traveller in Italy* (London: Methuen).

MURARKA, D. (1971) *The Soviet Union* (London: Thames & Hudson).

MURARKA, D. (1974) *New Statesman*, 18 January.

NAGEL (1973) *Moscow and Its Environs* (Geneva: Nagel Publishers).

NEIZVESTNY, E. (1984–5) *Studies in Comparative Communism*, Fall/Winter.

NEWTH, J. (1964) *Soviet Studies*, January.

NFAC (National Foreign Assessment Center) (1979) *An Analysis of the Behavior of Soviet Machinery Prices 1960–73* (Washington D.C.: Central Intelligence Agency).

NIKOLAEV, R. (1985) *Radio Free Europe Research, Bulgaria/10*, 2 September.

NOREN, J. H. and E. D. WHITEHOUSE (1973) in J. P. HARDT (ed.) *Soviet Economic Prospects for the Seventies* (Washington D.C.: Joint Economic Committee).

NOVE, A. (1974) *The Times*, 31 October.

OLDBERG, I. (1985) *The Annals of the American Academy of Political Science*, September.

OŢETEA, A. (ed) (1985) *A Concise History of Romania* (London: Robert Hale).

OWEN, R. (1985) *The Times*, 27 June.

Oxford Student's Dictionary of Current English (1980) (London: Oxford University Press).

ØYEN, E. (1982) *Current Sociology*, Summer.

PAKSOY, H. B. (1984) *Central Asian Survey*, vol. 3, no. 1.

PALLOT, J. and D. J. B. SHAW (1981) *Planning in the USSR* (London: Croom Helm).

PARKHOMENKO, A. (1968) *Ekonomicheskaya gazeta*, no. 27.

PEARSON, K. (1937: 1st edn 1892) *The Grammar of Science* (London: Everyman).

PETERS, B. (1940) *Industriya*, 3 February.

PINCHER, Chapman (1984) *Too Secret, Too Long* (New York: St Martin's Press).

PIPES, R. (1974) *Russia under the Old Regime* (London: Weidenfeld & Nicolson).

PLOSS, S. (1972) *Problems of Communism*, July–August. (The reference is to *Voprosy istorii KPSS*, no. 5, 1958, p. 159).

PORTIK, K. (1985) *Policy Review*, Spring.

POURNELLE, J. (1982) *A Step Farther Out*, part 2 (London: Star).

Pravda 1912–1914, 1917, Bibliograficheskiy ukazatel' (1962) (Moscow: *Gosudarstvennoye izdatel'stvo politicheskoy literatury*).

PRINGLE, P. (1974) *The Sunday Times*, 7 July.

PRUTKIN, Z. (1931) *Finansy i sotsialisticheskoye khozyaystvo*, no. 9.

PUSHKAREV, L. (1985) *Vodnyy transport*, 30 July.

RADIO FREE EUROPE RESEARCH (1975) *Bulgarian Situation Report/33*, 4 December, item 2.

RAMSEY, W. G. (1981) *The War in the Channel Islands, Then and Now* (London: *After the Battle* magazine).

RAUD, V. (1953) *Estonia* (New York: The Nordic Press).

RAVETZ, J. R. (1971) *Scientific Knowledge and Its Social Problems* (New York: Oxford University Press).

REED, D. (1934) *The Burning of the Reichstag* (London: Victor Gollancz).

REES, B. S. H. (1980 and later) *Soviet Studies*, 1980, 1981 and 1982 (July in each case), and 1983, 1984, 1985 and 1986 (October in each case).

RICE, C. (1985) guest speaker at NASEES, Cambridge.

RIGBY, T. H. (1968) *The Stalin Dictatorship* (Sydney: Sydney University Press).

RIGBY, T. H., A. BROWN and P. REDDAWAY (eds) (1980) *Authority, Power and Policy in the USSR* (London: Macmillan).

RIVIN, E. I. (1983) *Mechanical Engineering*, April.

ROACH, J. C. (1979) *United States Naval Institute Proceedings*, June.

RONAY, G. (1983) *The Times*, 4 March.

ROSENFELD, S. S. (1976) *The Washington Post*, 12 November.

ROYAL UNITED SERVICES INSTITUTE AND BRASSEY'S (1986) *Defence Yearbook 1986* (London: Brassey's Defence Publishers).

ROZMAN, G. (1986) *A Mirror for Socialism: Soviet Criticisms of China* (London: I. B. Tauris & Co.).

RUDBERG, P. Y. (1985) *Naval Forces*, no. IV.

RUSBRIDGER, J. (1985) *The Times*, 17 May.

276 *Bibliography*

RUSBRIDGER, J. (1986) *Encounter*, January.
RUTHERFORD, M. (1974) *The Financial Times*, 11 June.
SACKS, M. P. (1981) *Slavic Review*, Summer.
SALISBURY, H. E. (1969) *The Siege of Leningrad* (London: Secker & Warburg).
SANDAUER, A. (1965) *Kultura*, 16 May (in Polish).
SAVOVA, E. (1982) *Georgi Dimitrov, Letopis za zhivota i revolyutsionnata mu deynost* (Sofia: Izdatel'stvo na Bŭlgarskaya Akademiya na Naukite).
SCHAPIRO, L. (1960) *The Communist Party of the Soviet Union* (London: Eyre & Spottiswoode).
SCHAPIRO, L. and J. GODSON (1981) *The Soviet Worker* (London: Macmillan).
SCHIMANSKI, F. (1973) *New Scientist*, 20 December.
SCHMID, Karin (1985) *Berichte des Bundesinstituts für ostwissenschaftliche und internationale Studien, Summaries* 1–20/1985.
SCHOELWER, M. A. (1986) in B. W. WATSON and S. M. WATSON (eds) *The Soviet Navy: Strengths and Liabilities* (Boulder, Col.: Westview Press/Arms and Armour Press).
SCHÖPFLIN, G. (ed.) (1983) *Censorship and Political Communication in Eastern Europe* (London: Frances Pinter).
SCHULTZ, R. and GODSON, R. (1984) *Dezinformatsia* (Washington D.C.: Pergamon–Brassey's).
SEGAL, L. (1946) *Russian–English Dictionary* (London: Lund Humphries).
SERGEYEV, F. (1970) *Nedelya*, 16–22 November.
SETON-WATSON, M. (1986) *Soviet Analyst*, 22 January.
SHABAD, T. (1971) *The New York Times*, 16 October.
SHANOR, D. R. (1986) *The Daily Telegraph*, 3 January.
SHATROV, T. (1984) *Rabotnichesko delo*, 25 November.
SHEARS, D. (1970) *The Ugly Frontier* (London: Chatto & Windus).
SHELDON, W. (1969) *Soviet Space Exploration: The First Decade* (London: Arthur Barker).
SHLAPENTOKH, V. E. (1984) *Problems of Communism*, September–October.
SHORT, N. M. *et al.* (1976) *Mission to Earth: Landsat Views of the World* (Washington: NASA).
SIPRI (Stockholm International Peace Research Institute) (1975) *The Arms Trade with the Third World* (Harmondsworth: Penguin Books).
SIPRI (Stockholm International Peace Research Institute) (1979) *Yearbook*. (London: Taylor & Francis).
SMITH, A. H. (1981) in K. DAWISHA and P. HANSON (eds) *Soviet–East European Dilemmas* (London: Heinemann for the Royal Institute of International Affairs).
SMITH, H. (1976) *The Russians* (London: Sphere Books).

SOLZHENITSYN, A. (1963) *One Day in the Life of Ivan Denisovich* (Harmondsworth: Penguin Books).

Sotsialisticheskoye narodnoye khozyaystvo SSSR v 1933–1940 gg. (1963) (Moscow: Izdatel'stvo Akademii Nauk SSSR).

SPRING, D. W. (1986) *Soviet Studies*, April.

Staff Report of the Senate Select Committee on Intelligence United States Senate (1978) *The Soviet Oil Situation: An Evaluation of CIA Analyses of Soviet Oil Production* (Washington: US Government Printing Office).

STEVENS, E. (1974) *The Times*, 8 April.

STEVENS, E. (1975) *The Times*, 22 September.

STEVENS, E. (1985) *Sunday Times*, 17 March.

STRUMILIN, S. (1952) *Vestnik statistiki*, no. 1.

STUART, G. and TAYLOR, L. (1986) in SCHOELWER, M. A.

SUMNER, B. H. (1944) *Survey of Russian History* (London: Duckworth).

SUTHERLAND, I. (1986) Address at the Royal Institute of International Affairs, 10 April.

SUTTON, A. C. (1968) *Western Technology and Soviet Economic Development 1917 to 1930* (Stanford University, Hoover Institution on War, Revolution and Peace).

SUVAROV, V. (1985) *RUSI Journal for Defence Studies*, June.

SUVAROV, V. (1986) *RUSI Journal for Defence Studies*, March.

SZULC, T. (1975) *Penthouse*, November.

TARSCHYS, D. (1985) *Soviet Studies*, October.

TAYLOR, P. B. (1972) *The Russian Review*, April.

TAYLOR, R. (1980), in T. H. RIGBY, A. BROWN and P. REDDAWAY, *Authority, Power and Policy in the USSR* (London: Macmillan).

THOMPSON, E. M. (1986) *Policy Review*, Winter.

TOUR DESIGNS INC. (1986) *Independent Travel in the Soviet Union* (brochure, place of publication and publisher unspecified; Tour Designs Inc. is an Intourist-appointed tour wholesale-operator).

TOYNBEE, A. (1969) *The Hecettepe Bulletin of Social Sciences and Humanities*, June.

TREML, V. G. (1982) *Alcohol in the USSR: A Statistical Study* (Durham, North Carolina: Centre of Alcohol Studies, Rutgers University/ Duke University Press Policy Studies).

TREML, V., D. M. GALLIK, B. L. KOSTINSKY and K. W. KRUGER (1972) *The Structure of the Soviet Economy* (New York: Praeger).

TRIBE, D. (1973) *Questions of Censorship* (London: Allen & Unwin).

TSOURAS, P. (1986) see SCHOELWER, M. A. (1986).

TSVIGUN, S. K. (1973) *Taynyy front. O podryvnoy deyatel'nosti imperializma protiv SSSR i bditel'nosti sovetskikh lyudey* (Moscow: Izdatel'stvo politicheskoy literatury).

TUCHMAN, B. W. (1980) *The Guns of August* (New York: Bantam Books Inc.).

UTECHIN, S. V. (1961) *Everyman's Concise Encyclopaedia of Russia* (London: J. M. Dent).

VERE-JONES, D. (1964) *Survey*, July.

VERNADSKY, G. (1930) *A History of Russia* (London: Oxford University Press).

VERSTAKOV, V. (1986) *Pravda*, 9 December.

VIDALI, V. (1984) *Diary of the Twentieth Congress of the Communist Party of the Soviet Union* (London: Journeyman Press).

VIOLETTE, A. J. (1974) *The Slavonic and East European Review*, October.

VLADIMIROV, L. (1971) *The Soviet Space Bluff* (London: Tom Stacey).

VLADIMIROV, L. (1972) *Index on Censorship*, Autumn/Winter.

VOSLENSKY, M. (1984) *Nomenklatura* (London: Overseas Publications Interchange).

VOZNESENSKIY, N. (1948) *Voyennaya ekonomika SSSR v period otechestvennoy voyny* (Moscow: Gosudarstvennoye iz'datelstvo politicheskoy literatury).

VUCINICH, A. (1963) *Science in Russian Culture: A History to 1860* (London: Peter Owen).

WALKER, G. (1978) *Soviet Book Publishing Policy* (Cambridge: Cambridge University Press).

WALLIN, L. B. (ed.) (1982) *The Northern Flank in a Central European War* (Proceedings of a symposium). (Stockholm: The Swedish National Defence Research Institute).

WANLESS, P. T. (1985) *Taxation in Centrally Planned Economies* (London: Croom Helm).

WARD, P. (1983) *Albania: A Travel Guide* (Cambridge: Oleander Press).

WATTS, A. J. (1985) *Navy International*, March.

WELLS, H. G. (1920) *Russia in the Shadows* (London: Hodder & Stoughton).

WEST, N. (1986) *GCHQ: The Secret Wireless War 1900–86* (London: Weidenfeld & Nicolson).

WESTIN, A. F. in J. R. PENNOCK and J. W. CHAPMAN (1971) *Privacy* (New York: Atherton Press).

WETTERN, D. (1976) *The Daily Telegraph*, 14 June.

WHALEY, B. (1984) *Covert German Rearmament, 1919–1939: Deception and Misperception* (Frederick: University Publications of America).

WIGG, R. (1976) *The Times*, 19 October.

WILCZYNSKI, J. (1974) *Technology in Comecon* (New York: Praeger).

WILES, P. (1974) *Distribution of Income East and West* (Amsterdam and New York: Professor Dr F. de Vries Lectures).

WILSON, E. A. M. (1982) *The Modern Russian Dictionary for English Speakers* (Oxford: Pergamon Press).

WINSOR, D. (1976) *The Daily Telegraph Magazine*, August, no. 610.

WINTERBOTHAM, F. W. (1974) *The Ultra Secret* (New York: Dell Publishing Co.).

WISE, D. and T. B. ROSS (1967) *The Espionage Establishment* (New York: Random House).

WOLF, T. A. (1984) speaking at Ohio State University, 4 May.

WOLF, T. A. (1983) in G. K. BERTSCH and J. R. McINTYRE (eds) *National Security and Technology Transfer* (Boulder, Col.: Westview Press).

WOLFF, K. H. (trans. and ed.) (1950) *The Sociology of George Simmel* (Illinois: Free Press).

ZALESKI, E. *et al.* (1969) *Science Policy in the USSR* (Paris: OECD).

ZAND, N. (1974) *Le Monde*, 31 March.

ZELENOVSKIY, A. (1941) *Planovoye khozyaystvo*, no. 2.

ZIMMERMAN, W. and G. PALMER (1983) *The American Political Science Review*, June.

STATISTICAL SOURCES

Narodnoye khozyaystvo SSSR (1956) (Moscow: Gosudarstvennoye statisticheskoye izdatel'stvo).

Narodnoye khozyaystvo SSSR v 1972 g.

Narodnoye khozyaystvo SSSR v 1976 g.

Narodnoye khozyaystvo SSSR v 1977 g. (1978) (Moscow: 'Statistika').

Vneshnyaya torgovlya SSSR v 1971 g.

Vneshnyaya torgovlya SSSR v 1973 g.

Narodnoye khozyaystvo SSSR 1922–1982 (1982) (Moscow: 'Finansy i Statistika').

40 Années d'Albanie socialiste (1984) (Tirana: La Direction des Statistiques près la Commission de Plan d'Etat).

Council for Mutual Economic Assistance Secretariat (1976) *Statistical Yearbook of Member States of the Council for Mutual Economic Assistance* (London: IPC Industrial Press).

Index of Names

Abouchar, A. 84
Adamson, D. 221
Aleksandrov, A. M. 88
Amalrik, A. 148–9
Amann, R. 77
Andropov, Yu. V.,
  President 142, 149–51,
  172, 181
Annenkov, Yu. 41
Arendt, H. 61
Asselain, J.-C. 78
Atahualpa (Inca Emperor) 14

Bacon, R. 42
Bahushevich, F. 131
Bailes, K. 142
Bakule, V. 77
Bankuti, G. 205
Barman, T. 61, 178
Bauman, R. 186
Beck, F. 228
Beermann, R. 16
Belinkov, A. 127
Beneš, E., President 173
Bentley, R. 206
Berg, G. P. van den 70–1, 91
Beria, L. P. 129
Bernal, J. 62
Bethell, N. 121
Birman, I. 78, 138, 142
Bonavia, D. 202
Bracy, J. 255
Brezhnev, L., President 93,
  100, 140, 142, 146, 150–1,
  172
Bridge, A. 234
Brown, A. 17, 67
Browning, R. 63
Bukovsky, V. 109
Bulganin, N. A. 143

Calder, N. 144
Calvert, P. 111
Campbell, F. G. 135
Carell, P. 197
Carlyle, T. 29
Catherine the Great
  (Tsarina) 36
Chernenko, K. U.,
  President 150–1, 172, 245
Choldin, M. T. 39, 128–9, 136,
  205
Churchill, Sir W. 33, 217, 261
Citrine, Sir W. 178
Coleman, A. 194
Cowen, R. C. 144
Crane, J. 184, 215

Daniel, Yu. 146
Daniloff, F. 53, 169, 257
Davies, J. E. 145, 260
Dawisha, K. 141
Delbridge, R. 215, 220, 223
Diéguez, D. 213
Dimitrov, G. 110
Divine, R. A. 23, 217
Drasinover, J. 207
Durham, E. 14

Edward, Prince 2–3
Eichmann, A. 186
Einstein, A. 20
Elizabeth I, Queen 160
Ellingsen, E. 131
Engels, F. 244
Erenburg, I. 145

Fainsod, M. 126–7, 179–80
Fedorenko, N. P. 255
Feshbach, M. 147
Fishlock, D. 129

Flegon, A. 139
Fleron, F. J. 61
Fock, J. 28
Francis, P. 46, 233
Franco, General 213
Frank, T. F. 6, 15, 29, 165, 215
French, R. A. 75
Friedman, N. 73
Fukuda, Aiko 251

Gaddafi, M., President 250
Gandhi, I. 221
Garbuzov, V. F. 252
Gardiner, L. 59
Garmashev, A. F. 62
Genghis Khan 127
Gibbon, E. 4, 193
Glazov, Y. 51
Glezer, A. 66–7
Godin, W. 228
Godson, R. 8, 78, 95, 98
Gogol, N. V. 37
Gorbachev, M. S. 49, 93, 136,
    150, 172, 231–2, 238, 265
Gorbacheva, R. 47
Gordievsky, O. 12, 219
Gorshkov, A. 252
Gowing, M. M. 173, 195–6
Gregory, P. R. 76
Gromyko, A. A. 252
Grossman, G. 78, 138, 235
Gunther, J. 6

Hanson, P. 78, 87, 141, 212
Hardt, J. P. 6
Heseltine, M. 31
Hewett, E. 78
Heymann, H. Jr. 65
Hibbert, Sir R. 187
Hilton, R. P. 74
Hirszowicz, M. 74
Hitler, A. 10, 71, 261
Hobbes, T. 120
Hoffmann, E. P. 61, 234

Høistad, O. M. 108
Holloway, D. 6, 10
Hopkins, M. 164
Hopkirk, P. 66
Hoxha, E. 146
Hutchings, N. 189
Hutchings, R. 8, 26, 43, 61,
    63–4, 70, 74, 77, 79–81, 84,
    101–2, 109, 112, 126–7, 131,
    133–4, 136–7, 139–41,
    143–4, 156, 159, 168, 179,
    209, 235, 237, 242, 254
Hutchinson, R. 115

Ioffe, Ya. 78

Johnson, H. 10
Johnson, Samuel, 165
Jones, P. 46, 233

Kadar, J. 111
Kahn, D. 188, 196
Karpov, L. I. 63, 143, 256–7
Kaser, M. 50, 142, 210, 262
Katkoff, V. 145
Katz, M. 221
Kaufman, W. 200
Keep, J. 82, 129
Kellner, P. 216
Keneally, T. 23
Kennedy, J. F., President 192,
    225
Khrushchev, N. S., 32, 50, 53,
    56, 60, 70, 95, 140–1, 143,
    145, 148, 151, 157, 172, 174,
    193, 234
Kirov, S. M. 110, 146
Klochko, M. A. 143, 179, 256
Knightley, P. 10
Kohout, P. 205
Komarov, B. 69, 78
Kosta, J. 8
Krizanc, J. 125
Kun, Bela 37
Kurchatov, I. V. 143

Lacey, P. 120
Laird, R. F. 234
Lamont, N. 77, 214
Laqueur, W. 6, 157
Lebedinsky, N. 249
Lee, W. T. 146
Leitenberg, M. 80, 261
Lenin, V. I. 40–1, 193, 213
Levy, J. 120
Lewytzkyj, B. 126
Limpinski, E. 135
Louis, W. R. 217
Lycheva, Katerina 250
Lysenko, T. 143

Mackintosh, M. 52, 146
McMichael, S. 186
McNeal, R. H. 174
McPhee, J. 45, 194, 212
Maillart, E. 109
Maleter, P. 204
Malile, R. 212
Mandela, W. 221
Mango, A. 14
Marcos, F., President 49
Markov, G. 205
Marx, K. 50–1, 120, 244
Mason, R. 181
Matthews, W. M. 39, 78, 101, 112, 138, 146, 209
Medvedev, R. 170
Medvedev, Zh. 96, 101, 106, 127–9, 134, 170
Meetham, R. 257
Mellor, R. E. H. 75
Mickiewicz, E. 135, 155, 236, 247
Middleton, H. J. 217
Mikes, G. 111
Millar, J. M. 6
Miller, J. H. 128
Milsom, J. 75
Mirsky, J. 102
Molotov, V. 129, 193
Momirski, M. 205

Monas, S. 130
Moore, J. 218
Morton, H. V. 47
Mosley, Sir O. 217
Murarka, D. 76, 146

Nagel, 105, 148
Nagorski, A. 103
Nagy, I., 204
Neizvestny, E. 131
Newth, J. A. 71
Nicholas II, Tsar 14
Nikitenko, A. 119
Nixon, R. President 47, 226
Nikolaev, R. 211
Noren, J. E. 142
Nötel, R. 142, 262
Nove, A. 78

Oldberg, I. 184
Orwell, G. 61
Oţetea, A. 203
Ovid 118
Øyen, E. 5

Pallot, J. 76
Palme, O. 213
Parkhomenko, A. 64
Pasternak, B. 132
Paul, Tsar 136
Pearson, K. 62
Peter the Great, Tsar 119
Peters, B. 127
Pincher, C. 25, 180
Pipes, R. 60, 136
Podrabinek, A. 148
Ponting, C. 217
Popiełuszko, Father 112
Portik, K. 228
Potemkin, Prince 36–7
Pournelle, J. 180
Powell, E. 217
Powers, G. 183
Pringle, P. 183
Prutkin, Z. 79

Rakosi, M. 111
Rankovic, A. 206
Ravetz, J. 62
Reagan, R., President 131, 231–2
Reed, D. 110
Rice, C. 52
Rigby, T. H. 110, 173
Rivin, E. I. 176
Roach, J. C. 74
Roosevelt, F. D., President 20
Ross, T. B. 216
Rudberg, P. Y. 184
Rusbridger, J. 43, 217
Rutherford, M. 30

Sadat, A., President 183
Sakharov, A. 82, 100, 104, 136
Salisbury, H. E. 145
Sandauer, A. 205
Sasso, C. 186
Schaff, A. 78
Schapiro, L. 78, 173
Schimanski, F. 206
Schindler, O. 23
Schmid, K. 149
Schöpflin, G. 121–4, 134
Schultz, R. 8, 95, 97, 98
Seton-Watson, M. 163
Severtsev, V. A. 63, 143, 256–7
Shabad, T. 75
Shaw, D. J. B. 76
Shcharansky, A. 136
Shlapentokh, V. E. 154–5, 169, 249
Short, N. M. 46
Simmel, G. 5, 11
Sinyavsky, A. 46
Smith, A. 141
Smith, H. 6, 146, 234
Smith, M. 215, 220, 223
Smith, Samantha 250
Solzhenitsyn, A. 82, 131
Šoóš, E. 146
Spinoza, B. 120

Stalin, I. V. 14, 21, 50, 143, 157, 173, 192–3, 244
Stevens, E. 67, 146
Strumilin, S. G. 80
Stuart, R. C. 76
Sukhodrev, V. 172
Sumner, B. H. 240
Sutherland, Sir I. 153
Sutton, A. 83
Suvarov, V. 185–6
Szulc, T. 188

Tarschys, D. 192
Taylor, R. 41
Tereshkova, V. 144
Tisdall, S. 198, 217
Tokaty-Tokaev, G. A. 169
Toynbee, A. 94
Treholt, A. 108
Treml, V. 90
Tribe, D. 118–19, 130
Trotsky, L. 40, 61, 84, 110, 192
Truman, H., President 173
Tsouras, P. 74
Tsvigun, S. K. 249
Tukhachevsky, Marshal 173

Utechin, S. V. 120–1

Vere-Jones, D. 65
Vernadsky, G. 6
Vidali, V. 174
Violette, A. J. 136
Vladimirov, L. 75, 125–6, 147
Voslensky, M. 94, 169, 193, 215
Voznesenskiy, N. 139
Vucinich, A. 136

Walker, G. 219, 242, 246
Wallin, L. B. 185
Wanless, P. T. 205, 210
Ward, P. 207
Watts, A. J. 225
Watts, D. 227

Weisband, E. 6, 15, 29, 165,
    215
Wells, H. G. 68
West, N. 127
Westin, A. 27
Wettern, D. 195
Whitehouse, E. 142
Wilczynski, J. 77, 144, 174
Wiles, P. 89
Wilson, Sir D. 216

Winsor, D. 215
Wise, D. 216
Wolff, K. 5
Wynne, G. 186

Zamyatin, L. 103, 150
Zelenovskiy, A. 138
Zhivkov, T., President 236
Zielinski, J. 210

Index of Subjects

Åland Islands 131
Academy of Sciences 101
accidents 234, 245
addresses of citizens 59
addresses of industrial
    plants 139
Admiral Nakhimov 152
advertising 22, 162
Afghan war 247
Afghanistan 94, 103, 131
Aeroflot 69, 109
affirmative action 116
agrarian history 82
AIDS 65
air freight 44
air passenger traffic 44
airfields 45, 194
Akademgorodok 44
Albania 14, 45, 47, 142, 193,
    203, 207–12, 222, 227, 246
Alma Ata 89
Amur River 46
anniversaries 245–6
anonymous letters 162–3
Antarctica 228
ANZUS Pact 225
Argentina 222
Armenia 103, 132
arms exports 35, 84, 141
arms production 77
art 66–7
Asian 'flu 65
assassination 110, 206
Australia 219–20
Austria 94–5, 99, 210
Austria-Hungary 203
Aviamotornaya station 67
avtorskoye svidetel'stvo 62

Baltic Fleet 43

Baltic Republics 104
BAM 75, 100
Baykonur 75
BBC 10, 147, 159, 198, 209,
    218
Belgium 165
Belorussia 103
Belorussian language 133
Belzec 23
Berlin Wall 95–7
*Black Book of Polish
    Censorship* 121–2, 210
Black Sea Fleet 43
Bolshevik Revolution 39, 117, 230
book output 243–4
Borodino, Battle of 177
bottom crawling vehicles 184–5
Britain 12, 25, 32–3, 40, 53, 57,
    73, 127, 154, 165, 175, 181,
    214–19, 225, 227, 230,
    259–60
British Airways 30
British Land Utilisation
    Survey 194
British Telecom 99
British Trade Exhibition 156
Budapest 92
budget 26, 81, 88, 136, 139,
    247
Bulgaria 46, 84, 149, 203, 205,
    211, 236, 246, 251
business secrecy 13
Byzantine Empire 14, 63

Cairo 97
Canada 219, 223
Captor mines 180
cartography 10
censorship (Tsarist) 39
censorship 16, 114–33

Cetinje 162
Channel Islands 33
chemical industry 85
Chernobyl disaster 68–9, 150, 152, 158
Chess 161, 247
Chief Administration for Affairs of Literature and Publishing 39
Chief Administration for Guarding Military and State Secrets in the Press 39, 143
'Chief Designer' 65
China 46, 109, 197, 202–3, 249, 260
Chita *oblast'* 149
Choybalsan 45, 60
CIA 183
classification 19–22
CMEA (Comecon) 211–12
CMO classification 21
Coca Cola 59
codes 11
coding and decoding machines 42
Cold War 145, 238
collectivity of authorship 115
Committee for Cultural Relations with Foreign Countries 125
Communist Party, history of 40
compensation, principle of 16
computers 23
copiers 198
corruption 152
counter-intelligence 25
Coventry 33
cremation 157
crime 91
Croydon 163, 215
cruise liners 109
Cuba 105
Cyrillic alphabet 131–3

Czechoslovakia 94, 146, 158, 188, 203–4, 207–8, 210, 259

Decembrist plot 119, 191
Decree on the Press 39
defence innovations 6
deportations 104
détente 260, 263
Deutsche Welle 147
diplomatic bags 179
diplomatic compounds 103
diplomatic travel, restrictions on 104
dissident opinions 91
dissident slogans 163
Divulging a State Secret 40
domestic service 82
drug-taking 91
drunkenness 91, 152
Duma 37

East Berlin 96
East Germany 96–7, 199, 206, 251
economic information 55
Economic Plan for 1941 138
Egypt 72–3, 222
emigration 124, 148, 151, 167–70, 176
engineering books 176
entry passes 102
environment, protection of 140
epidemics 65
Eritrean liberation movement 121
espionage 40, 49, 180–4
Estonia 100, 104, 147, 239
Ethiopia, 41, 121
executions 72, 129
expulsions of diplomatic staff 180–3, 186–7, 218
exiling 170

Falklands War 198, 216
falsification 8–10

FAO   261
fiction   160, 241
field patterns   46
Finland   94–96, 98, 100, 106, 131, 133, 138, 195
Finnish-Chinese aviation agreement   104
First Five-Year Plan   137
food prices   78
force de frappe   30
forced labour   82
forced labour camps   91
foreign trade   83, 141–42
'Foxbat' fighter   175
France   15, 53, 99, 136, 165, 175, 218, 259–60
funeral goods   78–9
fusion   143

GCHQ   218
General Belgrano   195, 217
geography   38, 43–4
Georgia   103
Georgian language   132
German language   134
German Foreign Ministry   83
German rearmament   217
Germany   37
glasnost'   251
Glavlit   39, 125
GOD   21, 92
gold   77, 235
Gorky (city)   103–4, 107
Gosbank   79
Gostekhnika   63
graffiti   163
grain harvest   3
Great Purge   162
Great Russian   133
Greenham Common   185
GULAG   112

Harwell   143
Helsinki   14

Helsinki Agreement   113, 141–2, 149, 238
High Treason   40
Hindus   53
Holocaust   120
homosexuality   91
Hungarian uprising   204
Hungary   28, 37, 86, 95, 111, 203, 204–5, 208, 210

icons   67
ideology   236
IMF   262
immigration   171
Inari, Lake   98
Inca Empire   14
INCSEA agreement   74
India   53, 221, 260
Indonesia   72
input–output analysis   90–1
Institute of History of Natural Sciences and Technique   131
Institute of Nuclear Power Operations   262
Intelligence Service   217
intelligence ships   182
internal passport system   101
internal waterways   68
interpretership   171–2
Intourist   109
IRA   219
Iran   35, 47, 98, 103
Iran-Iraq war   110
Iraq   222
Irish Republic   219
Irkutsk   109
Israel   13, 15, 41, 249
Israeli maps   194–5
Italy   189
Izvestiya   244

Japan   32, 156, 226–7

Japanese industrial
     exhibition 156
Jews 41, 53, 148, 168
Judaism 21

Kaliningrad 99, 103
Kama river plant 65
Kamchatka 75, 103, 184
Karelo-Finnish SSR 76
Karlskrona 184
Katyn murders 32, 157
KGB 12, 95, 108, 110, 125,
     181, 214, 219
Khabarovsk 109
Khrushchev's secret
     speech 145, 174
Kiev 100, 158
Kirghizia 92
KOR 135
Korea 128
Korean airliner, destruction
     of 111, 183
Krasnodar 147
Kremlinology 246
Kuzbass (explosion) 69

Landsat imaging 189
large-diameter pipe 85
Large Soviet Encyclopaedia 129,
     147
laser 17
Latin alphabet 131–2
latitude and longitude 75
Latvia 254
Law on Criminal Liability for
     State Crimes 39
laws, decrees, decisions, orders,
     instructions (in date order)
     27 October 1917 39
     30 June 1919 62
     6 June 1931 39
     5 March 1941 63
     8 June 1947 56
     18 June 1955 63

     28 April 1956 55
     25 December 1958 40
     January 1984 150
     1 July 1984 150
     30 October 1985 163
LBJ Library 23
Leningrad 100,166
Leningrad *oblast'* 45
Lenin's Mausoleum 177
lectures by foreign visitors 135
Leipzig Trial 110
letters between USSR and
     USA 170–1
Library of Congress 176
Libya 223
light waves 17
literacy 40, 132–3
Literaturnaya gazeta 247
Lithuanian language 131
living standards 158
Loss of Documents Containing a
     State Secret 40
Lutherans 178
Lysenkoism 63

Mafia 191–3
Magna Carta 106
Magnitogorsk 147
map-making 64
Mars 144
Marxism or Marxism-Leninism
     41, 50–2, 54, 199, 246
Marxist classics, allusions
     to 244
masons 191–2
May Day 72
May Day slogans 241
MBFR 262
mental hospitals 110, 148
microfiche 23
microwave transmission 44
Mikhail Lermontov 109
Milan Institute of Statistics 207
military casualties 234

military information 55
military spending 255–6, 260
ministerial censorship 215
Ministry of Aviation
  Technology 64
Ministry of Foreign Affairs 103
Ministry of Foreign Trade 86–7
Ministry of Radiotechnique 64
Mojahedin 224
Mongolia 45, 60
Mongols 36
Montreux Convention 43
Moon 53
moral grounds of
  censorship 224
Mordvin autonomous
  republic 103
Moscow 100, 127, 147–8, 156
Moscow *oblast'* 103
Moscow sketch map 76
Moscow underground 150
Muscovy 36, 38
Museum of technology 64
MVD troops 111
MX missiles 14

Nakhichevan 103
Nakhodka 65
'national financial plan' 89
national security 232
NATO 189, 215
Nazis, Nazism 8–10, 23, 31–33,
  60, 110, 138, 157, 178
Nazi observation flights 197
Nazi secrecy 261
Nazi-Soviet Non-Aggression
  Pact 145
Negriz 97
negroes 248
NEP 42, 137
New Zealand 14, 189, 219, 228
NFAC 142
NKVD 110
nomenklatura 169

non-ferrous metals 254
non-Russian languages of
  USSR 172–3
Northern Fleet 43
Northern Ireland 218
Novoexport 67
Novosibirsk 44
NPPD 107
nuclear deterrent 196–7
nuclear test site 152
nuclear weapons 13

observation points 94
Odessa 45
Official Secrets Act 152,
  215–16, 224
OGPU 112
Olympic Games 100, 106, 186,
  210
oral censorship 118
Orthodox Church 10, 130
Ottoman Empire 234
out-of-bounds areas 109
*Oxford Students' Dictionary of
  Current English* 128

P.2 secret society 191–2
Paris 136
patent law 59
Pergamon Press 242
persona non grata
  declarations 106
Philippines 47, 49
photography 64, 105
Pirin population 205
plastics 254
'Pobeda' cars 129
Poker 161
Poland 47, 84, 86, 96, 99, 112,
  121–5, 144, 154, 175, 119,
  204, 206–7, 210–11
Polish censorship list 117
Politburo 60, 149
pollution of Volga 93

population totals 70–1
pornography 128
Pravda 244, 247
printing capacity 242
privacy 15, 27, 50–1, 134, 199
private secrets 11–12
public opinion 15
Public Records Act 216
purges 113

quarterly statistics 140–1

racism 91, 248
Radio Free Europe 98–99, 158–9, 226
Radio Liberty 98, 158, 226
radio-electronic industry 78
radio jamming 98–9
Radio Moscow 98
radio waves 17
Ramenskoye airfield 233
Rapallo, Treaty of 37, 60
receptacles for documents 166
reconnaissance flights 197
Red Square 2, 18, 115
registered mail 120
Règlement Organique 203
religion 47, 92
reporting thresholds 58, 81
residence in cities 100
'residuals' 82–3
restrictions on tourism by Soviet citizens 105–6
Revolution of 1905 37
Revolution of 1917 39
Ricin 206
Roman Catholic Church 158
Roman Empire 193
Romania 70, 83, 198, 205, 208–10, 259
Rostov-on-Don *obkom* 149
Royal Ordnance Survey 195
riots 89
Royal Air Force 215, 217, 232

Royal Navy 73, 215
royalties 144
Russian language 134, 172

'sacred' 46–7
safe rooms 107
Sahel 189
St Valentine's Day massacre 192
Sakhalin 103, 184
SALT II agreement 263
SAM-6 missile 183
samizdat 152–3, 163–4, 199, 243
satellites 197–8
Saudi Arabia 16, 25, 223
scientific espionage 257–8
'scientific' towns 101
seasonal influences 80–2
'second economy' 152
Second World War 29, 34, 45, 71, 139, 214, 217, 261
secrecy legislation 237
secret ballot 59
secret-keeping, purposes of 12–13
secret police 111–13
secret service 74
secret sharing 173–5
secret societies 6
secret treaties 60
self-censorship 114–15
self-criticism 244
Sevastopol 73
Severomorsk (explosion) 69
Shaddock missile 97–8
shadowing 74, 106–7
shipbuilding 77
Shkodër 14
Siberia 38
SIGINT 188–90
SIPRI 84, 161
Smolensk 99, 179
Smolensk Archive 126–7, 180
snow 46
Sokolniki Park 85

Solidarity 96, 99, 199
SOSUS 73
source references 129
South Africa 159, 220–1, 243
Soviet Embassy in London 105
Soviet Far East 176
Soviet Foreign Ministry 176
Soviet Navy 72–3
Soviet space research 33
Soviet spies 181
Soviet trade agencies 85–7
Soviet warships, appearance
of 74
Sovietologists 106
Soya Strait 185
Space Shuttle Mission 51-C 41
Spain 213
Special Air Service (SAS) 215
special reporting days 245
specialisation 257
Spetsnaz 185
Sputnik 183
Stalingrad, Battle of 157
State Farms 101
State Planning Commission 42,
138–9
state reserves 78
statistical handbooks 57, 79,
82, 242
Straight Flush (radar) 183
submarines 43, 73, 111
Sudan 223
Suez Canal 15
Supreme Soviet (USSR or
RSFSR) 147, 163
surveillance 107
Sverdlov *oblast'* 103
Sweden 96, 111, 178, 213, 228,
261
Swedish language TV 131
Switzerland 187, 194, 212–13
Syracuse 63

Tajikistan 103

'Talmud' 125
tape recorders 199
Taras Shevchenko 109
Tashkent 70, 99
TASS 241
Tbilisi (flood) 70
'technical aesthetics' 134
telephone calls 170–1
telephone directories 74
tenure of appointments 252
Terror, the 146
Third World 221–3
30-year rule 217
The Times 117–18
Tirana 14
Top Secret classification 19–20
trade unions 218
Transylvania 203
Trieste 174
Tsugaru Strait 185
Tsushima, Battle of 120
Tsushima Strait 185
TU-95 65
TU-114 65
TU-144 65, 69
Tuaregs 16
Turkestan 109
Turkey 25, 46, 94, 103, 206
Turkish language 132
Turkish rule 203
Turkish-speaking minority in
Bulgaria 205
turnover tax 78, 89, 205
TV sets 243
20th Communist Party
Congress 32, 145
27th Communist Party
Congress 242
25-km frontier zone 103, 105
types of decision not to supply
information 114–17
typewriters 44, 198

U-2 flights 183

Udmurt autonomous
    republic   103
Ukraine   36
Ukrainian language   133
UKUSA pact   175
Ulan Ude   127
unemployment   82, 132, 163
United Nations   212
Universal Convention on
    Copyright   179
Universal Postal Union
    Convention   120
Urals forest fire   205
Urals nuclear disaster   68
uranium   196
USA   14, 27, 32, 40, 43, 53, 57,
    61, 156, 165, 180, 187, 195,
    200, 218, 224–6, 230
US Army   179
US Congress   170, 196, 225
US Embassy in Moscow   182
US President, personal life
    of   27
US, trade with   84
US Navy   96
US State Department   83, 147,
    181, 233

Uzbekistan   92

Vechernaya Moskva   247
Venice   194
Versailles, Treaty of   38
video   199
Vietnam   222
Vietnam War   45
VINITI   126
Vladivostok   73, 109
Voice of America   98, 147, 158
Volga-Don Canal   76

warship shapes   16
Watergate   49, 226
West Germany   99, 207–10
women   48–9, 91
World Youth Festival   132

YHWH   21
Younger Committee   200
Yugoslavia   47, 195, 203,
    205–8, 210–11

Zagorsk   47
ZIL   66
ZIM   66